"Own a business & enough money that lives forever."

Zayd's Rules: Business & Money For Life.

ZAYD HAJI
AUTHOR

ZAYD'S RULES:

BUSINESS &

MONEY FOR LIFE.

Written by Zayd Iqbal Haji

"Own a business & enough money that lives forever."

Dedication

To my loving parents,

Father - Late. Iqbal Haji RIP (26th January 1965 - 21st March 2020)

and **Mother - Almas Iqbal Haji**

In memory of my **Great-Grand-Father, Late. Ismail Haji RIP (9th April 1999)**

Grateful acknowledgment made to **My Mum and Dad**, who mentor me to Self-Educate and some of the essential life lessons used in this book.

The Support that you gave me — made all of this possible

I wish Daddy were alive to see me succeed with your taught life lessons.

✳ ✳ ✳

Acknowledgments

Al Zayd Corp

www.alzaydcorp.com

Self-Published Book

Author: Zayd Iqbal Haji

www.alzaydcorp.com

Foreword

A life lesson has strife with trauma, pain, and difficulties. Yet, what emerges from all of this is a person with immense grit, courage, and acceptance.

Iqbal Haji My Father. I've grown up with his taught lesson. He is no more recently expired on 21st March 2020. He was suffering from a Brain Tumour a year ago, and that tumor spread in his chest speedily. I went through financial depression a year ago. I was in depression because I never faced any financial losses until daddy was fine and in good health.
Daddy said, Work hard; I know you will succeed one day. That stuck in my subconscious mind, and till now, I follow his rules.

I've gone through many difficulties in life; I have experienced being authentic, practical, focused, yet empathic. There are sensitivity and acceptance towards life that is very rare to come by. I roused to become introverted and concentrate on my goals. I am now the CEO of Al Zayd Corp that we set up to provide corporate services in Financial, Marketing, and Production in Dubai and India.

When starting my business at a young age and with the life experience of how the business and finance world works, I have set some rules for myself, and I would like to share them with you. I have addressed this book's provisions that put you to grow your knowledge. As you know, having plenty of knowledge and experience is excellent for us. Many of us are on our journeys of self-growth or strive to be successful. This book has something for all of us to connect. More importantly, this book delivers business, money, finance, and hope for people struggling with various sorts of business and money fortune concerns.

It is a citation from Zayd's Rules: Business & Money for Life.
- Zayd Haji

Preface

How will this book help you?

Do you prefer yourself to be an Employee or Employer?

Question yourself, what would you prefer to be, an employee or an employer?

You might think I am asking you this question because you will get whether you have an urge to start a business and be an employer or get employed as an employee.

As an employee, you work for others. You create money for others and receive a salary, usually a hard and fast amount of cash for every hour you worked for a set monthly amount.

As an employer, you're employed for yourself and hire people. It allows you to enhance your financial condition and earn far more money than an employee. Since you're the owner of your business, you'll probably work harder, make more, and have more reliability.

For some personalities, the thought of being their boss is intimating. They might instead work for others because they feel safer and don't worry about running a business.

As an employee, you'll be able to make progress and reckon where you're employed, and you'll be able to reach a high position and earn well.

As an employer, you continuously seek out customers, increase your orders, and improve your business. However, if the corporate succeeds, you'd earn far more money.

"Own a business & enough money that lives forever."
- Zayd Haji

Do you like to work for others, as an employee, or want better to work for yourself and be the boss?

Some people are better as employees, and a few can become employers.
Most people start to figure for others as employees. Some still do so all their lives, but a smaller percentage, at some point, contemplate quitting their job and starting their own business.
Others start directly being their boss, but this a small percentage of individuals.
The decision to remain as an employee, quit your job, start your own business, and obtain employees to work for you requires deep thought and taking into consideration many things.

The lifetime of an employee and, therefore, an employer's presence is different. Which one does one choose?
- Do You Possess the talents for growing an Employer?
- Are you confident enough to be an employer?
- Do you have experiences for the business you would prefer to establish?
- Do you have tolerably perseverance and patience to drive on, although you lose?
- Do you have enough urge?

- Do you have the money and means to start your business?
- What skills does one ought to acquire?
- Are you assertive enough and hold enough faith in yourself and your plans? Are you able to continue, despite ridicule, failure, or discouragement?

Whatever you select, attempt to choose wisely. Consider the pros and cons of your decision. Believe whether you want and may become an employer, or even it's wiser to remain an employee.

There is a choice if you would like to possess a business of your own without becoming an employer. It is often the business of 1 person. You'll be the boss and therefore the only worker, and there many such jobs.

Now, think, what does one want to be, an employee or employer?
If you would like to be the boss or be an employer, what are you doing about it? Does one have detailed plans?

To achieve business success, you need desire, visualization, decision power, leadership skills, and marketing skills, and you need to use your all with perseverance.

To achieve money success, you need to try and do smart work, have financial literacy, tax knowledge, and pension plans, and never hand over attitude in life.

All these rules and practices authors have addressed within the book have ways in his life.

"Make one goal in your life and work on it."

Contents

Chapter-1: RULE NO.1 DESIRE

Nowadays, there is a developing enthusiasm for self-development and personal growth strategies. There are several self-improvement books, articles, and sites managing these subjects.

It appears that individuals turn and attract them to discover the answer to their issues and life problems. They look for information, webinars, consultation, talks, and educators to show them the right way of living.

Individuals understand that personal growth and self-development can improve the nature of their lives.

The process of inner growth requires developing and improve the inner self.

It isn't sufficient to read understand words written in articles and books. Best practice what you learn and read. Inner growth and change require inspiration, ambition, desire, diligence, and devotion.

When you begin with a personal growth program, it expects to experience internal obstruction from your old habits and your inner mind and obstruction and restriction from the individuals around you.

The craving to change and grow in your life, build and acquire new habits, and develop yourself must be sufficiently able to resist sluggishness and laziness, lower the tendency to surrender or quit, and dread disparagement of opposition opinions from family, companions, or associates.

Let me disclose to you something important about Al Zayd. Al Zayd has been pulled into personal growth from an early age and has viewed it as a wellspring of inner quality and joy and a path to improve his life.

One of the most reliable methods I found and utilized was a straightforward, successful strategy. It comprised observing how individuals act and act in different circumstances or situations and afterward looking inside themselves to see if I moved similarly under similar conditions.

When I saw individuals with specific characteristics of the character, or a particular sort of behavior that I didn't care for, I inspected myself to see if I had those qualities of nature as well.

If I did, I envisioned in my mind another kind of behavior. I saw myself with the opposite qualities of character in my inner being. I imagined myself in a different situation, in which I showed a new kind of behavior.

When I experienced character or behavior attributes, which I enjoyed, I considered their favorable circumstances and benefits and their significance in my life. Here, I utilized perception and confirmations and strived to authorize them in my day to day life.

Along these lines, I took in and profited a great deal from the behavior and activities of the individuals around me, at home, in the city, and elsewhere.

This activity was never to pass judgment on others or exploit them, yet to figure out the proper behavior, respond, and carry on excellently.

This lesson had another advantage. It expanded my insight and comprehension about how the mind and feelings influence individuals' behavior and activities. It gave me all the more knowledge of individuals and their conduct and how to coexist better.

The Beginning Stage of All Achievements and Successes Is Desire

The author stated, "The beginning stage of all success is desire."

Each accomplishment needs to begin with want. It is essential, and if you don't have a powerful urge, you won't try to put any exertion and time into accomplishing any objective. You will not care enough.

If you look at your life and consider the things you have accomplished, you will see that your wants and desires were behind all that you did. Indeed, even the littlest and most secondary purpose expects to want to make it work out. Each activity you make requires desire, from getting up from your bed, preparing a cake, perusing a book, learning another expertise, or building a business.

Al Zayd said it right, "The beginning stage of all success is Desire."

Would you like to turn into an active competitor and win decorations?

Would you like to claim your own business?

Would you like to turn into a notable entertainer or artist?

Would you like to turn into a head administrator or a president?

Would you like to be a successful author?

Would you like to be a decent spouse or a virtuous wife, a generous dad or a noble mother, or a good buddy or friend?

Would you like to communicate in smoothly a foreign dialect?

You have to have a powerful urge on the off chance that you do.

Why the Beginning Stage of All Achievements and Successes Is Desire?

It is fundamental. Desire inspires you, driving force, obsession, and vitality, to seek after any objective and not surrender or give up when you meet snags, resistance, or challenges.

Desire keeps you on target regardless. A feeble want, wishing, and fantasizing, are not sufficiently able to convey you forward, for a long time, until you accomplish your craving.

Desire resembles a hydro that produces power. Without this force to be reckoned with, you will presumably not accomplish a lot.

When there is a powerful urge, you see the objective before you and direct your consideration and exertion toward it.

Al Zayd comprehended what he was discussing when he stated, "The beginning stage of all success is Desire." He investigated the progress and met successful individuals in his life experiences.

Achievement Is More than Money, Possessions, and Status

When discussing achievement and accomplishment, individuals regularly consider cash, assets, and status. True, these are the indications of accomplishment and success. However, growth and progress are, likewise, numerous different things.

There are achievements and accomplishments in training, artistry, sports, composing, personal growth, reflection, and numerous territories. You can get familiar with the different implications of achievement and success by pursuing this book, "Business Money & life route to success – What Are the Definitions of Success."

It was a desire that incited Bill Gates, Steve Jobs, Warren Buffet, Mark Zuckerberg, and numerous others to make enormous progress.

It was desire and urge to become successful that made Madonna and Oprah so successful.

Only one out of every odd individual tries to reach so high and is eager to put the time into such tasks. The vast majority don't have an enormous want and gigantic desire to get so high. Each fantasy, each objective, regardless of how little it is, needs the intensity of desire to fuel it.

Your longing may be to exceed expectations at your specific employment, get an advancement, get more cash-flow, be well known inside the hover of your companions, get a new vehicle, or purchase a new house. These are the "typical" desire of many people, and they must have craving as their beginning stage.

Continuously recollect Al Zayd's words, "The beginning stage of all success is desire." Desire, in this sense, implies strong desire. It isn't something that is here today evaporates tomorrow. For success, you need a continued want. It must be robust to the point that nothing can dishearten you and stop you from following your goals.

It isn't sufficient to be inspired or enlivened by something you read or something you saw. The beginning stage of success is desire, yet it must be supported and proceeded, despite any deterrents on your way. It must be strong and sufficiently able to help you move towards progress.

"On the off chance that you can't do incredible things, extraordinarily do little things."
– Zayd Haji

"Exertion just completely discharges its prize after an individual will not stop."
– Zayd Haji

"Desire is the beginning stage of all achievements and successes, not an expectation, not a desire, yet a sharp throbbing wants which rises above everything."
– Zayd Haji

"Value your dreams and your fantasies as they are the children of your spirit, the plan of your definitive successes and achievements."
– Zayd Haji

FAITH

The Power of Faith and Positive Thinking

Positive thinking is a psychological and passionate demeanor that focuses on the splendid side of life and anticipates positive outcomes.

An individual with faith and a positive thinking mindset foresees satisfaction, wellbeing, and achievement and believes that they can defeat any impediment and trouble.

Positive thinking isn't an idea that everybody accepts and follows. A few think about it as rubbish and laugh at individuals who tail it. In any case, a developing number of individuals acknowledge the intensity of positive intuition and faith as a reality and have confidence in its viability.

As proved by the numerous books, talks, and courses about it, this subject picks up popularity.

To utilize it in your life, you need something other than to know about its reality. You have to embrace the demeanor of positive thinking in all that you do.

How the Power of Positive Thinking and Faith Works?

Rachelle's Story

Rachelle went to a job interview; however, she didn't accept she will get it since her confidence was low, and she viewed herself as a failure and worthless of success.

She had a negative mentality toward herself, and in this way, accepted different candidates were preferred and progressively qualified over her.

Rachelle's brain was busy with negative considerations and fears concerning the entire week's activity before the prospective employee meeting. She has foreseen disappointment.

At the time of the interview, she rose late, and to her wrong fear and shock, she found that the shirt she wanted to wear was messy, and the other required pressing. As it was at that point past the point of no return, she went out wearing a wrinkled shirt and without having breakfast.

During the interview, Rachelle was tense, full of negativity, eager, and stressed over her shirt. It occupied her psyche and made it hard for her to concentrate on the interview. Her general conduct established an awful connection, and therefore, she materialized her dread and didn't land to get the position.

Mike's Story

The following story is about Mike, who went after a similar position and alternately moved toward the issue. He was confident and sure that he would land the job and had a decent confidence level.

During the week before the interview, Mike frequently pictured himself establishing a decent connection and landing the position. He likewise and rehashed confirmations with that impact.

The night before the interview, he arranged the attire he would wear and rested somewhat prior. On the day of the meeting, he woke up sooner than expected and had a fair chance to have breakfast, and afterward to show up to the interview before the scheduled time.

Mike established a decent connection and landed to get the position.

The Businessman Al Zayd's Faith

Three years back, Al Zayd surrendered the non-profit and academic world to turn into an independent marketing specialist, a man whose objective was to help organizations impart their stories to the world. I liked myself something of a writer specialist, a skilled author who could outline the speaker's best arrangement, message, and the crowd.

I told individuals I was a marketer or composed of blogs, sites, and newsletters for organizations. Every so often, I would reveal to them I "had my own business." It was valid; however, I made some hard memories saying it.

My advisor likes to discuss the stories we let ourselves know how those stories may lie dormant or work unknowingly for quite a while until some occasion inspires them. Afterward, we wind up responding to the anecdote instead of the truth.

One of the more unusual stories for me had been the United Arab Emirates Dream (and I've written in Good Letters about how I needed to get over that one). Another fantastic story went something like this: Businesspeople are effective either because they know the suitable individuals, start with the sort of investment that places them in the perfect spot at the correct time or are happy to sell their spirits. I don't have the foggiest idea about suitable individuals, have an investment in any case, and am not available to violate my soul. In this manner, I won't be effective in business.

It wasn't a straightforward lesson from my childhood; it was increasingly a reality of our lives. My family never had a lot of cash, and we were consistently at the impulses of all the more remarkable business premiums.

I'll concede a piece of me considered riches as opposing my confidence. Relatives who valued riches appeared to have abstract thinking that disregarded their social points of interest, such as growing up with cash and in the correct circles, whatever one may think about their spirits.

Whatever "advancement" transpired in school instructed me that my moderate childhood qualities advised me to apply to family and legislative issues ought likewise to try investments. Yet, I would never entirely get one of those Shadow-Marxist Dynamic Relatives. I would not like to put together my economic confidence and faith concerning a hypothesis that didn't pay attention to sin.

But you know how these chapters and rules work. There's, in every case, some change. You may be leary of where this is going.

Imagine a scenario where I disclosed to you; I'm leary, myself. Imagine a situation in which I revealed to you I'm not happy with where I'm going, either.

I was late at a business occasion run by a man of confidence and faith who trusts God needs us to thrive. He acquired a speaker to enlighten us regarding God's "benefits pack" and our organizations.

It wasn't "wellbeing and riches." It indeed wasn't Marxism. It was a message from a region where confidence, faith, and capitalism private enterprise meet on the merriest of terms.

Since I felt disheartened about my business pieces, I pulled in to this present man's faith and confidence. He talked like one of my relative numerous charismatic haters, and he shared stories of the Spirit at work, for example, we frequently hear in the corporate world.

In the corporate world, we additionally know to be careful when we are powerless. It is both when God can do the most with us and when we can most handily drive off the track.

Anxious to accept, yet careful about allurement, I heard stories of the Spirit getting things done in individuals' organizations. The Spirit was associating them with the right individuals. It was placing them in the correct spots on the proper occasions. Some of the time, it was re-establishing their spirits so they could rededicate themselves to their employments.

I needed to battle to keep a receptive and open mind. These stories conflicted with those different stories, the ones where I am not an individual who makes a profit out of business. I needed to appeal to God to observe the reality of what these people talk about business.

I found that, by some mindful triangulation with different thoughts imperative to me, the particular words he expressed guided me away from the old story more than what he implied by them.

"Business," he stated, "is a vehicle for enhancing the world." That's a business-talk method of saying business is imaginative. In Al Zayd Corp's terms, it is a sub-creation type, lesser support in God himself's movement. That it is frequently crooked just methods, it requires reclamation like the remainder of our lives.

At that point, he said something that associated my religious philosophy to my wants: "On the off chance that you don't accept, where it counts, that what you are doing is acceptable, you won't give yourself entirely to it."

It's one thing to accept a job is worthy; another to trust it is acceptable. You can make do with satisfactory, yet you can live off the great.

When minding your own business, furthermore having faith in your business idea, you need all the food you can get. Yet, the world's profound rationale necessitates that you can't get a life until you have parted with your own—indeed, even in business.

Business, similar to religion or love, hints such vast numbers of various things to individuals that it feels cumbersome, a word I despise everything holds for the explicit organization in case I misperceived.

However, am I a businessperson? What's more, here, toward the start of these endeavors, I realize I have to grapple with the strict importance of my work in the case in progress. I become the very thing I looked to dodge by disappointment and failure.

The entrepreneur drives faith during pandemic COVID-19.

It possesses been exceptional energy for business visionaries and experts during the pandemic emergency of COVID-19. Nobody has been insusceptible to this quickly changing business sector scene, and many are harming financial and economical as ventures are drastically affected as a rule. If you follow me, the situation and circumstance have blended faith and confidence questions. At times of emergency crisis, uncover strengths and weaknesses, both inside our respective associations and organizations and the fear inside every one of us as people. It might even reveal the regions of our heart that we need the Heavenly Father to tend.

Maybe most altogether, these occasions make us fully aware of the little control we have and how urgently we need God. During this vulnerability period, I always reminded myself to incline toward the exercises this season has for me on a down to earth level for work and a profound level in my relationship with God. I continue hearing the guarantee from Bible Chapter 23, section 1: "The Lord is my Shepherd; I have all that I need.

Further consideration of how the worldwide pandemic has affected the economy and many of our vocations, work lives, and fates. I needed to compose an open letter to you, the faith Driven by Entrepreneur, with a couple of down to earth exercises to draw after this phenomenal time close by some otherworldly bits of knowledge:

VIRTUAL IS HERE TO LINGER: HOW WILL YOU USE YOUR TIME?

As an essential segment of the workforce is filtering through unfathomable change, it is clear working remote and virtual workplaces are digging in for the long haul. Regardless of whether you work in an industry that requests up close and personal interactions, figuring out how to adjust your work to a remote domain and environment is essential for the short-term and long-term future.

Like this, begin making sense of how to be productive and gainful in this remote condition. How you perform now can affect and impact your profession in what will surely be an undeniably virtual workforce to come. The web is creeping with work from home pieces of advice, so get your job done and be vital about building up a rhythm that works for you. There might be some new otherworldly schedules to notice as an adherent or follower.

For instance, a significant number of us aren't hurrying out the entryway for our everyday drive. We can be deliberate with reallocating this additional opportunity to our peaceful time (whatever that may resemble). Moreover, we can transform our new remote office spaces into a unique, raised area or virtual office space. Possibly your regular afternoon work break looks like meditating on God's promise or playing worship music. Oppose the need to occupy this recently gifted time with profitability. Let me state it once more, RESIST, the need to work during this pandemic freed time. Instead, begin giving this time back to God. I am sure He makes a big deal about our little, including the time we offer back to Him.

ADAPT FAST: GOD IDEAS OVER GREAT IDEAS.

As an entrepreneurial-minded expert, you are likely doing this - adjusting quickly! Numerous enterprises and professions confront unforeseen difficulties that will proceed for a continued length of time after the pandemic—your organization's reaction rate to change now and later on will direct its suitability and achievement. Start asking yourself: what would you do all alone to enable your organization to turn out to be progressively dexterous? How might you turn or tailor your services to make them essential for such a period as this? What new issues are rising that you can address as a business person? Times of emergency crisis require imaginative solutions that rush to advance in the midst of quickly moving real factors.

This season with the entirety of its hindrances likewise, implies there are numerous chances to step. However, you need not pursue down each smart thought that comes in your direction. I need to urge you to implore through ideas and approach God for His beliefs. I trust God can address us about our work. I regularly pray to God for "God's thoughts" over my best thoughts because my best never approaches His. I am praying to God for the psyche in the name of holy Christ. Ask actively for His driving on entrepreneurial undertakings you presently can't seem to try and consider!

ACQUIRE FROM LEADERSHIP: HOW DO YOU LEAD and FOLLOW CHRIST?

Regardless of your leadership has been model or disillusioning, we would all be able to gain from our leaders this season. If you have been satisfied with your leaders, let them know! Observe how they explore unfamiliar results or strategies and convey them to their representatives and investors.

On the other side, if you have undergone frustration, thoroughly consider regions that could be enhanced and lead or drive from where you are situated or positioned. Criticism during times of disorder, chaos, or emergency crisis isn't profitable and productive; innovative solutions are superior methods to help. Possibly sharing an empowering word in affection could favor your leadership in this season of trouble and stress.

In gaining from the initiative, it is fundamental to comprehend that you have to work on being a decent supporter before you can lead. Our way of life fixates on leadership, yet as Christ supporters, we should give unique consideration to that word "follow." I realize I have needed to ask myself how I would follow my leadership well during this season?

You may have various thoughts on how your organization ought to adjust. However, you also need to respect your leadership and be pious over their choices. If you are the leader at your association, make space to gain from your adherents and followers. Everybody is learning through this chapter, and humility is a crucial characteristic of Christ-like leadership.

I know many confront the exceptional individual and budgetary difficulties during this pandemic crisis. Many have lost their jobs and missed achievement occasions. If it is you, I need to expand my deep compassion. Let us lean toward network community (though for all intents and purposes), consideration, and liberality more than ever to give respect and wonder to God whose devoted loves always endures – suffering through this pandemic. Maybe expanding these ethics regardless of our conditions is the best-hidden exercise for us as faith Driven by Entrepreneurs and supporters of Jesus.

WORD FROM PSALM

I love the Passion Translation of Bible Chapter 23; I have it here to put in almost no time perusing and resting in:

The Good Shepherd

23 David's beautiful commendation to God [a] 1 The Lord is my closest companion and my shepherd.
[b] I consistently have more than enough. 2 He offers a resting place for me in his lavish love.
[c] His tracks take me to a desert spring of harmony, the tranquil stream of bliss.
[d] 3 That's the place he re-establishes and restores my life. [e] He opens before me pathways to God's pleasure and leads me along in his strides of righteousness
[f] to carry respect to his name. 4 Lord, in any event, when your way takes me through the valley of most profound darkness, fear will never conquer me, for you now have! You stay near me and lead me through it all the way. Your authority is my quality and my peace.
[g] The solace of your affection removes my fear. I'll never be forlorn, for you are near. 5 You become my delightful feast in any event when my foes set out to fight. You bless me with the scent of your Holy Spirit;
[h] you give me everything I can drink of you until my heart overflows. 6 So, for what reason would I dread the future? For your decency and love, seek after me all the times of my life. A short time later, when my life is through, I'll come back to your glorious presence to be always with you!

CONCLUSION

Longer than years into this faith lead entrepreneur approach, I have been honored to grow business and support base services, alongside leadership achievement in our business that contrasts nicely with our compatriots in the market. It is conceivable to apply a religious way to have faith in GOD, yourself, and your business idea and lead the leadership attitude. I am still on the journey of having faith in God's Word to the route of success. Being religious, God has contributed to my good deeds and provided me beneficiaries' assets, and helped increase business. That consolidates learning how to be better pursers of creation, searching for approaches to promote human thriving, and looking to be redemptive and opportunity acquirer in everything I do.

BELIEVE

Have faith and believe in Yourself (And Nothing Will Work If You Don't.)

"As I offer my thanks, I should always remember that the most noteworthy thankfulness isn't too simple words, yet to live by them."

I'm composing this chapter during Pandemic COVID19 in Mumbai, India. I'm sitting in my room, where I invest most of my energy secured by these four walls and contemplating life experience. My family has lingered out of the room, only a couple of short feet away.

As I sit back and consider what I'm grateful for during the current year, I've chosen one thing that appears to have made a difference in my life repeatedly. I'm thankful that I have faith and believe in myself.

This quality is somewhat who I am and halfway a consequence of the loved ones that have bolstered me for incredible life experience. Despite where it originates from, it is the one quality that lets me discuss what I'm grateful for and yet experience it.

No One Will Work for You Unless You Don't Work for Yourself

Not long ago, I posted a Book on Unlock Your Mind that offers simple approaches to get more open-minded and train your subconscious mind. The book generally welcomes all platforms; however, I also heard a grievance from somebody who recognized themselves as "Useless Won't Work with Me" (the internet and social is a strange spot).

That is what the Author needed to state,

"None of these methods will work for those people who think all these high-level thoughts in books are "Useless Won't Work with Them":

1. Let your plate control your bit.

My concern is that I eat until I feel full. Indeed, I can utilize a little plate; however, I'll simply prop up back until I feel complete.

2. Pick a shading that makes life simple.

In what capacity would generally be able to individuals perhaps do this? I would prefer not to have 3, 4, and 5 various dishes for each shading dinner.

3. Attempt the occasional version of discontinuous fasting. Truly. Mostly don't eat for 24 hours. This system is one type of irregular fasting.

What do I do about my craving torments? What do I do on the off chance that I need food? I'll wind up snapping at individuals around me and biting every one of my fingernails deep down."
— For That Person

I gave a valiant effort to address the statement with significant counsel that would enable the peruser to overcome the issues mentioned. Be that like it; there is a considerably more meaningful accomplishment.

Is it accurate to say that you determined to Fail?

Do you notice the topic all through the entirety of the questions? There is a propensity for self-uncertainty and defencelessness. The unspoken idea that drives these questions is, "I don't accept these thoughts will work for me." Or, expressed another way, "I don't trust I can make these thoughts work. I don't believe in myself."

Worrying over not having the option to execute a couple of diet changes is only one minuscule case of this dread. Yet, an absence of faith in yourself will restrain you regardless of how extraordinary the thoughts or opportunities are that you presented.

My most important question to the reader would be this: Why are you resolved to make these thoughts not work for you? For what reason would you say that searching for ideas, but these thoughts won't control instead of making sense of an approach to cause something meaningful to happen?

The most significant contrast between successful individuals and unsuccessful ones (in wellbeing, in business, in wealth, and throughout everyday life) is that successful individuals resolved to make the situation and circumstance work for them. They are opposed to assuming the person's job in question and searching for reasons why a scene or condition won't work.

No consideration will strive for any individual on the planet. However, numerous ideas can work for the vast majority of you believe that you can make them work. You must think unexpectedly, however, to likewise to try different things with new beliefs and confidence that you'll discover an approach to make them work.

Believe and Have Faith in Yourself

The most considerable difference I've seen between successful individuals and unsuccessful individuals isn't knowledge or opportunity, or assets. It's the belief they can cause their goals or aims to happen.

We as a whole arrangement with defencelessness, vulnerability, and disappointment, a few of us believe that if we push ahead in any case, at that point, we will make sense of it. As I stay productive here on the

Pandemic COVID-19 situation, I'm grateful that I'm one of these individuals.

When I began my business, I was the first young business person in our family. I didn't have anybody to gain and acquire skills. However, I believed that I would make sense of it and figure it out in any case.

When I commenced a flight in the night while traveling to Malaysia reaching there, I was lost and confounded. I could not discover any individual who communicated in English since most of them speak Bahasa there. Hence, as it is quite severe for me to reach my hotel, I ran close by, hopped back on, and believed that I would make sense of it at anyhow.

Whenever I've found an opportunity that sounds wonderful, however, that I'm not equipped or qualified for (which happens regularly), I believe that I'll make sense of it and pull out all the stops in any way.

I believe in myself, and this certainty has made a difference for me repeatedly. I didn't require intelligence or opportunity or assets—only a fundamental faith in myself.

Do You Think That Change Is Conceivable for You?

One of the essential beliefs of this social community is that you can become better with experience.

We accept that it is feasible for people to improve. We recognize that it is conceivable to increase current standards in your own life regardless of whether your general surroundings acknowledge normal. We trust in ourselves and one another. We accept that if you need better wellbeing or more joy or progressively significant activity, you can cause those things to occur.

What's more, in the story of this belief, I am always happy to test, trial, and attempt new things in any event when I feel dubious. If you don't accept that it's conceivable to make new ideas work, it's difficult to gain ground. I don't care how great the thoughts are; nothing will work for you if you don't believe in them. Furthermore, more significantly, nothing will work on the off chance that you don't trust in yourself.

The capacity to have confidence and believe in yourself can transform you.

Simply think:

Why might it matter in your life that you had a steady trust in your ability to achieve anything you surely set your consciousness?

What might you need and wish and trust?

What might you hope against hope if you have faith in yourself with such a profound belief that you had no feelings of trepidation or disappointment at all?

How to Believe in Yourself

Many people start with pretty much nothing or low fearlessness; however, they become stiff and bold and friendly independently. Furthermore, I've found that if you do very similar things that other self-assured people do, you, as well, will encounter the same emotions and get accurate results.

The solution is to be compatible with yourself, be consistent with the absolute best in you, and carry on with your life steady with your highest qualities and aspirations. It is the best way to genuinely figure out how to have confidence and believe in yourself.

Set aside some effort to consider your identity, what you have believed in, and what is essential to you.

If you need to transform yourself by turning into a creator, accept that you can do it. The hardest step in that excursion is finding the certainty to figure out how to compose a book. When you need a few steps to get back, some peace of a demonstrated plotting to plan, organize, and distribute your work, and the more meaningful objective gets simpler to accomplish.

By trusting in yourself, you will discover the boldness to make a prompt move on your goals. As you know, this is the way to grow and succeed!

I urge you to never bargain your honesty by attempting to be or state or feel some falsehood for yourself.

What's more, all the significantly – never bargain your ability to develop because of self-constraining proposals. Rather, grasp your certainty and trust in yourself since you honestly can do anything you set your attention to that.

Expose to Yourself You Have Faith and Believe On Your Decisions

Rehash affirmations, for example, "I trust and believe in myself" consistently.

Your musings become words, and your comments become your activities. If you keep on revealing to yourself that you believe in yourself, you indeed will have faith in yourself in the long run.

It's that reliable and straightforward.

Have the courage to acknowledge yourself as you genuinely appear to be—not to be, or as another personality might speculate you ought to be—and realize that, mulling over everything, you are a genuinely decent individual.

As a whole, we have our gifts, aptitudes, and capacities that make us uncommon.

Nobody, including yourself, has any knowledge of your abilities and capabilities or what you may, at last, go or turn. Maybe the most challenging activity in life is acknowledging how remarkable you indeed can be, believe in yourself, and afterward to join this mindfulness into your mentality and character.

SUBCONSCIOUS MIND

It Comes Down to Your Subconscious Mind

Both Warren Buffett and Bill Gates have ascribed their triumphs or successes to one straightforward standard rule: Focus. Yet, in a technology and innovation-driven society where moment satisfaction and performing various tasks are top king - and queen - our capacity to concentrate on any a sure thing, be it a goal, desire, objective, work, or habit, for a significant of time is decaying and deteriorating.

The average human's capacity to focus is just eight seconds. That may clarify why 80 percent of individuals neglect to keep their New Year's goals when February comes up. The explanation: not enough focus and short core interest. Often, individuals quit, asserting they don't have the self-control and willpower to achieve it.

Be that as it may, resolve is just 10 percent of the individual when you're acquiring or surrendering a habit. To prepare yourself to focus, you have to go further into your psyche, where the staying 90 percent of what you expect to yield or acquire new productive habit lives: inside your inner subconscious mind.

Furthermore, the chapter reading will become familiar with the term theta. Theta is the state between your subconscious mind and conscious world. Among staring off by daydreaming and sleep, this is our most profoundly loosened upstate, where innovativeness and creativity rule comes.

Yet, how would you get to theta while pounding ceaselessly at your console, running from meeting to meeting, and conversing with potential customers throughout the day? The appropriate response is Hypnosis.

It "wouldn't be called Mind control."

Presently, just to move it, Hypnosis wouldn't be called a Mind control - despite what society culture, including movies like 'The Wolf of Wall Street', attempt to persuade us. Recall that dreadful scene with Donnie Azoff cheating his way to the top? Difficult to forget, correct?

Indeed, that is not what Hypnosis is. Or maybe, what I'm discussing is a profoundly relaxed, exceptionally focused condition of mindfulness that permits you to make enduring change. As indicated by the many hypnotherapists, "Hypnosis can help you gain control over undesired practices or to assist you in adapting and coping in a better way with tension or torment. It's critical to realize that even though you're progressively open to the proposal during Hypnosis, you don't lose command over your conduct."

Every individual is independent. The individual you are may have been resolved initially by your youth or childhood encounters and experiences. However, the individual you could be is heavily influenced by you.

The special rule, "You become according to your opinion and what you think of more often," alludes to what exactly you're thinking today, at present. Your thinking about the past or your consideration for the future decides the course of your predetermination and destiny. All you are and all you will be is controlled by what you think every second. You can also assume total responsibility for those musings whenever you choose to.

You become a positive thinker by assuming responsibility for your words and statements - your self-talk. Resolve today to build up the productive habit of positively conversing with yourself.

For example, direct sentiments toward yourself, "I love myself!" or "I can do it!" repeatedly. If anyone asks you how you're feeling today, consistently answer, "I feel fantastic today!" When you think about or do your work, rehash to yourself, "I love my work! I love my work!"

Most analysts concur that altogether 95 percent of your feelings are controlled by the things you think and the words you state to yourself as you experience your day. Utilize your self-control and self-discipline to contemplate the things you need instead of permitting your brain to get distracted with the things you don't need or that you doubt and dread.

What you perceive is the point that you will be.

The most remarkable assertion or message you can send from your conscious psyche to your subconscious mind is a visualization or mental picture. Build up the habit of making clear, positive, energizing pictures of yourself performing at your best and dreams of your aims as though they were at that point achieve.

Each time you make a mental picture in your conscious psyche, you communicate something specific that actuates your subconscious mind. It triggers the law of fascination, animates your Imagination, and pushes you toward acknowledging that mental picture in your outer world.

Vivacious and successful individuals habitually visualize the results they want, develop their subconscious minds, and form their positive self-image and external performance.

The best of everything is when you join positive self-talk with positive mental imaging. You talk about the things you need, and you make energizing, visualizing the image of your goals and desires as though they previously existed.

Positive musings and words make you increasingly hopeful, give you more vitality, empower you to skip back quicker from dissatisfaction, and keep you pushing ahead for the whole day.

Feed your brain with mental protein.

Build up the habit of taking care of your psyche with festive mental food. Keep in mind, you're incredibly delicate to the impacts in your condition, regardless of whether they're radio, TV, papers, magazines, boards, or discussions with others.

Your psyche is your generally significant and valuable resource. You should secure it and keep it perfect, bright, and concentrated on what you need instead of permitting it to be contaminated by the negative impacts around you.

Refuse or Decline to watch dread or junk on TV. Try not to read much all the murders, thefts, assaults, and disaster news in the papers. Turn off the long hours of thoughtless radio commentary or time-wasting sources on all the issues on the planet. Decline or refuse to participate in endless discussions with individuals about all the political and social issues in your country or community. Keep your brain perfect, bright, cheerful, and free.

In addition to the fact that you become what you think about, you likewise become what you feed into your brain.
If you need to be confident, hopeful, and glad, consistently feed your psyche with informative and knowledgeable books and articles, listen to upbeat and motivational music. Fill in positive and productive info and data from different specialists in your field and listen to positive talks and discussions of other idealistic, goals oriented individuals who are heading off to someplace in their lives.

Get around the right and successful individuals.

Make it a habit to connect just with the sort of individuals you appreciate, regard, and need to resemble. Don't merely drink espresso with whoever happens to be sitting in the lounge. Seek not to reach out for lunch with the individual who has ambitions.

Try not to hang out after work with any individual who welcomes you. Be insightful and clear about the individuals you permit to impact your thinking and emotions with their positive opinions and words.

Dr. David McClelland of Harvard found that your "group gathering" would decide as much as 95 percent of your success or failure in your career and individual life. Your group gathering characterizes as the individuals you routinely partner with and believe to be one of them.

These can be individuals from your family, colleagues, or individuals from your congregation or social associations. The fact of the matter is, "Personalities with similarities tend to grow successful.

Al Zayd states, "You can't fly with the eagles if you keep on diving and hanging out with the crows and pigeons." — Zayd Haji

Chapter-2: RULE NO.2 VISUALIZATION

Your Imagination and Visualization Is Your Key to Success

For the most part, the creative mind and Imagination connect with daydreaming, wishing, and hallucination. The vast majority would not combine it with progress, achievement, and down to earth individuals. They, in all likelihood, think about it as unreasonable and impractical.

It is off-base. Visualization is a vital key to progress. Each desire, goals, and plan begins in the psyche, in the creative mind, and later transforms into the real world.

"Imagination is considerably more than fantasizing."

Imagination is the capacity to make mental pictures and scenes of occasions before and of imaginary future circumstances and opportunities to experience new things.

Imagination isn't constrained uniquely to seeing images in the psyche. It is conceivable to envision physical sensations, smells, tastes, sounds, music and hear individuals talking. It is likewise feasible to expect sentiments.

In your Imagination, you can make various circumstances and various conditions.

In your Imagination, you can carry on with a great life.

You can wander off in fantasy land or daydream, which would give you an extraordinary feeling. You can take some additional steps and transform your Imagination into the real world.

Imagination is the way to progress. Each goal and plan starts as a dream in the psyche. The initial step is to assemble a mental picture of what you need to do or accomplish. It resembles building a plan or drawing a guide.

At the point when you plan a vacation, you utilize your Imagination. You see yourself through your mind's eyes in the spots where you need to travel.

When you wish to heat a cake, you see the cake in your Imagination and aim to prepare it as per the picture in your mind.

Athletes utilize their creative minds to improve their performance. They picture themselves running, hopping, or tossing the ball justified and in an ideal way.

Actors, artists, painters, and journalists utilize their creative minds to deliver their best performance.

You utilize your Imagination when you expect to restore your home, plant a nursery garden, and plan a gathering.

Successful individuals picture their aims before achieving them.

Your Imagination is dependable, to a great extent, for your present life conditions. It also influences your future since what you envision now in your brain will be what you would encounter tomorrow and later on.

Creative Mind Is the Key to Success.

A creative mind or Imagination is the practice room, where you practice in your psyche for what you need to do or achieve. It is an approach to dispose of slip-ups and blunders and spare time when you continue with your activity.

Imagination has a lot to do with the real world. It shapes how we see our world and influences our desires, expectations, activities, and conduct. It implies you should be mindful of envisioning just what you truly need, not what you don't need.

Imagination is the way to progress since all you make, develop, and achievements start creating a creative mind.

At the point when you envision a specific desire, circumstance, or aims, for quite a while, the mental picture you assemble will pick up power and would be in your mind most of the time, in any event, when you don't know about it. It will drive you to look for data about the goal, make you mindful of chances concerning it, and become inspired to achieve what you are envisioning.

Imagination, Creative mind and the Law of Attraction

Imagination is the primary ability to utilize the law of fascination and attraction.

You build a picture of your aims and desires in your psyche, and you focus on this picture frequently. It develops the outline of your goals in mind.

This outline gets engraved on your subconscious mind, which thus, fortifies your inspiration, aspiration, and encourages you to perceive opportunities regarding your goals.

Rehashing your goals' mental picture sets the law of fascination or attraction energetically and pulls in what you want.

If you wish to make the law of attraction work for you, you should get familiar with a couple of mental rules and skills to utilize your creative mind and imagination successfully. It is known as innovative visualization, which implies that you use your creative spirit, Imagination, and visualization to create achievement.

This strategy can utilize broad goals and primary, common goals, such as giving a surprise to loved ones, getting tickets for a show, a parking spot, or getting more customers for your business.

Imaginative visualization and the law of attraction or fascination work together. Visualization gives the mental picture, the plan, while the appeal provides the interest within power.

After reading the chapter and becoming familiar with imaginative visualization, the time has come to figure out how to utilize it. Beneath, you will locate a concise guide for the means you have to follow to make it work for you.

It is a chapter for giving you the rudiments and understanding the most proficient method to succeed. Suppose you desire to find out further and discover everything about this intriguing power and how to utilize it in your regular daily existence. In that case, I suggest that you read the chapter and practice all the experiences shared in your everyday life.

Desire about What You Want

Although the sign of your goal may sometimes occur in an abrupt and anticipated way, it will happen naturally and continuously, one thing prompting another.

On the off chance that you want money, it won't drop on your head from the sky, and most likely, you won't win it in the lottery. It will more probably come up into your life through a job, a promotion in your role, a business deal, or different channels.

Our considerations, thoughts, emotions, and feelings, and the mental pictures we convey in our minds, influence our lives. By evolving them, we transform ourselves. By considering achievement, we draw in progress.

Be cautious about what you think and how you feel; else, you may draw in the circumstances you don't generally need. It is more satisfying to think and conceive just what you truly and genuinely need in every situation.

Approach this psychological work with an uplifting demeanor, genuineness, and confidence, and don't get disheartened on the off chance that you can't picture obviously, or if nothing happens right away. Give this method of time.

The principle ability is your Imagination. You can get results, regardless of whether you can't envision obviously.

Improving Your Imagination

Imagination is an ability to improve via preparing, similar to some other aptitude. Here are two activities to assist you with improving it.

Exercise Number 1

Sit serenely on a seat, in a spot where you won't be upset.

For example, grasp a fruit, an apple, an orange, or some other natural product. Please take a look at it mindfully from all sides for about a moment, smell it, and feel its surface.

After around one moment, close your eyes and attempt to visualize or imagine the fruit for a moment or two. Attempt to envision its shape and shading, smell, and surface, as you are taking a look at it.

On the off chance that the picture of the fruit gets obscured and you can't imagine unmistakably, open your eyes and take a look at the fruit for a couple of moments, and afterward close your eyes and keep envisioning the fruit.

Rehash this activity a couple of times each day. If you wish, you may utilize various fruits every day.

Exercise Number 2

As in the past exercise, sit serenely on a seat, in a spot where you won't be disturbed.

Close your eyes and find in your creative mind and Imagination an enjoyable get-away or vacation you had in the past. You may likewise picture a spot you like visiting or a gathering you delighted in attending. It could be anything you delighted in doing.

Cause the scene as genuine as you can, attempt to hear the individuals and the sounds, imagine the environmental factors, and feel the delight you had.

Do this for 2-3 minutes, a few times each day.

If you wish, you may picture better places or scenes consistently.

Utilize the Imagination to Achieve Goals

Your Imagination and creative mind can change your life when you utilized them perfectly. Imagination isn't merely wandering off in fantasy land or daydreaming and holding up things to change with no exertion. There must be a powerful urge, focus, determination, and readiness to make a move.

As said before, your Imagination builds the outline of your desire in the psychological world; however, you have to drive forward, envisioning your goals as of now achieved. You need constancy, an open mind to perceive chances and opportunities and utilize the options.

What you regularly envision in your mind gets engraved on the subconscious mind psyche, and afterward, the subconscious mind deals with your sake to make your desires work out.

You can exploit this procedure and make positive changes throughout your life. To do such, you have to figure out how to utilize innovative visualization.

Innovative visualization and the law of fascination or attraction can change your life when you use them effectively. You can figure out how they work and utilize them to make achievements and roll out the improvements you need in your life. It has been clarified obviously in the chapter.

This rule in the chapter is a finished seminar on innovative visualization, clear and straightforward to adhere to directions and guidance.

From Innovative visualization to Reality – Drawing Success with Mind Power

Innovative visualization is a psychological strategy that utilizes the creative mind, mental pictures, musings' intensity, and the law of attraction to make dreams and objectives work out as expected.

Utilized in the correct manner of innovative visualization can improve your life and pull in to your achievement and thriving. It is an influence that can modify your condition and environmental circumstances, cause the desire to occur, and draw in money, assets, work, individuals, and love into your life.

Innovative visualization utilizes the brain and musings forces and is the force behind each achievement.

By visualizing a specific desire, circumstance, or a thing, you draw it into your life. It may look like enchantment; however, there is no enchantment included, just the normal process of the intensity or power of contemplations, thoughts, and reasonable mental laws.

Some individuals commonly utilize this method in their ordinary daily affairs, not staying aware that they are using a type of intensity or power. Every single capable individual intentionally or unknowingly uses it, pulling in the achievement they need into their life by visualizing or envisioning their goals as effectively practiced.

Innovative Visualization and the Power of Thoughts

The inner mind acknowledges the musings and mental pictures you frequently rehash in your psyche. This psychological practice changes your attitude as needs be, just as your habits and activities.

These rehashed contemplations, thoughts, and mental pictures draw in and carry you into contact with individuals, circumstances, and conditions that will, in general, change what you thought and imagined into the real world.

It occurs because thoughts have a creative force that shapes your life and draws you what you think about in your daily presence.

Thoughts head out, starting with one mind then onto the next. If they are sufficient, they can unknowingly and unconsciously get by individuals who are in a situation to assist you in achieving your goals and desires.

We are a piece of the Omnipotent Power that has made the universe, and hence, we take an interest during the time spent in the world's process. It is one reason that contemplations or thoughts emerge.

Stop for a second and think – You are a solid piece of the incomparable Universal Power!

It implies your considerations and thoughts can work out as expected! Not every one of your musings, yet those that are focused, very much characterized and frequently rehashed.

The thought is a vitality, particularly an engaged idea splashed with passionate dynamism or energy. Thoughts change the equalization or balance of life around us and acquire changes to nature's understanding.

Many people think about their present situation and environmental condition, on their issues and challenges, and like this, make and reproduce a similar kind of circumstances and needs.

To transform your life, you have to change your musings and thoughts!

This procedure, of continually thinking about your present life conditions, protects the balance "world" and the norm. It resembles watching a similar movie on and on. Fortunately, you can turn the film by changing your contemplations and thoughts. You can imagine various conditions and circumstances, and along these lines, make an alternate "reality."

By changing your musings and mental pictures, you change your "Existence."

You can utilize the mental pictures in your mind to make an alternate reality.

You are not utilizing enchantment or heavenly powers. You are using just natural forces and laws that everybody has. It isn't something "Material" that you change. You just change your musings and disposition; however, they change and reshape your reality.

If, for the case, you live in a small condo or apartment and need a bigger one, rather than agonizing about your destiny and lack of cash, change your musings and demeanor, and pictures were living in a more fabulous garret. It isn't hard to do. It resembles wandering off in fantasy land.

Overcoming or Conquering Limited Thinking

Innovative visualization can do extraordinary things; however, for each individual, there are a few regions where the person in question may discover hard to change, at any rate in the short term. The power or intensity of visualization is a forceful and mighty force; however, there are a few cut-off points to utilizing it. These cut-off points are inside us, not in the strength or power.

We frequently confine ourselves and can't look past a limited circle. We restrict ourselves by our considerations and convictions. We restrain ourselves to the existence we know.

The more open-minded or receptive we can be, and the higher we set out to think, the more prominent are our chances and potential outcomes. Impediments are inside our minds, and it is dependent upon us to transcend them.

It might require some investment until things begin to change. Essential, little showings of this force may come quick, yet more exceptional outcomes may require a more extended chance to occur.

The time and exertion outlined in this chapter are incredibly beneficial. Have confidence and persistence, and results will begin showing up or appearing.

Innovative Visualization Example

Quite a while back, before I got into a relationship, I chose to visualize or imagine getting a date. I envisioned myself sitting in an eatery and conversing with a young lady. I concentrated on this picture a few times during the day, a few minutes each time.

The following day, women working in a similar spot where I worked allowed me to chat with her. I barely ever talked with her, perhaps trying to say hello. I went to her work area, asking me whether I had a sweetheart. When she heard that I didn't, she disclosed that she needed to acquaint me with one of her friends. I agreed, and she gave me the telephone number of her companion.

When I returned home, I called the young lady and requested her to meet me. We met around the same time in an eatery, precisely as I visualized.

It occurred within around 24 hours. Astounding right? This force can now and again work truly quick.

Gracious, you are interested to realize what occurred with that date?

Nothing, since she was not the type of young lady I admired for a soul mate or a girlfriend. I utilized the power of perception rather heedlessly, not contemplating the subtleties and what kind of individual I needed to meet. I just thought about a gathering or a meeting with a young lady, and it was a desire that worked out as expected.

It motivated me to think about the subtleties of what I need, and I must be explicit and transparent with my desires and goals.

"Without leaps of a creative mind or dreaming, we lose the enthusiasm of conceivable outcomes. Imagining creative ideas in mind is a portrait of planning."

"Creative mind is the air that breathes life into dreams."

"Creative mind and imagination can change the world."

"The creative mind is a brilliant pathway all over."

"Vision is the specialty of seeing things undetectable."

"A book is a big ocean to ignite knowledge in the creative mind."

Over the years, numerous individuals have addressed me about their business strategies and marketing needs, which are too early in their thinking to begin. While they may have thought about what they need to sell and whom, they haven't identified what will make them distinctive enough to succeed. They want to get on board with the fleeting trend only.

Many of the enormous success stories out there are called "disruptors" - where, through innovation and "out of the box" thinking, they created ways of making individuals' lives simpler and progressively convenient.

For instance, Airbnb permitted individuals to discover accommodation effectively or efficiently in their desired destinations and encouraged individuals to save space by utilizing it and making money. Uber took the opportunity of a populace of individuals ready to drive individuals around for less and gave travelers an approach to get around less expensive.

That gets many individuals encouraged and excited "that could be me!"

Indeed, it's an extraordinary opportunity to begin another business, yet numerous individuals have unrealistic thoughts on what it takes. They want to set up their new business and consider themselves successful as these substantial hitters.

Confidence is right; however, we should be practical here. There are such vast numbers of excellent services and products out there, and you should be truly clear how you're bizarre. If you avoid this significant step, you'll lose all sense of direction in the clamor, never gain traction and at last - fall for failure!

"A nitty-gritty proposal for doing or succeeding something is Planning."

Looking at this thought, this could mean various things to a lot of different people. To me, it implies direction. It involves knowing what I need to achieve through planning.

You need to have a plan. How often have you heard that before? However, don't make a plan only for making an arrangement or succeed. You make a plan to focus, to push you ahead. Your project needs to contain an activity or action to be acceptable. Else, you'll have desires and only dream of success.

To be prosperous, you have to apprehend what your subsequent step is. It ought to be an unmistakably characterized process unless everything descends to your plan. Achievement conceived by making plans for the future, at that point, following up on those plans consistently. If you have clarity, at that point, you can move quicker. It doesn't imply that things won't disrupt or disturb your schedule or make you change them. Your idea is your guide and your plan.

For what reason do you need a plan?

1. Provides you clear guidance

2. Eliminates interruptions and distractions

3. Forestalls empty mind

4. Permits you to keep yourself responsible, so you are moving toward your dreams and goals

As you figure your plan, ask yourself, what are your non-negotiables. Whom do you depend? The steps you exert daily and long haul premise should reflect your esteem and value. It appears to be sufficiently straightforward; however, individuals can act contrary to their confidence.

Three overall plans make you believe that you should be successful. They will help you classify your desires and goals and move you from one zone to the next with more certainty, confidence, focus, and speed. Each plan expands on the other and reinforces them.

Life Plan

Your purpose and goals are a major one to take a gander at what you truly desire throughout everyday life. What do you need in your vocation? For your family? For your life? For your wellbeing?

The plan gets you more like a finished pattern of action. Goals, targets, and dreams, the contemplations you think controls everything, and you have to focus on them. One little move can make a psychological trigger that drives new activities and actions according to your thought. Affirming what is conceivable every day makes the inspiration to act.

Deals Plan

It is the manner in how you assault the commercial marketplace. It is the plan that makes every single other plan of action conceivable. It takes care of everything else. If you possess a solid deal plan, it will help you accomplish your life plan. Many individuals go through 20 to 30 years with similar deals plan without evolving them. If you think out how to present, you can do anything at that point.

Day Plan

What do you have to do each day to achieve your life and deals plan successful? What are you going to do today? Note it down. Each time you work out your day, you'll have more conviction and direction. Planning your day gives command over your decision. At that point prompts control over your clients or contacts, who rises to pay and, this fortifies or strengthens your business plan.

If you can't apply control, you can't make an expectation. You need to assume liability for your life by controlling it. Utilizing these three plans will make a conviction in your life, which prompts more certainty. When you are confident, you feel persuaded or motivated - and that is the point at which you quit thinking and take action. Achievement is a process. Follow the rules and put them to work.

BUSINESS EXPERIENCES & ACHIEVEMENTS

Achievements for Successful Venture Planning

Business visionaries draw up business strategies for new ventures to make different showcasing, evaluating, financial, and various projections. However, as a rule, their evaluations bear a small relationship to the real world. These creators contend that anticipating new undertakings varies overall from planning for existing organizations, given new companies' inherent instability. How can managers launch new ventures expect adequately for the numerous unknown's experience?

Distinguishing achievements over the undertaking and project's life empowers organizers to learn about its viability and changes in procedure and fundamental goals. The creators depict ten run of the milestone achievements that new organizations pass, including concept and strategy testing, first financing, market testing, creation start-up, and customer feedback and responses.

Leaders must match their suspicions with positive results at each stage and decide if and how to continue to achieve.

Starting a business is mostly an analysis. Verifiable in the report are a few theories (usually called assumptions) that can be tried distinctly by understanding and gaining experience. The business person dispatches the undertaking and attempts to set it up while approving or invalidating the assumptions.

Since some will be dead wrong and others mostly wrong, a fundamental goal of business planning must be to create and expand on new knowledge continuously. Directors must legitimize moving to each new stage or achievement in the program dependent on knowledge acquired in the past advance.

Adapting growth is essential for venture chiefs and investors, senior corporate supervisors, and executives. It can help them settle on educated choices about whether to support each stage, as signs of the business's potential unfurl. They can utilize our achievement to measure the executive's performance by analyzing what acquires and how viably the venture organizers have adjusted plans to react to new knowledge instead of using projections versus versions and executions as the measure.

Achievement planning is not new. Customarily, however, such a plan depends on foreordained dates for audits or venture completions. The issue with date milestone achievement is that they are inconsistent with new ventures. Subsequently, we propose that chiefs taking on financing decisions instead as occasions are completed, utilizing what they have quite recently learned how to build, off-limits, or redirection decisions. New undertakings may require a few deadlines and limitations.

For example, ongoing enterprises for wellbeing and indoor tennis have incorporated a fulfillment date that would permit the club to open for the coming season—each achievement connected to complying with this time deadline.

For most endeavors, ventures, nonetheless, significant occasions—not dates—ought to decide achievements. The first hard times in the plan should be remotely forced, for instance, by factors like agreement understandings or competitive and opponent pressures.

This way of dealing with achievement planning has three interest points for ventures.

1. It stays away from expensive confounding mistakes.

2. It gives consistent and down to earth achievements for learning and for rethinking the whole endeavors.

3. It offers a strategy for "rethinking" because of a developing assortment of ever-harder data.

Composing the Plan

To give a milestone achievement, most extreme learning values the business strategy and plan must characterize the occasion's finishing with the goal that chiefs can test any assumptions they make. For instance, a schedule would not peruse:

"Achievement—consummation of business advancement." A superior, progressively specific proclamation would be:

"Achievement—fulfillment of business advancement. Finishing off a model device that costs close to $150,000; that can fabricate for an immediate expense of $12,000; that can create 40 gadgets for every moment at 30 cents for every gadget; that the FCC authority will affirm; and that secondary school graduates can work with three days of training."

As organizers arrive at every achievement, they can contrast results with the definite determinations to discover whether their different assumptions despite everything hold. At that point, they can utilize their experience to settle on choices about the subsequent stages.

For instance, assume you are dealing with the venture we have quite recently portrayed. After completing business product advancement, you learn that the assumptions show up all around established, then again; actually, the cost will be $30,000 rather than $12,000. You realize that you have to discover how you can change the value. Is there still a market at another cost?

Do you proceed with the venture, divert it, or prematurely end it? How does the new target market contrast from the one you originally anticipated? Does the model have some other highlights—negative or positive—you had not envisioned? By what means will you approach changing your plan? What will the progressions and change educate you?

Few entrepreneurs or business visionaries utilize such planning and anticipating their new ventures, unequivocally delineating a sequence of occasions. Progressively are astonishing results of not planning altogether: the attendant mistiming's, elevated income "consume rates," and the aggregation of misfortunes and losses.

All enterprises are unique, and keeping in mind that each occasion in a product's history can show something, our experience recommends a few significant achievements that are probably going to be generally huge. We depict them in this perusing, and for each significant event, we pose appropriate inquiries and offer exercises based on genuine and actual cases.

Milestone 1: Completion of Concept and Merchandise Testing

This level functions at a genuinely low cost relative to future steps and precedes real product improvement; indeed, it frequently comes before any development within the least.

This phase's reason is to parent out whether to continue with any more development. At now, planners remember whether an actual market want exists for the products as they have conceived it or the model they've evolved, or whether it is a doubtlessly fatal flaw. At this milestone, marketers may additionally have determined a unique opportunity because of the outcomes of testing their original concept and changing it.

The concept testing demands that situation assumptions make approximately desired product characteristics, target markets, pricing range, and the notion of need. Planners want to invite themselves to the following questions:

- Have we shown that an opportunity exists with a good upside advantage to warrant the specified dangers and charges?
- What has this check taught us that modifies our assumptions and, thus, possibly, product-development goals and target markets?

Concept and merchandise version testing is possibly the littlest amount of costly methods of avoiding expensive failure if planners link product-improvement selections to consequences. While some actual improvement, production, and test advertising may additionally appear cheap enough to warrant casting off this stage, it's splendid cost as a safeguard against self-fable and as a source of alternative-possibility identification in each situation.

For example, long before starting improvement work, marketers at some stage in a statistics processing machine assignment in the 1970s identified via interviews with ability users relatively perfect characteristics for the processor. They then verified important goal markets with special programming needs in law corporations and authorities' agencies.

Long earlier than they initiated expensive microprogramming efforts, the founders considerably revised the initial product concept, supported the study's outcomes to be a software package in place of a combined hardware-software product.

Milestone 2: Completion of Prototype

Entrepreneurs can achieve many beneficial facts from carefully reading prototype improvement. They ought to seem precisely at what brought about roadblocks and disappointments and, therefore, how they overcame them; the seeds of great, hidden possibilities dwell the creative answers to those frustrations.

For example, in one task to expand a specialized, interactive information retrieval service, the software programmer finally needed training sessions, notably new programming processes, to beat a substantial records-searching bottleneck.

When the entrepreneurs searched for training inside things, they realized that they had an essential invention on their hands, which they patented. The invention's profit capacity is ten instances extra than that of the number one enterprise and evolved at a fraction of the worth.

To apply classes from prototype completion, entrepreneurs have to answer the following questions:

1. What assumptions did we make approximately development time and expenses, and consequently, how have they changed? Why?
2. What effect have those modifications had on our plans and timing concerning new hires,

plant construction, advertising, and marketing, then forth?

3. How do they affect financial needs and schedules?

4. What have we read about laborers' supply, system availability, and expenses, and consequently, how does this affect our pricing plans?

5. Do our observations and assumptions approximately our goal markets nonetheless hold? If not, how have they changed, and therefore the way will the changes affect our plans—targets, timing, and resource utilization—for each subsequent event?

6. Do the product's characteristics match with the number one concept and idea? Does this create any new opportunities? How have we altered our moves as a consequence?

7. Are our assumptions regarding full-size competition and aggressive product traits nonetheless valid?

8. How ought to we revise our funding requirements?

9. Are our projections approximately crucial providers and restore distributors nevertheless accurate?

If planners anticipate product-development time to be lengthy, they will find it useful to divide improvement activities into sub milestones for review.

Milestone 3: First Financing

Whether the first outdoor financing is for capital to look at the concept's capability, start-up financing for development and market testing, or first-degree financing to provoke manufacturing or sales, the entrepreneur should understand how investors perceive the task.

Businesses ought to compete within the capital also as product markets to survive. Entrepreneurs ought to view securing financing as a possibility to are looking for out about their ventures' acceptable financial and expense shape because of the particularly aggressive monetary marketplace.

For example, a publisher searching for the budget for an alternative mag soon found out that traders objected to her plan because she had budgeted to purchase an oversized piece of the capital system. In the course of a revised policy, she estimated leasing the system at standard rates; over again, she encountered endurance.

Eventually, she assured a supplier to allow her the device for the first nine months of operations. In conjunction with her determination, this good help to cash-waft projections enabled her to secure the investment she needed. What becomes a vital way for such a situation changed that handled rejection as a possibility to ask why the plan failed. He or she found out what investors considered to be the perfect economic shape.

Milestone 4: Completion of Initial Plant Tests

Entrepreneurs must use plant exams (or pilot operation for a provider venture) to the task or alternate their assumptions and produce facts about the following:

- Material suitability and fees
- Processing expenses and skills
- Investment prerequisites
- Training needs for production personnel, reject probabilities and costs, and excellent control requirements
- Material uniformity from suppliers
- Processing specifications, run time, and maintenance

New information about these elements will enhance overall performance and fee estimates at some full-scale operations.

In one case, marketers who were pilot testing a new technique authorized the assembly of a frozen food product aimed at the conventional market for such products.
The meals-carrier market—found that the product became more durable than absolutely everyone had thought it would be. By asking themselves what new opportunity this difference created, the founders recognized the chance to patron advertising.

Because the product was sturdy enough, they might robotically produce it in small programs and deliver it excessive product visibility, which had never achieve earlier than in this product category. The planners had assumed that the brand new product, just like the old one, might be fragile and could require exorbitantly high priced manual packaging. Company executives revised the advertising plan to include patron and meals-provider advertising, marketing, and selling.

Providentially, the administrators had also decided not to enter any licensing negotiations until they had found out all they might from the navigator experience. They may increase projected royalties without ability clients accusing them of reneging on prior deals.

Milestone 5: Market Testing

The first worrying demanding situations of the venture's simple marketplace assumptions arise at this milestone. The questions managers ask themselves now are:

- Have customers confirmed that they'd purchase the product? Why are they buying it? Why are they now not shopping for it?
- Is it genuinely distinct from and superior to the competition?
- Are the pricing assumptions nevertheless valid, considering emerging information about charges?
- Does the product perform properly in diverse field applications? Where do the problems lie, and why?
- How must we modify estimates of conceivable marketplace share and size and target markets?
- Are our servicing-requirement assumptions accurate?
- What effect does this information have on plans and timing?

An institution of folks who had developed a new electronic device for beginner band musicians decided to construct a profitable small commercial enterprise. The first step turned into to produce some hundred tools for marketplace testing. The entrepreneurs determined to make no dedication to fixed prices until they had learned from marketplace checks at what volumes the product would promote.

So they subcontracted all responsibilities and progressed to test the market within reality, with no overhead. Test market consequences confirmed the enterprise capability to be marginal, and the inventors dropped the assignment with a negligible loss.

Milestone 6: Production Start-up

The first, an unbeaten production run, checks the revised assumptions generated from pilot operations. The first runs are likely to expose several issues that need solving. Most vital, challenge planners will research the actual charges of manufacturing a consistent glide of the product and meeting first-rate necessities. Unfortunately, marketers continuously miscalculate the time this manner takes and its effect on future events' timing, specifically plans to expand the advertising effort and financing requirements.

Selling and making shipping commitments in anticipation of plan manufacturing can lead to intense strain to get the product out. Attempting to squeeze the product out of a plant going for walks into start-up issues can compromise outcome satisfaction alongside manufacturing at massive rejection rates, both of which supply upward push to purchaser dissatisfaction and waste enormous quantities of supplies. This wicked culture can destroy a new enterprise.

In the baked cake store's start-up, a brand new shop estimated up from a pilot operation ran into first-class issues from looking to produce an excessive amount of too soon. Because the proprietors had already made sizeable transport commitments to customers, many of whom had in flip employed sales forces to promote the product, the brand new enterprise observed itself operating at full scale with rejects at 20 instances the planned level. The owners needed months to remedy the issues and years to recover from the losses.

Planners can satisfactorily control production start-ups by making up a separate critical-course milestone plan and imparting stock accumulation earlier than shipments.

Milestone 7: Bellwether Sale

It is the first great sale to a likely primary account in the industrial marketplace. In the client enterprise, that is the first crucial sale to a giant distributor. Achieving this sale is probably to provide the new enterprise a considerable push forward; failure to perform it can end up a stumbling block to income growth. Entrepreneurs analyze the following from this milestone.

- The product compares with the opposition in the real world place on limited attention on the basis.
- Whether the product is functional
- Whether to preserve or adjust the original promoting method.
- Information about carrier requirements on persevering with a basis
- Additional facts regarding high-quality controls and specifications

Ideally, the bellwether sale might be to a vital prospect who has been in touch with the owners in the course of the entire development of the brand new commercial enterprise and whose needs the proprietors have considered alongside the way. Further possibilities may also present themselves.

Federal expresses enjoy with IBM as an early huge consumer, illustrates the learning opportunities this milestone offers. Instead of congratulating itself on its good fortune, Federal Express investigated why IBM become such a strong customer and found out. That the enterprise becomes the usage of its carrier to lessen inventories of very high priced components that IBM service bureaus held to support patron service.

Federal Express then modified its advertising and marketing attempt. It targeted an enormous part of its advertising on its industrial clients' specific desires in the most effective promoting package deal delivery providers. Thus, the organization rapidly identified and secured a much larger industrial, commercial enterprise than expected.

Milestone 8: First Competitive Action

Entrepreneurs can't know how the competition will respond to a new product or service in advance. However, it is viable to plan opportunity responses to sustainable movements and observe them learn what rivals' exact competitive function is.

Consider the case of an instrument organization that, during early 1984, evolved a quite revolutionary microprocessor-primarily based device. Its entire marketing campaign relied on how close a giant competitor came to coming out with identical merchandise. The top businesspeople reasoned that the brand new product's reaction could reduce its existing products' fees to lessen inventories if the opponent were near.

On the alternative hand, the competitor would first strive to protect its share by growing its sales promotion, advertising, and different advertising efforts if it has been now not equipped with a similar new product. When the opposition did no longer cut expenses, the instrument corporation moved aggressively into the market, and by using overdue 1984, it nevertheless needed itself.

In another instance, a leading travel wholesaler added a series of tours to the Middle East however hoped to discourage its most significant competitor's widespread follow-the-leader reaction. The wholesaler deliberately held off from its most massive advertising and promotion activities until the competitor acted.

The wholesaler figured that if the competitor tentatively entered the market by offering the simplest one or two excursions, that could signify the most effective half-hearted commitment. If it came on a grander scale, it meant business. When the competitor presented the best one tour, the wholesaler replied with a blockbuster marketing campaign, which scared the competition away.

Milestone 9: First Redesign or Redirection

Entrepreneurs may also discover that they want to remodel the product or modify the target market at any factor at the milestone course. This redirection may recast potentialities for the entire venture or, at the alternative extreme, create whole new regions of opportunity via defining follow-on product or marketplace needs. At this factor, marketers examine the differences between what they have provided and what the marketplace wishes.

The redecorate or redirection decision is a time for re-examining all of the simple assumptions regarding market size, segments, funding requirements, pricing, and financing (both needs and availability).

An interesting example is the design and marketing of Apple Computer's Lisa to fight the IBM PC with enhanced features and capability. Although significantly renowned for its technical aspects, Lisa's sales lagged, and Apple discontinued it. However, the agency noticed a capacity market in the personal pc area for a lot of Lisa's capabilities. Apple consolidated several of them into its Macintosh at a far more economical price and reached a mass marketplace.

Another case includes Thermo-Fax, which failed when 3M introduced it for researchers copying library documents. The corporation redesigned the product for the office market, and it became reasonably profitable.

Milestone 10: First Significant Price Change

New venture planners should base all their pro forma activities on assumptions regarding expenses, costs, and opposition. The actual price of a service or product is difficult to know until the employer launches it in a competitive environment. Changes in competition, technology, and fees may additionally force a significant fee revision, which, because of its direct effect on the bottom line, could make this milestone the most vital in determining whether to abandon a task or redirect it. Entrepreneurs need to invite themselves at this stage:

- Will the price exchange be everlasting or temporary?
- Is the commercial enterprise possible if this modification is perpetual?
- If no longer, what can we do to restructure fixed and variable prices to make them viable?
- Can we isolate the charge alternative to a selected market division?

In one example, the electronics business administrators desired to deliver virtual switching gear to the telecommunications field. They encountered strong rate resistance from telecommunications corporations while providing the device for sale as a unit. The fee assumptions had been wrong because an inadequate incentive existed for replacing the current product. Management offered to put in the system and rate according to utilization basis; however, it still had no success. Their charge assumptions have been wrong because the new charge would be too excessive for the agencies' customers.

Finally, management unbundled the services and supplied fashionable switching at a low line with utilization value for the direct customers and specialized switching options (which include automatic catastrophe or other emergency signals) for the client's month-to-month condominium basis. This method succeeded.

Milestones, Millstones, or Tombstones?
Milestone reviews are needless, except managers use them for making selections. The decisions help planners decide what they can do to fulfill or reduce the fee of failure.

Each new task has a set of milestones. Descriptions of these critical activities need to be an assertion of the excellent proposals that managers need to request to examine their opinions at every stage. Such layout forces planners to research and re-plan the idea of what they have found out. The milestone method satisfies the dual need for planning and versatility and makes apparent the hazards of neglecting linkages between festive occasions.

Decision selections at every milestone not confined to pouring more money into making the exceedingly improbable arise or aborting the assignment altogether. Equally feasible possibilities consist of slowing down, speeding up, learning more, redirecting, converting scale, or suspending or resequencing precise movements.

The point is that milestone making plans take entrepreneurs on the lowest possible cost to the next crucial stage. They can make informed selections in preference to blunder along adhering to a hard and fast plan that, out of lack of know-how, they have based on faulty projections.

In summary, we advocate that new venture managers undertake the following process while growing an enterprise plan:

1. Identify the important events or moves that should occur to acquire your objectives.

2. Determine which activities are conditions to others: the crucial sequential hyperlinks among occasions.

3. Develop a critical-direction milestone chart that graphically shows the collection.

4. Identify the many assumptions on which the assignment's fulfillment depends.

5. Ask if an occasion on the milestone chart will look at every assumption. If no longer, layout this kind of step and insert it. Specify what facts will update the belief and how you may reap it.

6. Every occasion takes place and replaces assumptions with data, overview the planned future

activities. Where vital, trade their sequence and nature. Evaluate the commercial enterprise based on evolving and changing projections. Ask yourself alongside the way: Do the upside gain, downside risk, and feasibility assessment nonetheless justify transferring ahead?

7. Establish an evaluation time table that relates to the occasion final touch in addition to time factors. Evaluate performance based on what you have discovered and what you can apply.

8. Rather than argue about whether effects met projections, design financing rewards—and aid allocations and rewards—based on the consequences achieved.

"Stop challenging yourself. Work hard and make success fall for you."

"It never receives easier. You just get better."

"Tough times don't last. Tough human beings do."

"A small improvement each day provides massive results."

Chapter-3: RULE NO.3 DECISION MAKING

A real-life story of more suited decisions at practice:
From obscurity to an outcome

This real-life story on decision-making will help you
understand whichever problem-solving and decision-
making in management practices exist.
Making a decision has never been a senseless
practice. Every time it's a conscious attempt to deliver
high percentages of success.

It was a hot, bright summer day. A weary man was
walking by a desert. Not a cold drop of water was with
him anymore. He seemed weak and deemed he
would surely die if he could not satisfy his thirst.
However, keeping light of hope in intention, he was
walking forth. He was loosening his speed but couldn't
bear to quit. After all, he had lost his direction as well.

Swiftly, he saw a shelter. He could not believe his
sights. Was that a hallucination? He queried if he was
hallucinating. Finding his last dab of energy, he
arrived at the endpoint.
The hut destroys. No one was there; then, heart
leaped a beating fast. Surprisingly saw a hand pump.
What a miracle! But his over-excitement promptly
came down when he noticed no water it.

He was nearly to give up out of discouragement.
Then he superintended the room. Suddenly, he saw a
glass of water in the corner of the room. Would that
satisfy his thirst?

His gut sense drew him to that corner. There he noticed a piece of paper under that glass. It addressed, "Use this water to commence the pump. Do not forget to refill this glass and re-corked it carefully." Out of wonder, he turned the paper. There was a map on which the next place of getting water guided, distant from the shelter.
And here, the difficulty began!

What should he do momentarily? He paused and pondered for a while. He can drink that glass of water and conserve his life spontaneously. In that situation, he would not be worthy of bringing along any water on his way forward. Also, no one else who would turn up there will capture a drop of water to preserve their life. But if he aspired to follow the paper's guidance and didn't serve, he would die.
That single glass of water might serve his immediate necessity and allow succeeding or better the immediate and long-term expectations both.

In any matter, he had to exert a chance – sooner or later. The darkness of the decision gave beginning to confusion in his judgment. His palms were trembling; he closed his sights and lingered praying. He controlled the emotion, practiced his argumentation, and opted for the second opportunity.

Hurray! He yelled at the top of his decision.
To his great pleasure, cold refreshing water got out of the pump in glug-glug turbulence. He drank it similar to a thirsty crow, refilled the glass, and corked it as per guidance. Moreover, he continued following the command, "Believe me, it works."

He also refilled his bottle, relaxed a while, and commenced his journey again with a grin on his look. Is it pure luck or a simple thought structure that enabled him to execute such a complicated decision?

This story on decision making assures me of a real-life situation. I've understood it from a very senior person.

Yes, it was the right decision taken by the person at the right time when the time was a barrier, and the best choice was required.

Decision-making is expertise. It is also base on ability and manners.
We often challenge ourselves what decision-making is and how we can execute the 'right' decision?

The achievement concerning the decision-making rule ensures one's ability to interpret the condition (problem statement), predecessors of the practices, risks, and chances. Once we find out many options, a conscious decision has to exert. Decision-making plays a crucial purpose in all situations. That's what we acquired from this narrative on decision making, and it served in problem-solving.
Decision making in guidance practices plays an essential role in personal and organizational progress.

In everyday life, we ought to take our journey and execute our own decision. A knowledgeable choice is perpetually better than an instantaneous decision. Set aside delegates, unwanted opinions, and ideas from others and believe in yourself. Decision making is a practice as well as interpersonal abilities, which should sustain. The process promotes us to be responsible – honestly and emotionally.

- Decision making is a practice.
- Decision making can learn.
- Decision-making experiences can nourish.

Bettering decision-making abilities will get from the knowledge obtained from experience. Employing inspiration and thinking decision making can nourish.

Presenting the best decision is a vital ability at every level. What's our value of confusion and the importance of clarity? It is easy to conceive.

What's best may not forever be successful & what's popular might not perpetually be right.

We all execute decisions every moment in our life. We purchase a pack of chip lays instead of a chocolate cake from the bakeshop, and we pass when it's a red signal, and no cars are befalling even when we know it's not that secure. We decide to mislead personally with social media instead of going on with our job. We want to sleep until the alarm past even though we could be extremely productive if we grew up earlier. We decide to foster our failures at someone, intimately conscious that there are better ways to release our anger.

Why is it that our experiences' unusual decisions are so difficult to execute? As mentioned above, the findings are something I prefer to term 'impulse decisions.' These are decisions we deliver on the scene, which appear to have only short-term outcomes — I say it 'appears' here because these decisions' assumptions may well end up doing more long term than we believe.

For example, passing when it's a red signal could begin moving over. Likewise, continually misleading yourself with social media could start a life-long obsession or addiction, influencing your overall achievement and happiness levels.

For a decision to be reliable, we must be painstakingly conscious of its long term outgrowths. We must apprehend that the decision we make will create a trajectory enduring a year, decade, or longer in our lives, which is entirely divergent from the possible shed route. To cover it all, we better be pleased with it because there's no reversing back from hereabouts!

Particularly critical decisions in life cover:
- What to take for a career?
- whether or not to get wedded, whether or not to have kids,
- whether to live overseas, whether to explore,
- whether to invest capital here or there,
- Whether to linger in or move on over a relationship,
- whether to stay in this residence or that one, or whether to concentrate more on profession or life. Whether to consider so-and-so in our mind or not (Yes, decisions serve us to the grave).

The complexity of a decision may also steep down to its existing dilemma; in this situation, we can't decide because all the possibilities seem to be as immeasurable as each other. There is no prominent champion. We consequently plundered for the berry ice cream and chocolate ice cream decision.

If we try the chocolate ice cream, it will be delightful. We'll always get the flavor of cocoa on our tongues, yet ever experience in the knowledge that we could've had the fresh strawberry flavor loitering on our tongues. But if we preferred the strawberry, then no quantity of generosity could transfer the knowledge that we could've relished that delicious, milky chocolate preferably.

We may adapt to its language to acknowledge the toughness of choice; the word 'decision' arises from the Latin source 'Decidere,' literally anticipating 'to cut off' ('de' implies 'off' and 'Caedere' means 'to cut'). So we can expect every time you're executing a decision, cutting, and leading a possible opportunity or destiny that could've flown with that which you've chosen. Almost as if you've cut off and delivered away moiety of a delightful cake because you haven't got the chance or extent in your belly to digest it all.

Why, if decisions are so sensitive, do we require to make them? Why can't we float through life without becoming to prefer and have everything? The solution is easy; decisions clarify who we are and what we become. They proffer us as complete freedom as feasible, the kind of space we informed the generations ere we addressed their experiences for, and yet frightens us to the bone because we don't understand what to do with it.

Nevertheless, having a decision is a fastidious opportunity and allows us to experience our lives in the direction we surely want to live them. Yes, bizarre

relationships may have seemed more in the times when the arranged matrimony was ordinary.
That doesn't mean arranged marriages are satisfying than freely preferred ones.
I would reasonably infer that most parentally-concocted weddings create more suffering and distress than happiness.

I brought to address this chapter because I am, by nature, a very indecisive personality. That may well be due to my furnished knowledge — being honored amongst a generous family in a first-world nation, with my developmental route planned out for me from childhood, assured that decision-making was nevermore something in my being. I required to bother about too much.

When I left the house for university and grew face to face with the immense void of my independent will, I was a little shocked and bewildered. To get up, I had to enter the billions of others on this planet who have to deliver challenging decisions every day, and I have blown out admiring why they performed so much better at proceeding it than me.

But I'm not the only one who's doubtful. Indeed, in the times reaching up to a no-deal Sharjah, the UAE can't decide whether to linger in or move the Arabian Union. This fatal issue of indecisiveness displays on a corporate and individual system, and it all arises from one root — fear of anxiety.

Any judgment we make challenges courage since it involves accepting full responsibility for it (or else it wouldn't be our choice). Yet, not only do we assume liability for the decision itself, but additionally for the *outgrowths* of that decision. This single triggers the fear that our anxiety will be confirmed if, God forbid, we made the obverse decision and that there will be blank or no one to accuse in the outcome but ourselves.

Here's an understanding of indecisiveness, though, and why it's not in the slightest bit valuable: *By not addressing a decision, you choose.* Consider it.

The decision is yours to address, but not the reality that you ought to make a decision. As before-mentioned, if you decide not to make a decision, the outcomes of not achieving so will be *what you bought to allow to appear*, however much you doubt it. Another method to express it is that you will facilitate the decision to be prepared by not addressing a decision. The outcomes are far more dangerous, considering you become a sufferer of that decision, preferably than take charge of it.

The turn in the road resemblance only covers half the picture because you can persist still for as lengthy as you prefer on the road. Preferably, see it as a creek in a river, and you'll realize that even if you don't accept responsibility for and lead your decision, the flow will sweep you under one barrier, whether you like it. Moreover, because you're not in power, you'll probably crash the bank and get captured in the thorns.

Unluckily, this is how many personalities live their lives, empowering their most crucial decisions to other, often more potent beings, the organizations to which they are wage-slaves, the ministries to which they are victims of power. The offensive associates to whom they are sensitive crutches, the progenitors to whom they endeavor to resolve their most profound concerns, and the stores to whom they are roots of revenue.

Since it appears, then, that indecisiveness isn't the most reliable way, how precisely do you compose a decision? It is the way I've been exploring with, and I would prefer you to try it out too for any decision you're striving to conceive in your lifetime:

1. **Compose down the different options you need to decide between**; Alternative A, Alternative B, etc. If like with most of the utmost decisions, you deliver them in your mind, then you may be unclear or doubtful about what you're leading. This initial step is an essential one because it drives you to enunciate precisely the options in a clear-cut, non-woolly approach. Then the difficulty is considerably correctly addressed out before your perceptions.
2. **Evaluate your options upon your top ten most leading purposes in life.** It is necessary to examine your choices to what you consider is essential in life because these purposes serve as your inner-compass; addressing any decision more manageable. For you, what are the ten most vital interests in your life? Address these ten things down and try to win them to one view or idiom, e.g., affection, creativity, knowledge, family, voyage, open-mindedness, etc. Then take each alternative, place them against each value, ask yourself; how harmonious is this alternative with this purpose? Afterward, respond to the following

questions: Which choice is congruent with the most benefits and why? Do any claims negotiate your utilities, and why?

3. **Estimate the pros and cons of each alternative**. Hook/form a table: Form two lines for 'pros' and 'cons according to how many words you require for each choice, and then fill in the areas. Conclusively, re-read everything you've composed in the table, asking the issues: Which pros will deliver the most pleasure? And, which cons will provide the most distress? It gives you a thought of what each alternative has to endeavors.

4. **Conceive and journal about the outcomes of each choice**. The preceding step proffers you a famous portrait and a more detailed prospect on each option's decisions. To conceive, solely shut your eyes for about two minutes (set a timer if you prefer), and visualize your response to these decision options:

If I [prefer alternative A] …
If I [prefer alternative B] …
After several visualizations, compose down your answers.

5. Examine your most profound feeling/gut/heart and address the decision based on its interpretation. Re-read everything you've considered to capture a big-picture prospect of your choices. Then shut your eyes. Take a few deep breaths in and out. Practice contact with that more in-depth, more tranquil side of you, the part you might command your' most profound feeling,' 'gut,' 'heart,' or something else (it doesn't express what you request it because you perceive what I'm talking about — it's not logical or emotional, it's just that *deep* part of you). Then the question is, "what choice should I prefer? [A] or [B]?" The solution it perceives is the best decision.

It's the result that feels more trustworthy and reliable to you. If you deem you don't answer, you need to sit with it longer. And don't worry, because your intuition grasps the answer — and it has seemingly known it for a long time. Once you have arrived at a decision, open your eyes.

6. Enunciate the decision you've executed by composing it down. As with enunciating your choices, you also aspire to be transparent about what judgment you've achieved. So compose it down using the resulting support: "I choose to… [decision]."

7. Imagine and journal about your decision. It may appear like a repeat of step 4, but instead of considering the alternatives, you're now generating a sharp image for the choice you've executed. Again, shut your eyes and imagine what your knowledge will shortly be similar with this decision. Then, compose down your image, highlight why you executed the judgment, and how it's performing to influence your life positively.

8. Question insecurities and confining convictions. Depending on how doubtful you are, you may find yourself wondering or mourning the decision you've arrived. Begin by acknowledging the subsequent questions hunt:

- Limiting convictions that deter me from performing to this decision are.

Practice these questions to each position:
- Is this thought genuine?
- How do I feel when I consider this decision?
- Who would I be without this belief?
- Could I let this opportunity go?

9. Delegate to the decision you've executed and taken 100% blame for it. Assert to yourself the knowledge by composing it down and seeing it plainly:

"I make completely to [decision] and accept full accountability for the outcomes of this decision while believing my foreknowledge that it will lead me towards the most profound delight."

10. Interpret everything you've composed here if you encounter yourself querying or grieving your decision.
This ten-step rule is clearly a long one, and you can exert as long as you need to achieve it for each uncertain or crucial decision you want to make in your life, or even simply try out a few steps willingly than all of them (the solution is to experiment). If you force to perform a challenging decision very promptly, I will infer completing step-5, which is seemingly the most crucial step.

The drive from indecisiveness to decisiveness is the totality of self-esteem. You'll notice that the more engagement you accept for your decisions, the more you trust your factual self, and the more confident you consequently appear. As far as anxiety and failure are involved, you can't deliver a perverse decision in your life. Realize that you obtain something valuable for each 'immoral' or 'wrong' decision you receive in your life.

You can constrain yourself, believe your foreknowledge, and ease once you've achieved a decision since we do not reckon to perceive all the answers correct for the first chance. It's only the perfectionist who strives to do that, and the perfectionist's decisiveness to be this approach was a misconception. We reckoned to make blunders, since that is, after all, how we get to obtain the right decisions.

"Don't give your sentiment to make your decision."

"The wellbeing of your marriage will determine by the decision you make today."

It is a story about the thinking youthful age generation. The age generation gap is consistently a matter of misconception among the young and old age generation. Why? Because of reality, individuals from the new age generation need to follow the old traditional custom, with no knowledge and proper understanding. However, "Youthful Generation of Today is competent in decision-making with an appropriate sense of logic," which considered in this chapter:

Sarah was an educator in a private school whose mother was a widow who used to stitch the lady garments for her work. After Sarah's dad's demise, her mom was expelled from her wedding house and started to sew garments with her savings fund's help.

One day, a relational matchmaker woman went to her home to discuss her daughter's marriage. She demonstrated a few pictures of Sarah's mom to choose the ideal perfect match for her girl. Sarah's mom needed to get her daughter wedded soon because she was her mom's only child.

Sarah's mom chose a boy (named James) from a wealthy family since she needed to see her daughter happy in a wealthy family like a Queen. After the decision, she chose to meet the family one day.

When she met with the boy's relatives with her daughter, Sarah understood that other than the dissipation of that family, the family's male individuals were alcoholics. Sarah met with James to learn about his family. James advised her, "We believe inappropriately appreciating life. In my family, the ladies additionally have the opportunity to drink. Along these lines, you can say OUR FAMILY IS MODERN".

Sarah answered, "My dad was an alcoholic in nature. Because of the utilization of liquor regularly, his wellbeing started to fall apart step by step, and one day, he passed on and left me and my mom alone in this world. Concurrently these words, I would choose not to marry you". Sarah refused to wed James and returned with her mom at home.

When Sarah's mom started to scold her girl, Sarah said to her mom, "Dad was likewise to a drunk and alcoholic individual. He has squandered all his cash in liquor and passed on by liver disappointment. Liquor is the silent executioner and makes humans into a fallen devil. You became a widow at an early age; how might you see a similar condition to me?"

Sarah's mom said, "I am the mother of a young girl. Guardians of a young girl are always inferior substandard before Boy's Parents."

Sarah asked, "What do you mean? My maternal grandma had made you wedded with an alcoholic individual since you are four sisters and one brother, and you had seen a hellfire life. You are attempting to give me a damnation hellfire life, which you had just endured after marriage. You have finished my studies, and now I am an educator. I can decide as regards right or wrong".

Sarah's mom answered, "I need to give you an extravagant life, not a damnation hellfire. Thanks, you have shown me James and his family's actual image. I was just twelfth pass because my parents had almost no cash for their broad family. That's the reason my sisters and I considered a burden in my parent's home.

I needed to instruct you to turn out to be financially free because, after the passing of your dad, my parents in law removed me out with you, and my parents had not given me any help because of my two unmarried sisters and one brother. But, I am pleased to realize that you are educated and free. My parents make me wedded with a tipsy drunken person who has given me a damnation hell life. In any case, you are not weakling or coward; you have demonstrated that young matured girls are not sub-par or inferior to young men."

Sarah said, "I am happy to perceive that you can comprehend and acknowledge everything. The age generation gap emerges when older people want to adhere to their own choice without acknowledging whether they are correct or wrong. Your young age generation is proficient in self-dynamic and self-decision-making. It can make the correct move to choose the correct way since marriage is a significant piece of our life, not a trade-off between two families".

Sarah's mom concurred with her decision and grinned.

"When you ought to take a hard decision, flip a rupee coin. Why? Because when the rupee coin is in the air, you swiftly acknowledge what you're hoping for."

HUMANS ARE BORN IMPATIENCE

"Patience is the power within you that controls anger, intolerance, and impulsiveness."

"Whoever can rise above patience gets closer to emotional peace."

"Patience heads to common sense, dignity, and peace of mind."

"Who controls who? It is the Soul – your inner self, controlling the lower strength."

Why People Are Impatient

For what reason are a few people impatient? For what purpose do a few people become impatient rapidly?

A few people are more impatient than others. Some show impatience in specific circumstances, and others show it in various conditions.

There are different reasons why individuals are impatient. Knowing the ideas can help you manage the individuals you experience and meet at work, in the town, and at home. This comprehension can likewise assist you with seeing if you are quick to get impatient, and if you are, do something to take care of it.

The Reasons Why Some People Are Impatient

1. Individuals who will, in general, get angry rapidly typically need tolerance. Impatience prompts anger and the other way around.

2. An individual with limited ability to focus is quicker to get impatient, particularly when the individual needs to concentrate on something over a few moments.

3. Standing by too long stirs impatience. It happens when one waits or hangs for the transport bus, trusts that a companion will show up, or is deferral at the air terminal. At the point when you have to stand by an excessive amount of time for something to occur, impatience regularly sneaks in.

4. You may become impatient when watching a film or showing that you don't care for or read a book.

5. If somebody makes a guarantee and doesn't satisfy it, you may become impatient. For instance, if your manager guarantees you a promotion, however, nothing occurs, or if somebody doesn't return a book or cash, which he obtained from you, you would most likely get anxious and impatient. It may prompt anger, unhappiness, and an absence of fulfillment.

6. When you are around individuals who move or act gradually, you may get impatient. For instance, it happens while paying at the store, and the individual in front of you is slow, or when the driver drives gradually.

7. If you have numerous assignments to complete, you may get impatient when things go gradually, or you face obstacles.

8. A great many people need moment gratification. They need results on urgent; however, this isn't generally conceivable. They would prefer not to pause, and they would choose not to contribute time, effort, and exertion.

If they study foreign dialects, they need to have the option to banter in a short timeframe. If they need particular expertise, they need to have it instantly. They need to get muscular promptly and get wealthy in a short timeline—everything humans need urgently and impatiently.

It isn't the correct approach since everything advantageous in life requires some time, effort, and exertion.

9. A few humans are brought into the world impatient, as a personality of their character. If they don't do anything about this propensity or habit, in time, as they develop or grow older, this habit may get more robust. Such an individual is regularly impatient with others and causes them to feel stressed. As managers, they demand a lot from their representatives and make pressure, disdain, and unhappiness.

10. Individuals these days search for quick techniques to get what they desire; however, that isn't generally the insightful activity and wise thing to do. This disposition prompts superficiality and triviality in whatever they do.

11. Another explanation is the quick pace of present-day life, long working hours, and the desire to get speedy outcomes and achieve many aims or goals. This sort of life leads to not only eagerness and impatience, yet to stress, pressure on the mind, and absence of inner peace, and might hurt one's wellbeing.

12. Impatience can likewise be because of feeble wellbeing and sickness, and for this situation, expert assistance would require.

In the wake of portraying the purposes behind impatience, you most likely ask, is there a cure? Is it conceivable to back off, quiet down and get patient?

The appropriate response is correct; it is conceivable; however, this requires some work on your part. It is safe to say that you prepared to accomplish this work? Is it true that you are prepared to liberate yourself from this habit, which prompts anger, intolerance, nervousness, and broken relations?

All individuals who came to far in life needed to develop tolerance and patience

Athletes need to rehearse for quite a long while to become champions.

Extraordinary leaders in each and everyday life needed to trust that their turn will pick up power.

Entrepreneurs of industries needed to work for a long time to pick up what they have

Actors, directors, writers, and individuals in each and everyday life, who arrived at the top in their field, must show patience.

There are different approaches to develop persistence and patient. One of the techniques that work and conveys results has to do with improving one's self-control. The more self-restraint and self-discipline one has, the more patient the person in practice becomes. This chapter strengthens your willpower and self-discipline.

You can likewise aim to be progressively understanding when you figure out how to calm down your psyche's anxiety. To achieve success with these techniques, you have to rehearse them for quite a while. The prizes are extraordinary and beneficial and can help you in each part of your life.

"Patience is an ability you can learn."

It's high time, isn't that so?

Not if you must be out on the world- waiting in line at the post office, standing in the queue at the ATM, struggling at the weekday traffic, and surrounding the shopping center parking lot to discover a space in a similar ZIP code as your destination. It's sufficient to make you wish every one of those other people would simply move. If it's not too much trouble

But, hang on. What you need this season are persistence and patience, says Irene McMullin.

McMullin, an associate educator of philosophy at the University of Arkansas, recently introduced a paper about patience at an academic conference. Presently customarily, this isn't such a thing reported in your daily newspaper. In any case, McMullin's thoughts regarding patience - which she calls a "disregarded virtue" - appear to be pertinent to everybody's lives, particularly in this period of an excessive number of individuals doing such a large number of things.

Despite having finals to review, McMullin patiently responded to our queries. It is what we found out about building patience in this challenging season.

"Patience is an ability."

Numerous individuals consider ability an intrinsic character trait, accepting that you're either born in the world with patience, you're not.

"They kind of relinquish duty by portraying it that way," McMullin said. "I feel that is wrong."

Instead, she says, patience is an ability. It's something we can work on, something we as a whole can improve. What's more, that implies we are entirely answerable for showing patients toward each other - regardless of whether it's simple for us or not.

Being impatient doesn't make you significant.

We endure a daily presence such that it's cool to be impatient, in vogue to occupied, and in a hurry. Also, "occupied" frequently means "excessively occupied for you." It implies impatience is OK, even rewarded, and the old, the moderate, the not brilliant, and the cumbersome are the ones who need to change.

It's nearly Christmas. You have the stuff to do. That implies you don't have the opportunity to grin at the agent who needs to talk instead of counting out change. You don't have the time to linger for the post office person who takes 10 minutes to mail twelve Christmas cards. They ought to move or face your fierceness, isn't that so?

"When [impatience] is encircled that way, it is anything but a bad habit," McMullin said. "It's the only sort of like, 'Well, I'm occupied and intriguing and confounded, so it doesn't make a difference that much that my behavior toward you are discourteous and harmful."

In any case, stop. If it's not too much trouble, no chance is you more significant than those individuals.

Rather than defending your impatience, practice showing patients. Here are a few methods.

Put yourself in the other individual's shoes.

It is what happens when we are in a rush, McMullin says: People become disturbing objects that are moving too gradually, taking an excessively long time, disrupting the general way, and slowing your way.

What's more, when you stop considering individuals to be individuals, at that point, it's anything but difficult to exhibit your impatience. "Seeing individuals that path kind of inconspicuously takes into consideration abuse," McMullin said.

So, instead of murmuring boisterously or making a snarky comment, attempt to envision what that individual is experiencing.

The person in front of you is possibly recouping from a stroke and can't work out a check as quickly as he used to.

It's conceivable that the clerk just got employed seven days prior, hasn't been prepared, and is going ballistic.

"Possibly, they truly are simply awkward," McMullin said. In any case, concocting some story - and perceiving that others have struggles, as well - "kind of powers you to step over from the circumstance and consider them an individual and not only a thing in your way."

It likewise gives you something to do while you're pausing. What's more that, it takes your mind off yourself for a moment, which is never an awful thing.

"What you're doing," McMullin stated, "recognizes the other individual as somebody who has an equivalent option to share the world with you."

Understand that everybody is in almost the same situation

You're stuck in rush hour gridlock traffic. You stuck in rush hour gridlock traffic for thirty minutes. Furthermore, you are beginning to despise the individuals around you genuinely. For what reason wouldn't they can drive properly? What's more, for what purpose do they insist on letting everybody access your path or lane?

Take a full breath. Consider every other person on the roadway. They all have destined to get to - work, home, the air terminal, the shopping center before it closes. Rather than foes, attempt to consider them partners in this excursion or journey, partners you have to work with to explain this traffic puzzle.

Or then again, suppose you're in line at the shopping center, and the sales register just came up short on receipt tape. Somebody needs to page the chief. Everybody must pause.

You despise everyone there, isn't that so? Be that as it may, stop. Some of the time, McMullin stated, if you crack a small joke (not a mean one about clumsy clerks) or start up a discussion with an outsider in line, everybody relaxes. The tension or strain shatters; out of nowhere, the individuals around you appear to be human once more.

"Out of nowhere, there's a serious move," McMullin said. "You're not, at this point, simply focused around how everyone is foiling or thwarting you, yet you consider them to be kind of accomplices in this struggle that is no one's flaw."

If you can't show the patient, be tolerant.

Suppose you're in line at the ATM. The individual in front of you is taking until the end of time. You have 10 minutes to get money and get your relative for last-minute shopping.

If you were feeling patience, you might get included. Is there an issue with the machine? Is the individual getting frustrated? Would you be able to help? If you were feeling patient, you might state, "Take as much time as is needed" - and mean it. You would care whether this individual at the ATM gets her cash.

If you can't keep that patience on a bit of yourself at present - when trying to be patient, attempt to daydream, turn away, give others their space and do whatever it takes to exacerbate the situation, make it worse.

If you should, step away.

You would possibly love groups, and you wouldn't mind lines, but spending a vacation with the family is the thing that abbreviates your fuse. Outsiders can't press your buttons the way family members can. How would you clutch your patience?

It returns to understanding that others are people, not obstacles, McMullin said.

If that doesn't work - state your sister's making you insane and your mom's nagging you - "once in a while, the best thing you can do is simply make a move or walk," McMullin said.

"Indeed, even the most prudent individual has such huge numbers of passionate reserves," McMullin said. "So you can't be ridiculous or unrealistic. You need to offer yourself a reprieve to recharge."

"You don't control harmful practices with power. You do so by growing new good practices."

"Be mindful of impatience; it drives to regret and unhappiness."

Patience Makes You More Productive

Hurrying around, getting to complete things done at the earliest opportunity, and attempting to complete more work in less time is how life has become productive. As we become more mature, and the busier our lives get, the more rapidly we begin growing patience.

Individuals go on a tirade or rant about how their endeavors have not indicated excellent outcomes, yet that is because they don't stand by well, so the results they get are not what they trust. By being anxious and impatient, likewise influences the nature of work.

Showing patience gives you sufficient opportunity to relax your psyche and to have the option to think obviously. What's more, the outcome, your errands will be better all through, and you will be happy with the result—not persuaded at this point? Read on to grasp how persistence can obtain you progressively propitious and more productive.

Better Time Management

However, it might be challenging to accept, showing patience can complete work quicker. It instructs you to sort out things in a progressively conscious attitude. As when you hurried, you wind up sitting around on things that are not significant. By driving and attempting to compete time, it can just influence the long-term process. Preferably, set aside an effort to do it with persistence or patience, and you will have a superior result.

The primary easy route you have to take is with consistency, do what you have to do, meet the desires, and afterward give it time.

Decreased Stress Levels

This one is no surprise that when you get anxious or impatient and race through completing work, you stress your psyche to an extreme; without freezing for every detail, set aside some effort to think with a clearer mind. Having persistence and patience causes you to relax and focus on everything occurring in your life. It keeps you settled, and with a serene, calm psyche, your work can just show signs of improvement.

Clean up the Mind

We want to do an excessive number of things and end up not giving enough concentration for any work. All this is performing various tasks, and meaning to complete everything simultaneously can just mess or wreckage up your head. It only forms disappointment and prompts more errands that have begun; however, none finished or completed.

Continuously remember that absence of tolerance and patience can just bring about mess and business, but not viability or effectiveness.

Upgraded Creativity at Work

Did you ever see that when you take as much time as is needed to accomplish something, it generally turns out how you need it to be? That is because you are giving your psyche the time it needs to perform at its best.

Showing patience prompts increasingly creative thoughts, as when the brain is very still, it thinks of the best ideas. Working allows the intellect to be intelligent and not give its full endeavors. Patience encourages you to be increasingly insightful about what you are making without being in a race to complete it.

Completing Tasks

Speed might be significant for specific tasks; however, persistence prompts better answers for problems. In this way, as it were, it winds up completing your undertakings for you.

When we need persistence, we wind up relinquishing errands, as even the smallest obstruction can bewilder us, and we proceed onward to something different. In any case, we attempt to discover answers with patience, and we finish what we didn't begin anything, is left fixed. It makes you progressively insightful as not to rush to hop all through a circumstance to hold up until it arrange persistently.

Improved Focus and Direction

Showing patience is frequently lost expertise, and it is one of the fundamental reasons why many people are worrying excessively.

By being progressively understanding and more patient, you can discover more bearing towards your aims. It helps your presentation at work, and the outcomes are satisfactory. It builds up a focus, as the mind is permitted sufficient opportunity to complete what work began without forgetting about what must finish. Showing patience can make you considerably more productive in your actions.

The absence of patience can make a terrible general involvement with any project or task since you are not living. While you are hurrying and worried, you pass up the beneficial things in front of you.

The continual rush can prompt disarray and incapability, and except if you delay down, you will suffocate in all the work and stress. Showing patience not just makes you increasingly powerful at what you do, yet also makes life simpler. The more significant part of us would be progressively gainful if we only hindered a piece and became increasingly insightful and thoughtful.

"Controlling patience is of exceptional concern to anyone desiring to have good relationships."

Chapter-4: RULE NO.4 LEADERSHIP

"Allow me six hours to cleave down a tree, and I will spend the initial four honing the hatchet." - Abraham Lincoln

A little more than 150 years back, the USA experienced one of its most influential and rousing presidents. The 16th leader of the United States, Abraham Lincoln, is associated with his exceptional visionary drive for reform and change. He completed it during the four years of his office.

Lincoln regularly motivated those age generations who trailed or followed him, and he will continue serving as such for the long term into the prospect. Be that as it may, this motivation that stays in each American's heart isn't just for his long years of administration and presidency; however, it is likewise because he was an exceptionally insightful businessperson.

Liable for the achievement of his dad's business, Filene's Department store, he was both a remarkable president and a master of marketing. His brilliance usually has contacted, and enlivened individuals over varying backgrounds due to his identity and because those enduring words make complete sense.

The statement above is noticeable to any project yet considerably more so for those undertakings which wish to develop and catalyze change. On account of ICOs, marketing is at its tallness, and frequently the words "development" and "change" are simply the selling talks about their product. It is a straightforward consequence of this that measuring an ICO, for example, Productivist can, now and again, be exceptionally challenging.

What could be more satisfying than retreating to the times of yesteryear and allude to the expressions of an older adult of wisdom who has stood the trial of time as well as whose activities both in business and governmental issues were so practical? To be sure, Lincoln's words bode well or make perfect sense, and they go in all cases of life's experiences.

Similarly, as a mountain climber doesn't climb Everest without a guide, the football trainer trains his group for the World Cup without a technique. In like manner, no business task can be useful without a practical success map. All lies in a very much idea out, efficient approach, and planning — after all, the tree won't fall if those four hours spent checking the tree's height and weight when the hatchet stays gruff.

The success map is the core of each task and should be one of the first things alluded to while checking a project. Questions such as the timescale reasonable? Is each progression tended to coherently? Are there adequate stages to its turn of development, and is the timeframe suitable or excessively aspiring? These can indicate the great or for sure awful administration of a future project.

Taking, for instance, Productivist's success map (a successful planning solution for supply chain management), we can perceive what must portray as a positive example of what an active success map ought to resemble. We can rapidly gather that the project's group has thought of most consequences. The first quarter plainly shows that the group has set aside an effort to see all points of their project before setting out on their experience. Besides, they have conveyed this phase, as indicated by the plan.

The three years of their planning have also perceived the work's sufficiency expected to conquer it effectively. They have a reasonable execution timescale and have planned an equitable testing period, executed step by step to guarantee that their user involvement at the end is one that culminated or perfected.

The group kept steady; however, its players are crucial. It is just in 2019 that continuous recruitment is foreseeable, and their ancestors' reintegration won't perform in a rush. Everything has a coherent demand.

They have explored their business sectors and a system on how they will lead it. The guide is undoubtedly intriguing, and it gives one who isn't in a rush to move excessively fast.

Contemplating this plan is justified even despite an expected potential investor. It is effectively findable: an empowering factor and a marker that the primary players' aim isn't to deceive. I would positively suggest that any potential investor should take a gander at this success map.

After preceptors, my conclusion is that this project's pathfinders have unquestionably acknowledged Lincoln's savvy and wise words. Indeed, the hatchet will be exceptionally sharp, and along these lines, it concerns the aspiration and change that this venture and project guarantees.

Abraham Lincoln is known for his leadership qualities. The author inspired himself by the most exceptional leadership quality of Abraham Lincoln with a sense of reliability and strong confidence in the principles. Acquiring Abraham Lincoln's qualities and studying how leaders made, the author pointed to three main attributes.

The first is a person's qualities and shortcomings, and the aggregate experience an individual gets strolling their way. The second is that an individual perceives a moment or circumstance that has shown up that requests their leadership. The third is that the individual must intentionally choose "to grasp the reason and get in the game."

Lafley portrays making oneself into a courageous leader, is dangerous, convincing, and depleting work. It is the most fulfilling one can do, and it couldn't be increasingly significant today. Like the violent Civil War that Lincoln ended up at the focal point of, the mid-21st century shouts out for compelling, better than average leaders. Individuals of direction and responsibility need to have a result-oriented outcome and decide to rise: first inside themselves, guaranteeing their better selves, and afterward on the bigger stage by marking out the higher ground.

Abraham Lincoln has something to offer every one of us right now as we attempt to create lives of direction, respect, and effect.

Discernment

Lincoln had humble roots and no conventional education. By age 25, he additionally had a developing enthusiasm for governmental issues and required a profession to take care of that intrigue while helping him improve his abilities. Lincoln started getting the law books of a mentor from the Illinois state local army, a cultivated lawyer, and a state lawmaker. He studied without taking anyone else to help. A neighbor recalled Lincoln "was absorbed to such an extent that individuals said he was insane. Now and then [while he was contemplating, he didn't see individuals when he met them."

We don't know precisely how Lincoln supported his assurance to succeed. We cannot deny that he rehearsed extraordinary control corresponding to the things that made a difference since the beginning. A portion of the control centered around viable closures: setting himself up to be a legal advisor or bettering himself mentally. Some of it aimed at dealing with his feelings. As his possibilities extended, he attempted to comport himself with more prominent poise and restraint.

He earned notoriety for being a lawyer who was talented before a jury. Not because he aced the laws of evidence or better purposes of points of reference; he did neither. Instead, this notoriety laid on his ability to focus a jury's consideration on a couple of fundamental goals of a case while surrendering the less significant issues to his opponent.

Lincoln's ability to identify with juries gives valuable exercise about wisdom. Leaders are attempting to achieve a commendable strategy to develop the ability to recognize the one, two, or three fundamental issues confronting them at a given time. It is rarely five or ten that consistently a couple of possibilities of three problems truly matter.

Having recognized these, leaders must release the rest of the worries, either by allowing themselves to dismiss their consideration from all that isn't vital to their purpose or by giving peripheral issues to other people, including an opponent. Having the option to do this—to focus on the most significant problems while surrendering the rest—relies upon a leader his ability to perceive two things: first, the individual can't do everything, and second, by disapproving of that which isn't critical, one is saying yes.

Dissatisfaction

In the same way as other different leaders, Lincoln didn't blast onto the bigger stage at a young age. In any event, when he started to manufacture a lawful and political vocation, his way was set apart by the same number of disappointments as triumphs. The creation of courageous and gallant leaders is quick and smooth in decision making. Without a doubt, the mishaps and the times that Lincoln spent not satisfying his aspirations were significant fixings in the wisdom, flexibility, and sympathy he sustained and afterward performed successfully.

In 1846, for instance, Lincoln was chosen for the US House of Representatives by a vast majority. During his first year in Washington, he gave a large portion of his thoughtfulness regarding assaulting Democratic president James Polk's arraignment of the Mexican-American War. When his term in office finished in March 1849, Lincoln came back to Illinois.

He found that his political stock was lower than when he had left. His gathering had neglected to choose its contender for the congressional seat Lincoln pulled out. A significant number of his supporters accused him, and his difficult situation for the Mexican-American War for the destruction made him fall into a depression.

Although he returned to the act of law, Lincoln found the allure of legislative issues compelling and set about assisting with sorting out the youthful Republican Party in the province of Illinois. The Republican stage's focal component was a restriction to slavery's augmentation. Inside Illinois, Lincoln turned into a leading spokesman for this position (while tolerating its legitimateness where it previously existed). Conversely, numerous Democrats, such as the US representative from Illinois, Stephen Douglas, braced slavery's augmentation.

In 1858, Lincoln confronted Douglas for his US Senate position. The community pulled in national intrigue because Illinois viewed as a battleground state—in encounters among Democrats and Republicans, yet also among supporters and adversaries of slavery. Lincoln lost and was profoundly disillusioned.

Triumph and disaster

Late in 1859, papers referenced Lincoln as an expected presidential competitor in the 1860 political decision. At the Republican Convention in Chicago, no up-and-comer won most of the legislative votes on the first voting ballot. Backing for Lincoln developed as the show progressed, and on the third voting ballot, cast on May 18, he won 364 of 466 potential votes, turning into the Republican chosen one for president.

After a month, the Democrats met to select a chosen one. Gathering delegates split, with Northern individuals backing Stephen Douglas and Southern agents supporting John Breckinridge. This fragmenting of the Democratic party enormously expanded the chances of a Republican triumph in the general political race on November 6.

At around two in the first part of the day on November 7, Lincoln saw that people chose him, president. Lincoln didn't exult as he strolled back home in the too early times. Reviewing the second two years after the fact, he said he rested before daybreak. "I felt, as I never had, the duty that had arrived."

Lincoln's political decision accelerated a national crisis. Persuaded that the duly elected president would attempt to repeal slavery, numerous Southern leaders accepted the best way to ensure the foundation—and the lifestyle that laid on it—was to leave the United States and build up their nation. Toward the beginning of February 1861, delegates of South Carolina, Mississippi, Florida, Alabama, Georgia, Louisiana, and Texas met in Montgomery, Alabama, to frame another country, the Confederate States of America, and embrace a constitution.

On March 4, 1861, preceding a horde of 50,000, Lincoln conveyed his debut address on the US Capitol's means. He knew the destiny of the above Southern conditions of Virginia, Arkansas, Tennessee, and North Carolina, which had not yet withdrawn, might rely upon what he stated. He made careful arrangements to promise Southerners that he would disregard slavery in the states where it previously existed.

Despite Lincoln's endeavors, strains among North and South escalated. These reached a crucial stage with the president's choice of Fort Sumter, a government army in the harbor of Charleston, South Carolina. Government fighters inside the fort were coming up short on food. Yet, sending provisions into a presently risked area gambled Confederate assault. For a considerable length of time, Lincoln struggled with what to do. He didn't want his organization to seem powerless by not resupplying the fort and, along these lines, successfully giving it up. But, he additionally would not like to start an open fighting war.

After numerous restless evenings and discussions with his bureau, Lincoln requested government powers to cruise for Charleston Harbour with food, however, no arms. On April 12, 1861, Confederates bombarded the army with shells and gunfire with the government armada close. Within 36 hours, the stronghold boss gave up to Southern powers. The Civil War had started.

Lonesomeness

From the beginning, the Civil War resisted Americans' desires. Following Fort Sumter, numerous Northerners and Southerners believed that triumph was close and coming for their particular side and that couple of lives would be lost. In any case, after the Battle of Bull Run close to Manassas, Virginia, in July 1861, in which very nearly 5,000 Union (northern) and Confederate soldiers were murdered or injured. It turned out to be sure that the war would be longer and more bloody than most had foreseen. The day after the fight, Lincoln called for 500,000 volunteers; inside days, Congress approved an extra half million soldiers.

By late 1861, the Union's general in boss, George McClellan, had revamped troops around Washington yet wouldn't move them south to assault Confederate powers. His Army of the Potomac 120,000-men unbroken stayed in and close to the capital without seeing any sort of fight.

Stressed over the general's inaction, Lincoln visited McClellan at home during the evenings. The president and his secretaries on November 13, John Hay, announced at the general's house. McClellan was not in, and the two chose to delay. When the general showed up an hour later, he rushed upstairs, disregarding his guests. The president and his secretary remained for 30 minutes before Lincoln sent word up that he was still ground floor. McClellan sent his message back, saying he had headed to sleep. Hay was horrified at the general's impoliteness, voicing this to the president as they strolled back to the White House.

"It was better now," Lincoln reacted, "not to make purposes of manners and individual respect." As he came to comprehend, not all issues—including personal insults and abuse—preceded him were of equivalent significance. Lincoln acknowledged he needed to keep his eye (also his passionate vitality) on what was integral to his mission, not become distracted by what we would today mark "sweating the little stuff."

The president started to show himself military methodology, obtaining course books from the Library of Congress, poring over field reports, and deliberating with military officials. As he did this, it became evident that a Union triumph relied upon the North's capacity to misuse its more prominent assets. Human and monetary—in a progression of interrelated assaults on the Confederacy. But, how might he cause his commanders to execute this technique? McClellan successfully overlooked Lincoln's requests. Other officers, frequently acting without high-level coordination, followed their plans or permanently paused.

It was a lonely time. Lincoln's depression and loneliness spilled out of the authority and duty he conveyed. The president realized that sparing the Union laid basically on his shoulders—on the ability to lead on numerous fronts against numerous snags. This substantial acknowledgment detached Lincoln from family, companions, and associates.

Not could these individuals and not completely handle what he was managing, in addition to the fact that he had to be cautious about entrusting his contemplations and emotions to other people. Yet

Lincoln likely comprehended that nobody else could venture to every part of the internal way he was taking as a leader. None could see the things he was finding of himself and his effect, mind the manners in which he was changing as the war extended on, or, at last, experience his fears and doubts. These were fundamental aspects of his authority, and they were his alone.

Each leader will know absolute loneliness. It is natural for the work; it can be dodged or cleaned away by explicit activity once in a while. Instead, compelling leaders figure out how to acknowledge such moments of disengagement, utilizing them to support their more effective strategies keeping their guidance, thinking about cautiously a specific issue, or grappling with their contemplations and emotions.

Transformational change

Lincoln had no silver slugs to spare the Union. It was hard to acknowledge. However, as the war extended on, he started to comprehend that the conflict's complex nature, contention, and the greatness of its stakes made an individual, evident approach to end it incomprehensible.

It is an understanding of the present leaders. We feel the squeeze to move quickly, jump tall structures in a solitary bound, and significantly effect. But, the truth of attempting to achieve something genuine and great offers lie to the enchanting thought that there is one basic solution. Nearly anything along our life travels that merits putting resources into, worth battling for, and worth gathering our best selves have no silver projectile.

The higher the issue, the more outlandish it is that a leader can resolve it in a couple of quick strokes. Understanding this implies relinquishing the mission for the single authoritative answer. Abandoning this mission liberates leaders—emotionally and for all intents and purposes—concentrating on the numerous potential actions and approaches expected to have a substantial effect.

In the repercussions of the fight at Gettysburg, horrified by the human carnage, numerous Northerners figured the legislature should quit fighting and look for a settlement with the original states, one that perceived the legitimateness of slavery. Against this background, in mid-1863, Lincoln acknowledged a greeting from his old companion James Conkling to address an enormous gathering of Union supporters in Springfield, Illinois. As the discourse developed nearer, squeezing obligations kept the president from leaving Washington. As exposed to getting back to his old neighborhood, he composed a Conkling letter to introduce at the social occasion.

The letter, which was distributed in papers the nation over, spread out the harmony group's essential contentions and Lincoln's cautious reaction to these. Thinking back, we can see that Lincoln was accomplishing more than putting forth the defense for his policies. As any genuine leader occupied with enormous scope change must, he was likewise attempting to keep the pertinent lines of communication open.

Lincoln comprehended that far-reaching change consistently releases waves of aggregate dread, discontent, and uncertainty—feelings that frequently convert into vocal, and possibly increasingly damaging, resistance. He likewise realized that enemies could wreck even the worthiest endeavors at change whenever left unacknowledged. In this way, a leader must recognize and, when fundamental, kill their most powerful or impressive critics.

How is the individual at the focal point of the change to do this without appearing frail, making other foes, or conceivably legitimating the very assaults the person is attempting to mitigate? These are confounded issues, so it isn't astonishing that leaders frequently maintain a strategic distance from head-on commitment with their challengers, trusting instead that the revitalizing cry of the crucial excitement of supporters will overpower naysayers.

It is risky and unsafe, mainly when the stakes are on the line. It was shocking that Lincoln comprehended the intensity of Northern elites, who would not like to battle a war to end bondage. Likewise, the president understood that to defuse this "fire in the back," he needed to talk straightforwardly to the American public. Required to do this by addressing the particular arguments his rivals were making against him. At long last, he needed to clarify his activities as far as his more significant reason.

Lincoln did the entirety of this in the speech for James Conkling. That seen from a change leader viably speaking with applicable partners and attempting to reduce genuine threats to the more extensive change, the president's letter was a visit of power

Willpower

As the late spring of 1864 wore on, without a Union military triumph insight, Northern confidence fallen. Journalists and politicians called for a prompt end to the war, with many foreseeing that Lincoln would lose the forthcoming presidential political election. "The individuals are wild for Peace," said New York government official Thurlow Weed. They won't bolster the president, he included, because they told that he would just listen to terms of tranquility and peace on condition [that] slavery surrendered."

The president started to waver. Maybe, he let himself know as he paced the White House passage late around evening time, he ought to go into harmonious talks with Southern leaders.

On August 19, he drafted a possibly pivotal letter to a Democratic legislator and paper editorial manager, finishing the correspondence with this suggestion. "If Jefferson Davis wishes to realize what I would do if he somehow happened to offer harmony and re-association, saying nothing regarding slavery or bondage, let him attempt me."

Having composed these words, Lincoln delayed. He didn't send the letter; instead, he put it away in his work area while pondering what to do. After two days, when the escaped slave and abolitionist Frederick Douglass visited Lincoln at the White House to talk about helping slaves arrive at Union military lines, the president read the letter so anyone might hear to him.

The dark extremist emphatically asked the CEO to remain quiet about it. Douglass stated that if he sent it, the message would be deciphered "as a total surrender of your abolitionist bondage or anti-slavery strategy, and do you serious harm."

Lincoln restored the letter to his records. With recharged confidence, the president concluded liberation would stay a primary state of any Confederacy negotiations. In the sweltering summer of 1864, Lincoln had thought to move in the opposite direction from his crucial. But, at long last—right now, it truly made a difference, and he held the line.

History specialists and biographers have highlighted Lincoln's qualities and their job in his authority. However, one of the most noteworthy of these qualities isn't mentioning, and this is Lincoln essentially continued onward. When he settled on a crucial choice, he oversaw it, even when everything around him appeared to stack against such dedication when for all intents and purposes.

This adherence was not merely the aftereffect of tenacity or honourableness. Or maybe, it originated from the consideration that Lincoln practiced in settling on decisions, including the gradualness with which he acted when stakes were on the line. From his developing profundity as an ethical entertainer, his sheer will to get up every morning and do what he could in the administration of his mission.

The Civil War finished over 150 years back. But, it appears, are not gotten done with the man who drove the nation through it. By no stretch of the imagination, Lincoln's excursion was one of learning by doing, the continuous duty to bettering himself, sharp insight outfit to similarly intense enthusiastic mindfulness, and the ethical earnestness into which he developed as he achieved immense power. It was additionally a very rational way set apart by misfortunes, disappointments, and derailments.

Abraham Lincoln was made into a successful leader—first from the back to front and as he created and changed for a mind-blowing duration. As president, he would not overlook the more significant results of his actions on people who had practically zero offices that he saw beyond the imagination and claimed the responsibility of influencing a considerable future. He dismissed a moral insensitivity about the decisions he presented, a sign of leadership that we long for now. May all who try to lead with worth and nobility gain from the life and leadership of Abraham Lincoln.

"Leaders ingrain in their people an expectation for progress and faith in themselves. Productive leaders enable individuals to achieve their desires."

"On the off chance that your activities motivate others to dream more, find out additional, accomplish more, and become more successful, as you are a leader."

"The best leader isn't the person who does the best things. He is the one that gets the individuals to do the best things."

"The executives do things right; leaders do the right things."

"To deal with yourself, utilize your mind; to deal with others, utilize your heart."

"Each time you need to talk, you are trying out for leadership."

For being a successful businessperson, one needs to acquire leadership quality as leadership is vital to the achievement of all things considered. It is an excursion that requires reference to ensure leaders stay on course and keep on developing. Practically all organizations need progressively purposeful and focused leadership turn of success. They need leaders who rouse individuals to follow. It is particularly evident while actualizing fruitful work forms. This chapter portrays the required steps, just as the jobs and responsibilities needed, for achieving successful work forms and a leadership structure.

Building up a leadership structure begins with associations setting desires for their leaders. It is significant for all leaders in an association to comprehend and share a predictable message to every one of its representatives, starting from the top. Workers need to see guideline-based practices from their leaders. Leaders explain essential execution desires and connect them for preparing to ensure or guarantee an understanding of surpassing consistency.

Leaders must be prepared to use high-impact moments that typically happen each day to convey their vision. It likewise permits them to associate their choices with the association's built up core beliefs.

Leaders must practice zero capacity to bear deviations from these core beliefs.

In any association, the individuals are the secret fixing to its prosperity. Leaders must have individuals dealing with the right decision always. They do or don't decide the end of the game and the achievement or disappointment as leaders. Leaders must be energetic about close to personal ethics and process well-being and positive practices to accomplish this reality's shared vision.

The Leader's Roles and Responsibilities

Leaders must lead with a dream of things to come. It is challenging to get your kin where you need them to go on the off chance that you don't have the foggiest idea about the end destination. You could never take your family on a get-away by stacking up the vehicle and afterward asking them where they need to go. Representatives need to feel that their leader has clarity, certainty, and good faith about the future and has a plan with enough subtleties to show them the means they should take.

As the leader, you must keep up your people's concentration and heading while limiting interruptions. Lead with a can-do winning soul to drive constant improvement while fortifying advances change to support achievement. The leader must characterize ramifications for their employees' activities, with clarifications for each to ensure positive cooperation.

It is a respect and benefit to be chosen as a leader. As a leader, you must concentrate on others and care about them, just as their thoughts. But you can't do everything alone. Pick your colleagues wisely to have outstanding achievements. Your leadership components are critical to creating and using strong work ethics.

Steps to Achieving Successful Work Processes

Regarding work ethics, associations must permit time to carry out every responsibility securely. They should stay up with the latest and precise by consolidating continuous feedback from the field that proactively distinguish and dispose of dangers.

Leaders are answerable for expressly establishing the pace for greatness, with operations and support as evident partners. Connect all the frameworks and strategies, work ethics, regulatory methods, and instruments to lead all your business. Make and mentor a day by day work process discipline that anticipates proprietorship by the administrator, mechanic, and all gatherings engaged with the work ethics.

Defend against lack of concern and tolerating business as usual as sufficient. Show others how it's done, for example, wearing legitimate individual defensive tools or personal protective equipment (PPE) to show your representatives that everybody should keep an eye out for each other. All parts must function like a triumphant race group to pick up the triumph everybody desires.

Leaders ought to be accessible and open, however much as could reasonably be expected to give direction. They ought to impart at a level that their people comprehend. When things get incredibly intense, don't get debilitated; instead, attempt to recall this also will pass.

Lead by narrating to give individual instances of comparative occasions when you were successful. Keep in mind, giving encouraging feedback is the best way to improve execution. Negative fortifications will ensure consistency.

Build trust in your workers by perceiving and remunerating excellent practices and results. A necessary and accurate "Thank you" will go far. The approach gives time to make required adjustments and show gratefulness for enhancements.

Instructing is your activity in any place you are. You possess to cut out energy for training every day. Contribute time to know your people. Mentor for performance and lead with questions, not answers, to ensure your kin comprehend. Mentor your workers to consider the correct activity (i.e., think, act, confirm). Evacuate deterrents to their prosperity and success.

Request their contribution to what you can do or quit doing to assist you with being an increasingly compelling leader. Keep in mind and you generally get an enormous amount of what you measure and prize. Intercede where proper in a convenient way by understanding what occurred and what individuals thought. Rethink failure as something that transpires, not something you are. All individuals have essential commitments to make. Your workers will do what they train to do.

You must help to descend and challenge upward. You fill in as your representatives' channel for all the things moving downhill. Be a decent cushion to keep them concentrated on the stuff inside their control. Communicate a great deal, all over the association. Representatives need to detect good faith and certainty from you that there will be a superior future, just as clearness around actions in achieving it.

Estimating Leadership Performance

Your leadership performance is estimated by what your supporters do. It is crazy to repeatedly utilize a similar instructing and anticipate that they should accomplish something other than expected. Serve them with practicing thought of concerns and develop to ensure overall achievement and fulfillment. Try to comprehend before being understood. Your success as a leader relies upon your employees and people. Focus on building up your colleagues' entirety to their maximum potential through duty and assignments, instructing, and preparing.

Think about qualities and interests when making assignments. You will likely create yourself and other people in a consistent learning condition. Look for and esteem input about yourself, colleagues, and team performance. Rather than being a leader who completes work through individuals (i.e., the final product is task completion), make it your business to achieve individuals through work (i.e., the undertaking accomplishes changing and improving individuals).

Build up well-defined desires and set an excellent example of the desired practices to accomplish them. Transparent communication is of the utmost importance and vital key. Continuously verify understanding by the individual being address. This interaction and cooperation will upgrade your relationship, as well.

Make sure to assess what you anticipate. It includes responsibility for the exhibition. As you lead your people, be responsible for individual and authoritative outcomes, being mindful of giving them how they have had a beneficial result on each. Your workers are continually watching your activities, so all you do (or don't do) matters. Your model is the main thing that influences and impacts your people. Do what you state you are going to do.

Scoring Yourself as a Leader

How would you know whether you are working admirably? Get feedback from your workers and addressing the accompanying questions to yourself is an excellent indicator of a successful leader:

Do I realize what anticipated from me?

Do I have the materials, gear, and information to carry out my responsibility right?

Do I have the chance to do my best each day?

Have I gotten the opportunity for good work every day?

Does my chief or a co-worker appear to think about me as an individual?

Is there a co-worker who supports my development?

It is beneficial to look for these answers from your hover of impact routinely. To score yourself as a chief, answer these questions from your viewpoint and those who report them to you.

Your representatives will accomplish self-inspiration when they feel and accept that: I heard; my thoughts add to the business; I have a place here; I get acknowledgment; I am able at my particular employment; I am learning; I have command over how securely I decide to function; I effectively care about the well-being of others, and I acknowledge negative feedback and take activities to improve based on that feedback.

Being part of the Leadership Structure

All leaders are a piece of numerous groups all over the association. To be effective, your job as a leader is generally primary as a site leadership team member. Every individual from the site leadership team must be a victor for the association's core principles and values, built up processes, and the well-being and leadership of its people.

Site leadership team members must concentrate on results, just as leader/individuals ability advancement. They should be aware of the ability stream to work for potential compensation (with growth opportunities). They need to deal with today and tomorrow.

Site leadership team members likewise should:

Be a victor for change with appropriate prioritization to keep the association's limited resources focused.

Support an "act like a proprietor" point of view and conduct from all representatives.

Comprehend and influence representatives' qualities and interests to help them develop and adjust their energy to career paths.

Explain for representatives how they fit into the strategies for the organization's vision and association.

Succeed the realities in a helpful and respectful conversation to learn from mistakes and develop for what to come.

Supplant corrupt practices with positive ones to cause the bad ones to disappear.

Set up trust through a relationship-focused condition.

Acknowledge and influence the decent diversity inside the work gathering to ensure overall achievement.

Conclusion

What leaders don't have the foggiest idea in each circumstance, they ask. They settle on the correct decisions and consistently lead others how it has done.

Great leaders ensure they follow security rules, set aside an effort to carry out every responsibility securely, report all activity related drawbacks, recognize and dispose of hazards, and watch out for one another. They are focused on protecting their people's safety to return home every night and return the following day.

Great leaders work themselves out of occupation by building up their substitution. Leaders realize that the ideal path to the ext. The duty they want is to leave an association that keeps developing after they are no more. They ensure that learning, development, and consistent improvement are vital properties for an association's way of life.

"A leader is somebody who sees more ability and talent inside you than you find in yourself and brings it out of you."

"The mind isn't a vessel that needs filling, however wood that needs lighting."

"A leader is a seller in trust."

"Advice resembles snow; the milder it falls, the more it abides upon, and the more profound it sinks into the psyche."

"Each beginner has an extraordinary potential to be a specialist in their chosen field."

"Leadership is Bestowing Life's Experiences and God's Devotion"

"We are what our extraordinary Leaders have educated us."

"Gain from extraordinary leaders, become incredible!"

"The great mentors are extraordinary leaders."

Chapter-5: RULE NO.5 MARKETING IS AN ART

Art of Marketing

The art of marketing is a systematized procedure of making mindfulness and enthusiasm for a marketer or exceptional product that prompts a craving to engage the marketer, promote an organization, claim its products, utilize its services, or the entirety. Small and Large Businesses use marketing to convey their offerings, promote and advance their brands, recognize new possibilities, and strengthen bonds with existing clients.

Marketing can be chaotic and refined, requiring a great deal of information and learning, as proven by most large organizations seeking advanced degrees for entry-level marketing positions. Luckily, to be successful in marketing, an MBA in marketing isn't required. By reading journals, for example, being a business student in marketing, you can figure out how to use similar strategies to sell products.

Smart Art of Marketing Needs the Willingness to Learn and Do.

What you need are the desire and craving to be successful, the readiness and willingness to connect with your normal range of familiarity, the ability to apply relatively simple to-utilize marketing strategies, and the organizational skills to achieve basic, practical, effective marketing plans. A marketing career achievement ties in with identifying your goals, objectives, qualities, and the best marketing techniques to utilize on the business aspects. At that point, that done determinedly, routinely applying those strategies to achieve your business goals.

Art Must-Be Seen To-Be Sold.

The thriving art of marketing is vital to succeeding as a marketer. It tied in with building up a precise technique for getting your specialty seen and sold. The reality regarding art, or any product so far as that is concerned, is that nobody will get it except if individuals know about it. Envision if Apple made the iPod yet neglected to tell anybody it was accessible. They would have an immediate progressive product without any deals. To flourish, you need to sell products, and to do that, you need to get your work seen.

"A Marketer Career without Marketing Is Just a Pleasant Hobby."

There are endless living marketers who make convincing excellent products; however, their work isn't selling for the straightforward explanation it isn't being seen. Without the art of marketing to make mindfulness, there is no intrigue, no interest, and, therefore, no deals. If your professional goals are to live by selling your work, you have to utilize successful marketing strategies combined with active selling abilities.

Bolder, Braver, Better Marketing

How might you discover more customers on the off chance that you could not utilize traditional marketing strategies? If you failed to do any print, radio, or TVC promoting or utilize the digital platform, we've gotten so used to depending on it as an approach to drive business development. Where might you start?

My supposition is you'd start with individuals. You'd twofold down on serving the customers you previously had and talk with, not at, individuals who were not customers yet. You'd get truly adept at clarifying what you do and how it helps your customers.

You'd become a specialist at looking at individuals without flinching. You'd be bolder, more courageous, braver, and better. You'd make your enchantment.

It's not advanced rocket science, yet it's something we've disregarded in our digital age.

It is how most organizations marketed themselves fifty years back. Making the ideal item for customers, they knew and cared or minded to serve. We moved away from that bold marketing model, and from numerous points of view, that move has been to our weakness. Our focus on proficiency and scaling has removed us further from our customers and made us less gutsy marketers.

Is your marketing mindset constraining your ability to interface with and serve your customers better?

Marketing isn't Selling.

Deals happen simply after the art of marketing has carried out its responsibility to make consideration, intrigue, interest, and desire to claim the work. You naturally realize you can't assemble a profession on unconstrained product deals. Most marketers, particularly firsts, require a rehash introduction to your forthcoming buyers before consideration, intrigue, interest, and desire can prompt a purchase.

Desire alone is frequently insufficient to convince a client to purchase a product. Revealing and reacting to objections, introducing alternatives, giving consolation, just requesting the order, and different factors are, for the most part, making product deals. Your marketing art may lead them to the display; however, the association that happens after that is when selling skills come up in front.

Art of Marketing Matters.

Numerous specialists hold the mistaken conviction that marketing their work somehow or another downgrades it. The demeanor that innovativeness and quality can't exist simultaneously with economic achievement is widespread beyond the marketer network. It impedes the progress of numerous small ventures. In any event, when there is a considerate disposition toward marketing, the fear and dread of or indecision toward performing the vital task; for example, marketing frequently keeps entrepreneurs down.

It Is Nevermore Too Late to Get Lighted.

It doesn't address an unlikeness where you are with your art of marketing operations at present. When you begin putting a progressively extensive, increasingly informed effort into your plans, you head to a more fulfilling marketing profession. To turn into a successful marketer, you should focus on proceeding with long haul endeavors and efforts to bring issues to raise awareness and light for your work and yourself.

As I boarded for the long hour flight, I kept my fingers crossed that I'd rest before we landed. So it was a help when my kindred passenger, Michael, pronounced his goal to do likewise. We concurred that we weren't against social, only two practical people attempting to leave away from the excursion in the best shape we could. Be that as it may, part of the way through dinner, presumably as we were flying over Sharjah UAE, my traveling buddy appeared to alter his perspective.

Michael starts talking about the problematic gathering he was heading a beeline for when we landed the following hours. He and his colleagues ran a successful engineering design organization; however, they couldn't concede to the best strategy for guaranteeing its supportable development. Michael stressed over what might occur straight away. He detected difficulty ahead.

After he understood he'd been discussing himself for a long while, Michael apologized and asked the ques, particularly us marketers, love to despise. 'In this way, what do you do?' It's consistently simpler to respond to these questions if your duty title is your duty, regardless of the title, doesn't pass on your contribution to your locale and the world. As marketers, many of us have the additional issue of nearly feeling embarrassed about the appropriate response. When I revealed to Michael, I worked 'in marketing,' his stance moved.

'Goodness, that is all simply purposeful misdirection,' he said.

Is that we're all 'in marketing' Michael is as well. Marketing isn't just about selling. Marketing ties in with making a difference; it's tied in with courage and fortitude to appear with weakness. It's tied in with telling stories that change individuals' perspectives about the product. It's tied in with helping them settle on choices they won't later lament. Marketing done right is a demonstration or an act of liberality and generosity. It's work that matters for individuals who care. In any case, that is not the vast marketing adulthood experience and not the marketing numerous individuals practice. It's dependent upon us to improve. To do marketing, we're glad since we can.

In case you're on a journey to accomplish work that matters for individuals who care, and if you want to be a pleased and exhilarated marketer, at that point, this new chapter is for you.

It's challenging to evaluate the effect Al Zayd's work has had on a large number of individuals worldwide. Individuals like you and me. I wish I had a duplicate copy of Al Zayd's book that time to provide for Michael on that flight.
I realize it would have helped him and his associates arrive at the spot they needed to go. I know it will help you as well.

When you walk into the Enab Beirut Restaurant in UAE, you will witness more than cuisine sold by the restaurant, and you will see the art of superior ambiance built. An entrepreneur who goes to the difficulty of composing these sorts of depictions in their menus isn't only a marketer; he's a smart marketer, practicing with expectation and liberality and in all likelihood out of adoration.

Consistently business leaders ask the individuals who 'do' their marketing to make campaigns that will make individuals love their brand. The questing on each and everybody's lips is, "how would we get individuals to think about us?" The appropriate answer is that you don't sell them; you care about them first.

Your food and services should feel like a blessing.

However, you can market all you need at long last; it's your aim, not your marketing, that radiates through. In all actuality, individuals will know that it's a chance and an opportunity that is not a disadvantage.

We will consider marketing as to how we promote and sell our services. Marketing is almost what we do to take an expected customer on an excursion from attention to a deal. In any case, that isn't the leading thing marketing is.

Great marketing isn't only how we impart our message—it's also the methods for guaranteeing we pull in and devote our services to serving our potential customers.

What's more terrible than not drawing in enough customers is pulling in the wrong customers. These individuals will occupy time and vitality away from their ability to enchant your best customers.

Your message has four occupations to accomplish for your optimal customer:

1. Show that you comprehend their concern or neglected need.

2. Approach unanswered questions.

3. Alleviate their problems, fears, and doubts.

4. Please give the certainty that your answer will work for your needs.

Your marketing has one employment and a chance to accomplish your wrong customer to make them look for another option.

"Employment as marketers are to see what the customer needs to purchase and help them to do as such."

Marketing Skills in the New Decade and Stay Relevant

Ongoing reports have indicated that numerous organizations intend to reconsider their spending plans, emphasizing wiping out non-business essential marketing. Therein lies the keyword that will control marketing in the post-COVID time – business fundamentals. It's demonstrated that in a period of emergency, marketing financial plans are first to hack out, and now like never before, the spotlight is on exhibiting esteem. To prevail at driving business net worth, value and stay relevant, marketers need to upskill and cross-expertise. It's not, at this point, enough to be an expert. Confronting money crunch, organizations will be seeing groups double down and play out various errands to convey a result. It is merely the ideal opportunity for marketers to invest in themselves and become full-stack marketers. To accomplish that, they will require a few essential marketing abilities:

1. Storytelling

Marketing and client experience master Bryan Eisenberg was not far from reality in saying, "Realities tell; however, stories sell." Since ancient people painted their undertakings on cavern walls, narratives have been the magic that binds human development and civilization together. Nobody can oppose a decent story! Stories are significant – specialists state stories are 22x more essential than straightforward realities. Coca-Cola, Harley Davidson, Nike, and Apple are incredible and predictable examples of brand storytelling progressed nicely.

During a time of commoditization, it's significant for marketers to have the option to weave convincing narratives that line up with market conclusion and sentiment, client need, and their brand message. Marketers need to get familiar with the specialty of narrating to have the option to create drawing in and engaging, authentic, and trustworthy informing that builds and reinforces their client base.

Here are the assets to get familiar with the components of narrating:
- TEDx: Public Speaking Courses
- The Official TED Guide to Public Speaking

- Udemy Storytelling Courses
- Coursera Storytelling Courses
- Online Course on Storytelling from Pixar

2. Data Analytics

As we anticipate that marketing spending plans should lessen and concentrate progressively on esteem, marketers should rapidly utilize information to measure campaign viability and effectiveness. Data-driven bits of knowledge will help marketers understand clients better, settle on the correct choices, and course-right when necessary.

3. Design

They state an image expresses a thousand words—and research demonstrates it. As indicated by the marketing industry influencer Krista Neher, the human mind can process pictures multiple times quicker than words. Forefront design is likewise bound to get a campaign the insights it merits. But, considering the cut in assets, marketing groups will not help specialist design jobs. Marketers must become familiar with the design and art of plan and the specialty of putting out incredible visual narrating.

Some free, simple to-utilize, cloud-based tools such as Canva and Adobe Spark Post offer instant templates and make it simple for anybody to design imaginatively and creatively. What's more, Canva offers excellent tips and instructional exercises to gain proficiency with graphic design. Unlock your imagination and add significant marketing abilities to your tool kit with Canva's Design School.

4. Technology

Marketing innovation assumes a significant job in planning, executing, and estimating marketing programs' achievement. Today marketing is generally about change. From the robotization of processes to the client's journey and experience update to empowering better working and cooperation approaches inside marketing groups, technology and innovation are all unavoidable and play a critical job. A wise marketer should be comfortable with these instruments and changes and utilize them to improve their promoting skills and accomplish their goals.

5. Industry Knowledge

Today marketers are relied upon to have a solid comprehension of their industry, business, item, and clients. For example, innovative marketers must have the option to work out a solution to discover a chance for marketers and focus on ability. In light of that information, marketers ought to have the opportunity to characterize content and channel strategy to enhance the degree of profitability and return on investment. This data originates from effectively listening and gaining from cross-functional groups – like topic specialists, sales groups, and business leaders. Gain from all that you approach and distill that information to make campaigns that will resound and resonate.

6. Budgeting and Strategic Planning

Understanding budgeting and vital strategic planning are fundamental to marketing achievement. You can put the time in making a tremendous effort to understand later that you don't have the assets to run it. Discover a few hints on planning from the next chapter on Don't Work for Money.

The marketing scene is continually developing, and marketers need to upskill to remain essential and stay relevant continuously.

"Marketing is more than a trendy message. It is the most conspicuous trend in marketing; however, it is the deepest gap between what purchasers need and brands produce."

The Most Helpful Marketing Lesson Steve Jobs Ever Directed

Steve Jobs: Icon, Legend, Disruptor

Steve Jobs was the foundation of Apple. Without him, Apple could never have even existed, significantly less arrived at the statures it has. What's more, in October 2011, we lost a visionary founder and a motivational and inspirational person who changed the route billions of individuals do things every day.

Today, our purpose isn't to grieve the passing of a legend; we are here to praise his accomplishments and gain from the progressive lessons he shared.

The Three Words That Changed Marketing

In June 2011, Steve Jobs walked onto Apple's WWDC and gave his last key speech ever. In this speech, he shared a single phrase that has consistently been a characterizing normal for Apple's products under his initiative and leadership:

"It just works."

At that point, he was alluding to the iCloud and how customers never genuinely need to collaborate with it. It works quietly out of sight, the applications on the phone interfacing with it for you. You don't need to segment anything; you don't need to assign assets; you don't need to hire a developer or graphic designer to set it up for you. It just works.

And keeping in mind that he was referring to an only Apple service, this straightforward phrase truly reaches out past and into the entirety of Apple's products. It's one of the fundamental reasons why such vast numbers of individuals own numerous Apple products (myself included).

For what reason would you spend $2,000 on a MacBook Pro when you could spend a fourth of that on an HP laptop with similar specs?

Since it just works.

It operates with the iPhone that I pay a normal of three hours every day (as indicated by my week by week screen experience records). It operates with my iPad, operates with my Apple watch, and operates with my Air Pods Pro. It just works.

However, hold up a moment.

For what reason do I even have these Apple gadgets in any case? Why didn't I purchase the Android or laptop or whatever likeness each and spare myself a boatload of money?

The response to that question is a straightforward one. Furthermore, your answer is similar to mine.

Everything Started with an iPhone.

When it came time to purchase a smartphone, I usually needed the "cool" choice — the one with a smooth structure and interface, the one with intuitive or consistent user expertise, the one that I'd been gazing at with my companions since its launch. The decision to me was an iPhone, the highest smartphone level.

What's more, when I'd gotten my first iPhone, I had formally ventured out the Apple biological system. I turned into the glad proprietor of an Apple product, another individual from the clique, and a reliable adherent of the organization that exemplified all that I longed for turning out to be.

What's more, similar to me, when you possessed an iPhone, the choice to purchase different gadgets was most likely similarly as straightforward. Do you buy a laptop that is completely isolated from your new closest companion that lives nearby? Or do you purchase the one that talks and matches up straightforwardly with it? It even highlights many related design components along these lines leveling your expectation to learn and adapt. How convenient and helpful. What's an extra $1,500 in any case? Correct?

What's more, when I needed a tablet, I needed an iPad. It speaks with my iPhone. It even downloads the iPad-upgraded variants of all my iPhone applications, consequently!

Also, when it came time to purchase a smartwatch, once more, the decision was an undeniable one: buy the one that synchronizes with my telephone.

Last Thoughts

My purchasing choice was weighed vigorously by convenience and comfort in these cases.

The most magnificent spark in everyone was that it just works with my iPhone.

Furthermore, we can take that crucial marketing lesson from Steve Jobs: convenience is a definitive marketing strategy. Make things simpler for your customer. As long as that the perceived cost of that comfort and convenience is sufficiently high, the price of your product will just be a controlling factor in the model they purchase.

"It just works" may just have been unequivocally referring to the cloud service that day. When you cause a pace back and take a look at everything Steve Jobs did, it's clear that these three words were a compass that he went to conspiracy to manufacture and market Apple's uncontrollably productive and wildly successful products.

What's more, this simple idea is the specific reason behind why you've joyfully bought eight diverse Apple gadgets. A simple and straightforward mantra controlled every single one of those buys:

"It just works" In this case, you may have learned how much customer convenience is crucial.

"Great marketing isn't about great storytelling. It's tied in with telling a true story well."

The Future of Marketing

Working in marketing has, as of late, become one of the most challenging occupations. In addition to the fact that marketers need to have inventive and logical personalities, they must consistently update regarding continually changing marketing scenes. If you own a business, you have a hard nut to pop. Getting across to the present consumer is a mind-boggling process that requires changing your endeavors to developing trends. Yet, don't stress! I am here to help!

A week before, I was interested in the Al Zayd Corp Group Conference about organic marketing. Cool and expertly set one-day occasion with heaps of meaningful information, inspirational or persuasive thoughts, and valuable experiences about the present advertising. I made a couple of conclusions from all the talks, and I need to impart my contemplations and thoughts to you.

What might the eventual future of marketing resemble? Sit comfortably or serenely and keep perusing.

1. Disregard 4Ps; welcome 4Es

It would help if you heard on the off chance that you went through years of acquiring all marketing ideas to build valuable strategies. They are not substantial any longer. Famous and Renowned Product, Price, Place, Promotion from Marketing Mix are not successful, and you should manage it. The digital world is developing at a swift pace, and if you don't follow, you will simply lose.

Alright, so what do we have rather 4Ps at this point? Welcome, 4Es – the new way to deal with customer offer, which encapsulates Engagement, Experience, Exclusivity, and Emotion.

Let's confront reality. Individuals don't accept items any longer. They purchase experiences and emotions. You should change your "what would it be advisable for me to sell" or "by what means would it appear desirable for me to sell" into "For what reason would it be a great idea for me to market it?". Emotional marking is the thing that makes a business stick and stands out.

The best brands don't offer material products or services, however genuine experiences and emotions. Disneyland or Coca-Cola sell satisfaction, Adidas or Nike give you an act of mental courage to follow your fantasies, L'Oréal sells magnificence, and Apple offers a challenge to business as usual. That is the reason individuals purchase from them.

In this manner, disregard communication that begins with "what would I like to sell?". Buyers couldn't bother less about what you necessitate. They need a person or thing that would give them an additional worth.

2. Most buyers wouldn't give it a second thought if 73% of brands vanished for good

I realize it may be a hard certainty to swallow; however, manage it. The vast majority of purchasers won't be in trouble if a brand quits existing tomorrow, and it concerns about 75% of organizations. Individuals would divert to another from a full panoply of particular producers that work available and likewise satisfy a similar need.

Why couldn't individuals care? Since brands do not apply to them. The information transferred every year by the Internet will outperform one Zettabyte's round figure. Indeed, 2016 will be the time of Zettabyte. To place that in perspective, it is practically 1.1 trillion gigabytes (1,100,000,000,000). An enormous data measure, so doesn't be shocked that an insignificant message gets lost.

Brands ought to improve our lives, add to the neighborhood and worldwide networks, and respond to our necessities. Furthermore, they should move us on a more profound level than the vast majority of them do. You should give it a thought if you don't need your brand to stand up in this 73%.

3. Build coordinated personal connections

One-to-many marketing figures used to work very well before. The process was simple. Marketers did a top to bottom research about the target audience, characterizing a persona and its fundamental attributes. At that point, they built up a communication style and messages to send to the target audience. Conversion rates possibly were not extreme, yet the model worked.

With advanced digital media development, this model developed marginally. The Internet lets us accumulate information about clients or users, and marketers could then target their message to limit the audience of individuals with similar interests, socioeconomics, and propensities. It is an increasingly precise approach to reach purchasers, anyway not as successful as it used to be a couple of years back.

Cloud computing revolutionized promoting communication. These days, information lets us gather point by point data about purchaser conduct, inclinations, and interests. You can use it to make customized marketing messages to people.

You should take a step further on the off chance you need to recognize your brand and make customers faithful or loyal. The present purchasers need individual assistance, service, and personalized approach in each perspective. They can acknowledge when a brand goes the additional mile in client care and service. Demonstrating your customers that you care will help you build strong relations with them and afterward keep them with you and your brand. The most significant, however, is to make those relations personal.

4. Try not to be shallow

Do you know why most brands don't resound with the target groups they attempt to reach? Since they fail at building profound and firm relations with them. They contact them only on the superficial level on which you can't generally connect with an individual. Consumers are passionate and love encounters. If you need to pass on your message and win the audience, you must know their needs and touch their emotions.

The genuine engagement won't originate from a Facebook contest in which the audience gets prizes for likes. It's an investment not worth the exertion or effort. It will bring you just momentary impacts. Your follower or adherent base may increase; however, the individuals will leave if you don't draw in them on an enthusiastic level.

5. Influencer marketing is key to Millennials' reality

Vloggers, Bloggers, and influencers have the power of forming consumer assessments. Internet users are all readier to trust in the suggestion from a most famous YouTube creator instead of a brand. Influencers are real and dependable, so individuals rely on what they need to state.

More brands have begun to welcome the power of collaboration with influencers, and all the more frequently engage assessment leaders in their campaigns and general marketing communication.

They consider being of such activities as they do bring quantifiable outcomes.

There are many approaches to include well-known individuals in your marketing communication. You can just discover influencers who are conceivably intrigued by your organization or its value with the Internet analysis. Usually, they need to resonate with your brand and your audience. At that point, you can, for instance, shoot a promotion highlighting a famous person or draw in a blogger or vlogger in content creation. There are numerous alternatives, and it is up to your creativity how it would resemble.

6. Individuals crave essential stories about genuine people

We've presented an image of the world developing on fake reality. Media gives us ideal pictures of famous people, entertainers, and celebrity figures. We do like watching that; yet again, we hunger for the world near our own. We need to see individuals who are straightforward and genuine in what they do, and all the more crucially, they are much the same as us.

That is why a youngster with no expert background who shot videos in their room and posts them to YouTube has a broader audience than other brands that cater to the youth. It's because they communicate in a similar language as the community, present a direct message, and fans can personally connect with them.

As a brand, you should concentrate on your audience's genuine issues and needs on the off chance that you, as a brand, need to connect with your audience. Identify problems relevant to them right now. With such a message, you can be crucial to the consumers.

7. Coexist with new applications

Living in times of consistent changes may be tricky for a marketer. You become acclimated to one application or social media platform. When you become a specialist, it is replaced or supplanted by something new. If you need to keep steady over things, you have to adjust to innovations and follow your target audience on platforms they utilize.

Youngsters are not all that active on Facebook any longer. These days Snapchat and Vine are turning into leaders. Likewise, Periscope is making strides and the various applications that give disappearing content sharing. In any case, don't include too much; this scene will look unexpectedly in a year or so.

A couple of years prior, Snapchat or Vine campaigns were irregular, and no one truly paid attention to them. These days they are incredibly reasonable and bring quantifiable outcomes. Audi needed to connect with future purchasers, so they run the Snapchat campaigns. They shared news and fascinating realities from a somewhat alternate perspective, getting incredibly positive feedback on Snapchat and diverse social media platforms.

8. Youth customers don't trust or confide in brands

We live in an era when one thing alleges on traditional media and something individuals see through various channels. This conflicting picture summons considerable confusion among customers, particularly the youth. Information that communicates on conventional media is often grasping as falsehoods. It does not shock anyone; individuals don't trust in either press or brands that are unessential to customers.

For as far back as decades, we've been overwhelmed with untruthful promotional ads, so don't act perplexed when your crowd doesn't accept a message you attempt to pass on. Customers are increasingly distrustful and dubious about what they hear and see on the Internet and different channels. If you need to persuade them to your brand, then you, the vast majority of all, must be straightforward and genuine. On the head of that, to pick up customers' trust me, you have to give something first. You bring to the table a value that is valuable to your audience.

9. Music plays a significant job in promoting and marketing

If you think about any productive engagement now, there was likely a piece of decent music.

Melody has been one of the most dominant marketing and promotion assets for as long as decades. It causes brands to make an enthusiastic connection with their intended interest group or target audience and build a solid bond between them that enables brand acknowledgment and steadfastness. It is a widespread language that lets us communicate our contemplations, perspectives, and conclusions with a worldwide audience. It has a massive effect on our states of mind and emotions. You must try that!

You can use sound content to advance the stories you need to tell. The correct music joined with the right brand, and the privilege of visual content can expand your marketing endeavors or efforts.

Better Understand Your Competitors

Despite what your business's service or product provides, it will consistently confront rivalry or competition. Understanding your rivals or competitors and their strategic practices is the way to progress.

It's imperative to recognize what services or products they offer, how they market their business, the idea of their delivery and distribution system, how they execute innovation, and how clients see their brand. These factors are not generally natural to survey.

Competition comes in numerous structures. Direct contenders or competitors are anything but difficult to track down because they sell a similar product. Indirect contenders or competitors – the individuals competing for the same market with marginally various products – are sometimes harder to distinguish. Also, competitors can emerge out of anyplace; supermarkets didn't think they would need to contend or compete with Amazon. However, in 2017 the online giant bought the Whole Foods primary food item chain.

Understanding competition or rivalry is imperative in business. The accompanying offers a few different ways to understand how your competitors work and where you stand concerning or corresponding to them. As such, would you say you are winning or losing the critical business war?

Address Your Customers

It is a straightforward step; however, numerous organizations don't do what's needed. Nobody can give you a more precise image of the competition. If new clients once got their service or product from another business, ask them why they did the switch. Additionally, while it may be hard to hear, it's likewise critical to connect with former clients and discover why they quit utilizing your business and switched to a contender or competitor. You can't roll out necessary improvements without social gathering the correct information from the right source.

Address Your Suppliers

Like office executives and managers in the corporate world, suppliers know the inside secrets of each business they work. Becoming more acquainted with your supplier well is a keen move. While they may not be eager to share detailed secrets, you might have the option to get a general thought of what a competitor is doing. They may likewise give insight and understanding into new products or innovations, beating the opposition to quality and cost upgrades. All information is helpful when investigating the competition.

Address Your Competitors

You can gain proficiency with a great set of information about an organization by necessarily reaching them and posing the proper inquiries on the off chance that you utilize the correct approach. While they absolutely won't uncover the entirety of their business strategies, it's conceivable to get significant level data, such as the organization's size, current product contributions or offerings, and new markets they might be moving towards that. Once more, even little snippets of information are useful in assembling the overall riddle.

Go to Industry Seminars, Conferences, and Expos

At whatever point those in a similar industry meet at a show, expo, or class, a lot of valuable information shares through informative meetings, display stalls, and networking system events. Seeing your competitors in real action will give you essential knowledge of their business. If there is more beating than one competitor in your market, you can get accustomed to a great deal about the contrasts between contender A and contender B, and vice versa.

Direct Online Research

Competitor research starts by looking at Google for its site and afterward looking at each page in detail. For example, there likewise services there likewise, Ahrefs that permit you to determine the status of the keywords and Adwords that competitors buy, just as analytics, for example, Google Trends and Google Keyword planner.

Check Social Media

Just checking social media-based websites, for example, Facebook, Twitter, Instagram, and LinkedIn, can offer a great insight into understanding what clients and contenders are stating. One of the web's distinctive qualities is that individuals express their genuine thoughts. It is particularly true on audit websites, for example, Yelp or Trip Advisor. Google also offers clients the opportunity to survey organizations, all accessible for nothing on the web.

Watch Who Competitors Hire

It's anything but difficult to learn where an organization engages by looking at who they employ. Another web-based digital media marketing executive? A manager for a branch area? Jobs postings packed with data about an organization. What's more, on locales, for example, Indeed and Monster, among numerous others, you can find job postings from all the competitors in your market.

These thoughts can help you increase progressively nitty gritty bits of knowledge into what the opposition is doing. Use them to improve your position and brand. In a grim business world, you need each desirable place you can get.

"Competition is consistently something to be thankful for; It compels us to give a valiant effort. A business model monopoly renders individuals complacent and happy with average quality."

"Organizations that exclusively focus on competition will bite the dust. Those that emphasize on esteem creation will flourish."

Chapter-6: RULE NO.6 HARDWORK

Hard work is an essential key to progress. Without being eager to work hard and put everything into an endeavor, business achievement is almost unimaginable.

Regardless of what industry you work in, hard work is also the formula for a blossoming and productive business. As each entrepreneur, supervisor, and business person will tell you, every so often, days are essentially more productive than others.

No motivating business leader got to where they are without an eagerness to work hard and put everything into their business.

"Money is just an instrument. It will take you any place you wish; however, it won't supplant you as the driver."

"Work hard, have a great time, influence the world forever."

"Try not to run after money; let it come after you."

A high percentage of worries that people, families, private associations, and corporate firms, governments of countries have in quantum comes down to only MONEY. It is such a grand issue since it is a means of exchange for what individuals need to move throughout everyday life. Nobody can survive and make anything achievable without cash or money.

The lack of funds will, in general, cause people to lose trust in themselves. They feel less human and utterly perplexed. If you have never been in a place where such a significant number of things, however, have no cash to get it, you probably won't get this. Indeed, even the Holy Book says, "cash answered all things" and that "cash is a resistance."

Because of this hugely important job of money throughout everyday life, there is a distraught day-by-day surge after cash. Check the exceptionally dense populated zones in your city, and you will find that the spot is much populated every day since it is a high worth condition by which money can make. The busiest place in this world, I surmise the strict commercial center.

Many of us don't give close consideration; however, the primary language is cash whenever you go to the market. On the off chance that all the clamor around a specific city is to stifle except for the noise of cash talk originating from inside the city's market, you can hear the sound from 10 to 15 kilometers away. Everyone is talking simultaneously, and the entire object of that hullaballoo is cash.

The most meagrely populated territories in a city during the day are local public locations. The inhabitants have all gone to search for cash: work, business spots, and a wide range of places. Money is the inspiration for those lawbreakers who ransack banks and your homes. Money inspires the government official to look for political office.

The government official's aim may not be to steal; however, he accepts that he will feel satisfied with cash available to him to do ventures for the public good. Money is the main subject you can vouch for in your brain that over 99% of individuals think about each day.

The reality regarding money is this: money is challenging to earn. Not every person gets all the money he needs. Few individuals have it in abundance, yet most by far of individuals scarcely get by on the little they get. The inquiry presently is, "how might I get enough money?".

What will I be ready to do to move from the unfortunate circumstance to the wealthy club? There is a spot for having all that anyone could need money. That spot is where you don't pursue money, yet money comes searching for you. Until you get to that point, you will keep on being in need.

What does money look like for you?

It's as straightforward as ABC. Do you have anything of significant value that individuals need? If you do have it then, individuals with money will come after you to get that stuff while giving you the cash in your hand. It's straightforward for the innocent hearted to believe that they don't have anything of significant value. That isn't correct.

Everybody was brought into the world with a present for their age. Your blessing is your lucrative and money-making machine. You have to make that blessing into an aptitude. Expertise is the thing that individuals pay. God may have given you more than one grace and ability. Remember them and train in the regions of those blessings.

When you have prepared and created yourself to make the value sold, the individuals who need the services will come after you. It could be a product you have discovered, assistance that you render; as long as individuals need those things, they will come searching for you with cash in their hand. Rehash the hover in different territories, branch out and expand, and before you state "I am Rich," you have become super-rich and left the class of the "Never have Enough" to the club of "All that anyone could need."

You Have to Pay the Price

There is a cost to pay. It is anything but a stroll in the park. It's not as simple as strolling into a restaurant and requesting a beverage or driving past McDonald's for a cheeseburger. It will require your time, vitality, and brain. Finding your blessings and possibilities could take an instructive interest, not really in a regular establishment yet through simple methods. It would imply that you should pursue more books and build up a constant learning culture. No one discovers wealth coincidentally; it accomplishes by purposeful and deliberate effort.

There are classes, workshops, and preparing programs that are bundled everywhere on all occasions, including your city. Look to discover what they are about and pay the necessary charge to realize what they need to educate. It identifies with your quest for uncovering your money-making and lucrative potential. If you don't learn through the accessible means by getting accurate info, you will remain whereby the majority of individuals who would prefer not to raise their fingers to live.

They might be competent individuals, benevolent, and intelligent in their specific manner, yet they will stay low. They might be strictly religious, prayer warriors, and blessed individuals, yet they will remain in religion, the battle in prayer, and become priests in destitution.

If you need to be agreeable, comfortable, ready to address your needs, leave a fortune for your kids as a legacy, the time has come to get yourself, dust yourself up and discover your bearing in the race for earning money for a good reason.

This chapter will be useful to you, and you are getting angry with where you are standing in your life journey and earnestly need to take care of it, I can get you to begin to consider your business and money goals. I have composed this part for you to start to prepare yourself.

The chapter may cost you to spend a little active time on yours; however, it will be worth spending your time and energy. You might be excited to read; further, I will get you on the most intriguing excursion of your life towards money and financial knowledge.

"Time is more important than wealth. You can get more wealthy, yet you can't get additional time."

"Hard Work Won't Get You Be Successful - But Doing This Surely It Will."

I don't accuse any individual who has gotten disappointed and frustrated with the working corporate world. It is a tremendous frustration to grow up with and understand that the more significant part of what we've learned about success is flawed guidance.

We educated, "Simply work hard at whatever specific employment you get, and things will work out." That's bogus. Working hard at your specific employment doesn't get you much. When you work hard at a job where the manager doesn't esteem or value your endeavors and efforts, all your hard work gets you underestimated. Directly working hard by yourself will deplete you and abbreviate your life expectancy with no advantages for you.

There must be more to progress than just working hard, or many individuals around the globe would be significantly more effective than they are!

Consider the investment of time and vitality you are giving if you are working at present. Envision that you returned home to rest for four hours a night and surrendered the rest of your opportunity to complete more work. Envision that you practically sat at your work area and worked your tail off for five years. What might that extraordinary exertion or effort get you?

In case you're working for a fixed pay or hourly based compensation or wage how a great many people are, you won't see economic advantages from pouring your vitality into your job. Your manager might be thankful to you for all your additional exertion or effort;

however, the person won't give you a salary increase each month since you're placing in extra hours.

You're not going to get paid all the more since you have extraordinary thoughts or ideas. None of those investments, on your part, convert into substantial career achievement. You could give each waking hour to your job and still get a one percent pay knock toward the year's end, or get laid off when the organization understands that you've tackled the entirety of their most significant issues. They needn't bother with you any longer.

We can see that there's more to career accomplishment than merely hard work - so what's the enchantment element?

The enchantment element to progress and success isn't the good fortune to originate from a wealthy family. It is anything but an incredible instruction and education, either, as a lot of underemployed yet highly-educated studied individuals can bear witness. The enchantment element for career success, achievement, and fulfillment is self-assurance. When you are the boat commander, you get the opportunity to choose what direction to cruise. That is the best way to be successful in your profession and career.

Career self-assurance doesn't expect you to go into business. My companion, Mike, has been madly successful in his profession, working for notable managers. Mike's success is that he chooses what he needs to do next instead of letting the job promotions or latency choose for him.

When one employee has given Mike all it must provide, he proceeds onward. He doesn't generally mind what his manager thinks about his presentation. He cares what sway he's making at work - an impact that he can discuss later, with other employers, when it's an ideal opportunity to proceed onward!

That is the only thing that is meaningful because his manager's just influencing Mike is the manager's impact while Mike is working for that manager. Mike never anticipates remaining at any association for over five years.

Mike is independently employed as far as he could tell, even though he works for others. He cherishes his profession, has a lot of downtimes, gets paid well indeed, and the best part is that it is healthy and cheerful.

Mike isn't a suck-up or somebody who needs to get an outside endorsement to like himself. He recognizes what sorts of Business Pain he understands for managers, and that information and knowledge makes him entirely important, just as content in his covering.

Mike didn't originate from a wealthy family or go to a top-level school. He adheres to these guidelines for professional achievement or career success, and you can do something very similar.

Rules for Achieving Career Self-Determination

1. You'll begin by making a plan and vision for your life and career. Your imagination can change after some time, and it without a doubt will; however, at

each point, you'll be following a way that you spread out for yourself as opposed to another person's plan for you, or no idea by any stretch of the imagination.

2. When you want the money and can't get professional career-type work, take an endurance job. Try not to wrongly decide, "Since I have this low-level job, I'm a low-level worker. I'll need to ask and crouch to show signs of better work." Use the endurance job to win enough cash to live on while looking for a superior job. Never at any point turn off the "accessible" light on your taxi!

3. Choose for yourself what you need to do next at each point in your career. Try not to be enticed by a manager who lets you know, "You could have an incredible career in this organization!" Talk is modest. Remain in charge of your forward movement, and if it eases back down to an unsuitable degree, proceed onward!

4. Know yourself. Most people depend on others to tell them what they ought to do expertly. If you need to succeed or achieve career self-assurance, you must be honest and loyal with yourself, and you need to glance in the mirror. You don't require to feel bad for circumstances in the past, as it's challenging to commit unethical as long as you gain from experiences.

5. When you accept another job, ensure this is because you like and trust the individuals, not because they offer you an extravagant title or a significant compensation or salary. Many occupations and jobs that look great from the outside are spoiled

and will make you wiped out. Listen to your gut over each other, guide!

6. Remember, you are an advisor and the CEO of your career, regardless of whether you work for a major organization, a small start-up, or yourself. How you get paid is detail. Mike remained the CEO of his profession through six or eight job changes, and he's not prepared to surrender that title yet!

7. Get a counseling business card and start to consider yourself an expert who tackles issues for customers, regardless of whether you're not prepared to take on customers yet. Give out your counseling business card rather than any business card your manager gives you. Make a plan for your youngster counseling business. What sorts of services will you offer? What issues will you tackle for your customers? What amount will you charge them for your services?

8. Get a diary and write in it consistently or as frequently as you have time. Expound on your career and your plans for your life. Expound on your objectives and difficulties. Expound on your emotions and your dreams and thoughts. You are concocting something brilliant. Get it off of your mind and onto the page!

9. Choose cautiously with whom to invest time. Your time is your most valuable asset. However, invest much energy as reasonably expected with individuals who grow your fire and keep away from individuals who suck your life power or force away.

10. At long last, discover your voice and support yourself. Each successful individual has needed to

confront plenty of naysayers and haters, and they've to walk away from circumstances that were not a solid match. You won't be successful by attempting to satisfy everybody or by letting yourself become a mat. Make some noise and state what you feel. Not every person will like it. You may even get terminated on more than one occasion. It is anything but a severe deal, and getting completed will make you more grounded and more sentenced. To be effective, you need to surrender the possibility that you can avoid any risks and still achieve your dreams.

"It isn't the man who has close to nothing, yet the man who wants more, that is poor."

Life is transitory or temporary. Each job is quick, as well.

You can conclude how to go through every year, every minute, and each moment of your valuable time. You get the chance to choose when to let others steer your boat and grab the wheel.

This second is the perfect chance to assume back responsibility for your career and begin your working life as a business - For what are you sitting tight and waiting?

"Too much hard work could be bad for your career."

You would feel that working ridiculously hard is the best assurance of advancement and headway in your profession or career. If you put in massive amounts of exertion or effort, at long last, you will get noticed, correct?

The fact of the matter is unique. However, here is why representatives depend on working around 40 hours per week and get paid for having vacations. (Even though the number of weeks differs per nation).

Here are the reasons why buckling or working too hard could hurt your career:

1. Working too hard will harm your wellbeing

On the off chance that you work too hard and spend an excessive number of hours at your particular employment, you will have no time and vitality to take appropriate care of yourself. You won't discover an opportunity to work out, eat nourishments that fuel your body, or get enough rest. Skipping on these three components of a healthy way of life is a formula for ailment or illness. Besides, investing an excess of energy at work will forget about you feeling worn and stressed. Once more, elevated levels of pressure are a formula for stress. Over the long haul, no one can keep up an insane work routine. Despite whether it appears at some point or another, you will get sick— and working yourself until your breakdown isn't something that will dazzle anyone at work.

2. Working too hard will harm your imagination and creativity

You need downtime from work to reframe and pull together. If your work schedule is riotous to such an extent that you have no time left for any of your leisure activities, your creative mind will evaporate. In

The Art of Thought, Graham Wallace dissected renowned researchers' imaginative procedure. He discovered that a significant advance in the process is "incubation," a timespan during which musings are in the rear of somebody's psyche and set aside in such a stew. You won't concoct intelligent thoughts on the off chance you continue working on your tasks or projects without leaving existence for incubation.

3. Working too hard shows you are not working shrewd or smart

Working too hard is so 1980s formula. The way to progress is to settle on keen decisions in your career and duty, with the goal that you can hoist your profile. Slaving endlessly, the entirety of your waking hours at your specific employment shows that you are not working smarter. Working smarter is tied in with comprehending what tasks you are excellent at and designating the rest. Working smarter is tied in with energizing yourself with innovativeness and inspiration, rather than letting yourself get depleted by repetitive tasks. Most importantly, working smart is about self-reflection and streamlining your work process forms to benefit from superior productivity. By working more intelligently and more astute, you show leadership.

4. Working too hard shows that you can't delegate

If you are serving in a group or you have bolster or support staff, and you are placing in 80+ hours while your staff individuals are winding their work and returning home early, at that point, you have a trust issue with your staff. At that point, you need to figure out how to delegate your work. If everyone in your group is working 60+ hours a week and going around worried, you have to persuade your managers that the time has come to hire an additional staff member. As a whole, we have a restriction of what we can take.

5. Working too hard demonstrates that you can't prioritize

Try not to worry about your time by doing the small tasks that don't propel your career. Try not to spend a lot of potential answering emails, for instance. Attempt to reply to your emails once every day during an apportioned timeframe in which you decide if you can quickly respond to the request and ought to plan time in your schedule to manage the inquiry. Persistently changing tasks and answering emails in the middle eases you down and causes you to spend more hours at the specific employment to get similar work done.

6. Working too hard shows your role or job overpowers you

On the off chance that you need 80+ hours seven days to complete your project, this may impart off an inappropriate or wrong impression to your supervisors. They may decipher this as a sign that you overpower by the work, can't manage your tasks in a constrained measure of time, and are not prepared to assume greater liability and responsibility. Consider the amount of a different sign; this is from what you may see similar to an exceptionally devoted employee.

"The individual who doesn't have the foggiest idea where his next dollar is coming from as a rule doesn't have a clue where his only last dollar went."

"Hard Work isn't enough."

There is a whole other world to success than working hard every day.

It said hard work is just a single way to succeed. It turns out you need something beyond hard work.

Hard work isn't sufficient to succeed or prevail today and age.

Get it down, and become obsessed with your aim or goal. Work hard on it; however, you need to accomplish more than endeavoring.

That doesn't indicate hard work has no practical esteem and value.

Working hard raises your chances of accomplishment; however, you can't depend solely on placing in the hours.

Hard work is essential to progress; however, it's risky to consider it the most significant thing.

There must be more to progress than only working hard, or a vast number of individuals around the globe would be significantly more successful than they are!

Pause for a moment to think about the individuals you believe are successful.

Now pause for a moment to think of individuals who are not all that successful.

Everybody at the top is dedicated; however, many people at the bottom are working hard.

Along these lines, hard work is necessary to be wealthy; however, hard work itself doesn't mean you will succeed.

Hard work is vital to achieving an objective; however, it's anything but a characterizing factor.

Al Zayd addresses, "The individuals at the head of some random field didn't succeed just by working hard. Truly, hard work is vital, yet similarly as significant is being smart about the work you're doing and concentrating on doing the things that will enable you to improve."

Some of the time, hard work pays off, yet keen thinking joined with smart work, will consistently pay off over the long haul regardless of whether you bumble for the time.

Working hard doesn't imply you are productive.

In this chapter, Al Zayd discloses being gainful or productive:

"Productive, set forth plainly, is the name we give our endeavors to make sense of the best employments of our vitality, intellect, and time as we attempt to hold onto the most important rewards with the least squandered exertion. It's a process of figuring out how to prevail with less stress or pressure and struggle."

Input versus Output

Most worthwhile goals require hard work.

Here and there, they take days, weeks, even long periods of consistent exertion or effort.

Al Zayd contends in this chapter and if one has to turn into an expert, you have to place in around 10,000 hours (that is three hours per day for a long time).

Achievement isn't just about what extent or how hard you work – it's about what you accomplish, furthermore, why you continue working at it.

Is your exertion or effort moving the needle?

Achievement is totally about what you focus around and guaranteeing you utilize your time productively.

A vast number of individuals have gotten excessively engrossed with "the grind," It's burning them out.

In an imaginative interest, you can fill in as hard as could reasonably be expected and still not get similarly as somebody who works uniquely and on the right things at the ideal time.

Long hours don't rise to hard work. They simply equivalent long periods.

What's simply the story you keep yourself narrating on working hard?

The time you put in has zero to do with how hard something is.

Al Zayd says hard isn't sufficient to succeed or prevail in today's world.

He expresses, "When moving in the direction of a goal, everybody examines their input sources and then sees their outcomes. Many people have figured out how to see the significant contribution as an effort. As such, on the off chance that I need to turn into a tycoon, I'll need a specific measure of exertion to accomplish it."

Al Zayd contends that hard work is being supplanted by three different variables that will be an unquestionably increasingly significant future: innovativeness, connections, and learning.

"Effort should assume a lower priority concerning the measure of innovativeness, connections, or learning we require. So if you need to turn into a millionaire, you'll need a specific measure of innovativeness, connections, or comprehension to arrive," says Al Zayd.

Don't only work hard in separation. Build relationships and connections: questions your schedules, decisions, and actions. There is consistently a superior approach to deal with a similar goal.

Continually ask yourself, "Would this matter to any other individual; however, me?" If the response to that inquiry is genuine, yes, at that point, ask yourself, "Is it worth my time or cost to include it or change it?"

Try not to focus on perfection. This present reality remunerates the individuals who dispatch and complete stuff.

Focus on profound work as opposed to working hard on shallow work

There is infinite plenty of things you can do to accomplish a goal.

Profound work propels your goal, while shallow work is your specialty to keep away from genuine work. External work infrequently gets you closer to your goals.

Go for the most significant tasks – the ones that cause the most significant impact.

A significant number of us confuse being "occupied" with being compelling or productive.
Suppose you start your day by replying to emails. You could get sucked into addressing questions, answering each email, and propelling the reason for others' actions.

Being proficient at a wrong interest isn't equivalent to being successful at the correct undertakings. The two are not identical.

Somebody who tries sincerely or savvies and is efficient; however, invests all their energy in trivial tasks might be proficient yet not powerful.

Time is limited, and there are just such a significant number of hours in the business day. So the secret to working smarter is simple: Work more productively.

To be viable and useful, you should have the option to separate significant tasks from earnest ones and focus on completing meaningful activities when you are generally dynamic.

Dealing with your time isn't tied in with pressing whatever number of tasks into your day as could reasonably be possible. It's tied in with rearranging how you work, improving and quicker, and realizing when to take a break and invigorate.

Try not to become involved with responsive mode.

"The vast majority of us have no issue with being occupied, yet we frequently occupied with inappropriate things," says Al Zayd.

"You could rage through nine to five utterly emailing, yet that is not driving outcomes or pushing you toward longer, greater goals. When people state, 'I'm so occupied,' it truly signifies, 'I'm a helpless organizer,' or, 'I don't have the foggiest idea how to organize or appoint".

You will realize that you know how inspiration works for blasts and waves on the off chance.

It's impractical to keep up a 100% sufficiently motivated state every second. Consequently, you have to make/influence your condition to keep up your workflow.

Utilize the 80/20 guideline for your potential benefit.

The rule states that 20% of the causes proffers 80% of the impacts. So consistently spend your consideration on the top 20% of things that provide the most returns.

Take the 80/20 course.

There is consistently a wide range of approaches to accomplish a similar result.

80/20 course alludes to the route that requires the least effort; however, it gives you the most extreme outcomes. What's the best path to get you from where you are to where you need to be? Take that way.

Measure results to improve work effectiveness!

Audit your schedules regularly.

Do a formal review of what you have done in the previous week and the relating results.

At that point, examine the things that are working and the things that aren't working. With the previous, keep them; with the last mentioned, expel them.

Very soon, you will have an excessively smoothed out rundown of things that work.

Burnout is genuine.

It worries you, costs your money, and harms your wellbeing.

Being genuinely compelling (and not merely working hard) is the consequence of crucial thinking, focus, and deliberately applied mental or physical muscle.

Make time in your schedule to loosen up day by day, week after week, and month to month.

Try not to let your hard work disrupt the general flow of your prosperity and success.

The work you deliberately decide to do should make your work life more grounded and better—not merely busier and distressing.

"The wealthy people don't work for money. They don't get compensated for the hard work they do."

Possibly you know somebody that works for money and gains a great deal. It doesn't contrast the amount earned; it will conclude what's more if you do not make a lot if you put the size in some specific perspective.

Working for money will make you high-makers earners in the best-case scenario. That doesn't make individuals wealthy. Numerous game players and performers today are salary earners. What's more, most go broke after their playing days finished. Indeed, even while earning huge debts, they pay high taxes and spend the capital on things that lone increment their duties.

These high-revenue makers may resemble the rich; however, they are most certainly not. If you have grasped my work, you will comprehend that my definition of a rich person is certifiably not a high-revenue earner.

You are rich if you have paid off over $1M coming in consistently without busy (and your required costs isn't over half of that)

The income isn't a prize for any work. But, it is a framework set up to deliver income even while you rest or sleep. If you can't draw in money while you rest or sleep, it implies you will work like a donkey till you die.

Work should satisfy. But the competition for money is extraordinary. The most diligent individuals frequently have the least money. Furthermore, as long as you believe that you need to earn cash through work, you will never have a great deal of money.

Significant capital is not earning, and it made. Indeed, even top bankers and hedge investment managers don't deserve a great deal as pay rates. The most noteworthy gaining top of a national bank world full is the Bank of England's governor head. Furthermore, he earns pretty much $1.14M in a year. Most others earn considerably less. Only for some point of view, his US partner gains about $203K in a year. Furthermore, you know some properties are $20M, $50M, $100M, or more. Giving you that pay for work (even smart work) isn't the best approach to wealth.

Rich people have organizations. Rich people have money working for them. Rich people play the game of cash. Rich people work, yet they don't work for money.

Things being what they are, for what do they work?

Dependence on a paycheck creates destitution.

The issue with a paycheck is that it obstructs your psyche from thinking straight. Individuals are intellectually bound to the amount they acquire. It is the reason they require an attitude move to move to start with one pay level then onto the next.

Rich people consider how to make wealth. They believe in how to make a wellspring that ceaselessly delivers money for them. Yet, low and healthy individuals need to fulfill the present needs. They would prefer not to think about tomorrow.

The money game played with the psyche. When an individual's mind adapted to the paycheck, they don't see a need to do business or have other pay sources. The salary keeps on being comfortable until the day it quits coming.

With the idea of retirement plans, individuals have given that the paycheck will continue coming as long as they live. They never consider what they can do if there is no paycheck.

The paycheck is a psychological impediment. It is a factor that keeps individuals from what they can do.

The vast majority don't think except if their backs are against the walls.

Try not to exchange your future millions for the present pennies.

One of the essential contrasts between the rich and every other person is that the rich play a long game. A great many people just think of a present moment— many lives from month to month.

If you need to play the long match and dominate, you should manage losses or misfortunes in the short term. The setbacks or failures include leaving the instant advantage for the benefits following ten years.

Some deals and exchanges require instant benefits. In any case, if that is every one of them an individual partakes in, it is practically difficult to get rich. Multiple millions and billions are grown. They developed more than quite a long while, and now and again, more than a very long period.

Continuously consider the value of what engage you. In 10 years, what might it be worth? Trust me, and ten years can stop by so quickly. The main thing that will make you ahead in 10 years are the things you do any other way today.

Allow yourself to grow in riches for at least ten years.

Try not to consume all your future possibilities. Try not to exchange your next millions for a couple of bucks today.

Fix your look on the vast wave

There is a disturbing thing that happens when you simply focused on the paycheck. Huge cash moves will happen to surround you, and you wouldn't take it in the notice. Your psyche would simply narrow on that paycheck.

The second, the paycheck detracted from you, and you need to fight for yourself in the wild business world; you would be shocked by what you would see that you never observed.

Except if your look is on the enormous wave, you will pass up on the chances. If your stress is just on the compensation for your hard work, you won't get rich. Rich people figure out how to remove their eyes from their remuneration.

You won't see the master plan or big picture on the off chance that your eyes fix on the salary. If you don't grasp the master plan, you will miss clear opportunities.

Take a case of two development workers employed to deal with a large hotel in an average town. One fixed on the sum he earns every day for his work. The other is pondering the progressions that will happen to the city when it finished in two years.

One worker is considering how the construction organization can build his wages. However, the other worker believes how he can profit from the resort's progressions to the town. This subsequent worker (who is pondering the future) will find how to purchase lands nearby. He can even compose large organizations to be their official partner in the modest community to sell their products. There are bunches of things he can do.

Ten years after the hotel's construction, the principal worker is searching for another construction organization to employ him. The second worker is a vital businessperson in the (presently) large town used to be healthy.

Keep your eyes on the 10,000-foot view or big picture.

Work for free and make sense of stuff.

The story of Robert Kiyosaki in Rich Dad Poor Dad consistently comes to mind. When he needed to find out about money and went to his closest companion's father, the man advised youthful Robert to work for free.

His closest companion's father was a business entrepreneur. The man had comprehended the contrast between a representative and a business person. He said to youthful Robert, 'the second I begin paying you, and you begin thinking like a worker.'

So Robert consented to work for nothing and learn or find out about money. At that point, he asked his closest companion's father, 'so how am I going to earn money if I work for free?' Then the man furnished an excellent response, 'That is the stuff you make sense of.'

The wealthy mindset has an entrepreneurial attitude that makes sense of stuff.

Working with the expectation of free as of now places you in a tight position. It drives you to think. Indeed, you need to make money, yet not pay for your hard work. How am I going to make this work?

Make sense of things and grow rich.

Position, position, position

The three most crucial things in real estate investing are area, area, area. In becoming rich, is position, position, position.

Your position decides a lot of things as a matter of course. Individuals will offer what you resemble; you can deal with it. Likewise, your post decides how much reality and consideration give to what you propose.

In every case, it is excellent to position oneself as high as could be expected under the circumstances. Positioning is the vast mystery of the business world. I have seen two individuals doing likewise, and one individual paid twofold what the other individual gets. Strikingly, the two are women. The one paid double was coming from another organization while the other one was straight from school. They were almost age mates.

Positioning isn't just in appearance. It is in the individuals, things, and spots you decide to connect.

Figure out how to sell

If you desire to be wealthy, you must figure out how to sell. Regardless of whether you won't be a business entrepreneur, you need to realize how to sell yourself.

Selling tied in with making individuals purchase. Selling linked in with being sure about what you bring to the table. Selling tied in with making individuals sure about creating a purchasing decision in your quality.

When individuals need something severely enough, they find how to manage the cost of it. The vast majority of pondering is about selling. However, selling tied in with acing how individuals purchase. Take this example.

A youthful father strolls into a store where musical instruments sell. An accomplished sales rep sees him and asks him the question, 'what musical instrument is your child learning?'

That one question has just carried out the responsibility. It is precisely in uncommon cases that the youthful father won't accept something. Individuals love to purchase yet prefer not to sell.

It is why you have to figure out how to sell if you don't have the foggiest idea. All the rich people I know can sell. It seems to be the main thing they share for all intents and purposes (asides from money).

Conclusion

Wealthy people don't work for money. Instead, they see the master plan and position themselves for it.

The question you should pose to yourself if you are yet to be where you want to be.

What is the 10,000-foot view or big picture here? Furthermore, how might I have a piece of that?

I believe you have picked up something.

"Rich person is not he who has enough wealth, but he who gives a lot."

Chapter-7: RULE NO.7 FINANCIAL LITERACY

To be financially intelligent, a person expects to recognize the way to manage your money. It suggests learning how to pay your bills, the way to borrow and economize responsibly, and the form and why to speculate and prepare for retirement.

Practice the initiative to self-educate and grow your financial knowledge by beginning with the fundamentals of cash management and maturing into a conscious spender. Setting time for your economic improvement improves saving and investing decisions. By leveraging resources—like age, talent, money, and, therefore, the ability to determine good habits—you can build a long-lasting nest egg.

"Financial literacy is the ability to encounter a life approach to new circumstances."

What is Financial Literacy?

Managing your money may be a personal skill that benefits you throughout your life – and not one that everyone masters. With money succeeding in and going out, with due dates and finance charges and costs attributed to invoices and bills, and with the general responsibility of consistently performing the correct decisions about essential gains and investments, it's daunting.

You would deem that because the stakes are so large that this can be a profession practiced in high school, that's not the problem. Controlling your own money needs a fundamental perception of individual credit and an interest in embracing personal responsibility. You pay your bills in an exceedingly timely manner, and you don't drown yourself in debt. You accept the very fact that sometimes you have got to sacrifice immediate demands and desires for long-term gain.

Your budget. You save. You protect your savings. Once you spend, you spend wisely. Once you make big purchases, you are doing so for worthwhile things.

You acknowledge the variation between good debt and debt. And you continuously concentrate on your overall portfolio — earnings, savings, and investments. You furthermore may know what you don't know, and you arouse help once you need it.

To be financially literate means having the power not to let money – or the shortage of it – get within the way of your happiness as you're employed hard and build an American Dream complete with an extended and fulfilling retirement.

"Money is a horrendous master; however, an elegant assistant."

How to Manage Your Money?
Properly handling your finances should be a preference, and it should manage your daily spending and saving choices. Personal finance experts propose taking the time to find out the fundamentals and maintain a checking or debit account to the road to clear your bills on time and develop from there.

Controlling your money demands a common interest in your spending and accounts and not living beyond your financial means.

Money within the Bank

Developing financial awareness starts with opening a checking account. Once you've got a paycheck, found out about direct deposit. That keeps your money secure and saves you from paying interest to advance companies that charge a percentage of your check.

Having a checking account provides convenience, access to a choice of advantages and protection. Cheques and debit cards grant proof of payment, so you've got a record of transactions showing where your money goes. The FDIC insures cash in an exceeding bank account for up to $250,000.

There is an assortment of options for the sort of primary account for saving your paychecks. Most people choose a checking, debit, or bank account, or a combination of these. These enable you to line up automatic payments for monthly bills and offer the convenience of not holding cash around. Each option comes with certain benefits and drawbacks. Evaluate the different overdraft, monthly, withdrawal, and other maintenance fees accompanying account options.

Experts recommend you've got a bank account that you'll use to handle unexpected financial expenses and emergencies, like a broken arm, pneumatic wheel, or hike in class tuition.

Choosing only to open a checking or bank account is often a poor choice. Having the two sorts of accounts separate helps distinguish between the money accessible for instant spending and savings, expected to be kept for the long-term. Saving all of your money in an exceeding bank account means your savings are easily accessible and available to spend. You'll miss out on interest generated by a bank account.

With money in an account, you'll start spending—that where you would like discretion. Learn to differentiate between necessities and luxuries. For instance, you would like to buy your yearly dental cleaning, but you would like to afford the salon appointment. Cash in mobile banking to urge updates on what proportion you're spending and how much remains in your account.

The best thanks to leveraging the cash you've got in your checking account will be to start budgeting immediately.

Budgeting
One of the critical building blocks of a successful personal finance plan is the ability to budget. Although it's easy to know, it's also challenging to try because it requires a fierce look within the mirror and a willingness to check what stares back at you.

Budgeting requires that you analyze and, likely, change your spending habits. Rather than your money controlling you, you manage your money. Develop practices to save lots of, avoid a financial crisis, and maintain peace of mind.

A successful budget plan clearly defines:

- How to follow a monthly spending plan?
- Ways for lowering your monthly bills
- How to handle accrued debt
- Debt pay-off options just like the snowball and avalanche approaches
- How to differentiate between short-term, medium, and long-term aims
- A breakdown of family needs

Financial Literacy & Personal Finance Basics

How does one start budgeting? Simple: you plunge right in. You would like to ascertain how you're spending your money and identifying your financial holes precisely.

Some measures:
1. Commence tracking your monthly expenses
In a record or a mobile application, compose in wherever you spend money. Be careful about this, because it's easy to forget. It can be an incentive for your budget.

2. Identify fixed and variable expenses
You have fixed expenses: rent, mortgage, car payment, the electric bill, water bill, and undergraduate loan payment. Fluctuating expenses go up and down monthly, and ones that arise and go – supermarkets, pet groceries, headdresses, show tickets, etc.

3. Add up the totals
After three months, calculate what proportion you're spending, on average, per month. And the appearance at the categories.

4. Study your variable expenses

It is where most people tend to overspend. Decide what gives you the maximum pleasure from these monthly expenses that you feel these costs are worthwhile? And without which of them are you able to do? Be honest, and begin cutting. That can be the start of hard decisions.

5. Think about savings

A crucial part of budgeting is that you simply should pay yourself first. That is, you ought to take some of each paycheck and put it into savings. If you make it a habit, this one practice can pay dividends (literally in many cases) throughout your life.

6. Now, set your budget

Start making the required cuts in your fixed and variable expenses. Decide what you would like to save lots of weekly or every period. The leftover money is what proportion you've got to live.

Effective budgeting demands that you simply are honest with yourself and put together an idea that you can follow. The longer and energy you set into your budget today, the higher you'll be ready to have a life-long savings attitude.

Credit or Debit?

In interest to cash and a savings account, most personalities own some sort of substitute, debit card, credit card, or combination of the two. What you are doing with these tools has severe repercussions on your ability to determine credit history and evade taking or borrowing habits.

Formal financial experts advise having only a debit card or having both with the Credit Card reserved for special uncommon payments, then immediately paid off. This recommendation usually gives to people that have accrued a large amount of debt.

Starting with one among each card can assist you in developing responsible spending habits and supply assistance. Acknowledge the rewards granted by both cards, exceptionally if you travel or make large purchases often.

The main advantage of only employing a debit card is you spend money you have already got. Debit cards often tie to your bank account, where paychecks are automatically saving.

Debit cards have advantages like no limit on the number of transactions and rewards had on regular use. You've got the power to spend without carrying cash, and therefore the money is instantly withdrawn from your account.

Because using the card is very easy, it's vital that you simply don't overspend and lose a record of how often you're spending with this account. If you're not mindful, overdraft charges can drain your budget.

Some hotels, rent-a-car companies, and other businesses require that you use a credit card. Getting an account designed for infrequent use is often a wise decision. You'll establish your credit history and cash in the time buffer between making a sale and paying your bill. Another advantage of using credit is that the added protection offered by the issuer. For online shopping and more significant purchases, a credit card is often safer than a debit card.

Relying on a credit card can cause taking over serious debt. Do you have to prefer to own a MasterCard? The most effective method of action is paying fully monthly? Likely, you'll already be paying interest on your purchases, and therefore the longer you hold over a balance from period to period, the more interest you'll pay.

Saving

Saving is an essential component of excellent budgeting. Employing a bank account allows you to stop emergencies from draining the cash you would like for monthly bill charges and gradually increase saving for investing in large future purchases. This wealth is often used for car repairs, apartment deposits, unplanned surgeries, and other medical needs, even gathering funds for a home deposit.

Some facts about saving:
- Sixty-seven percent of American citizens have but six months of expenses in savings.
- From 2011-2014, 24 to twenty-eight percent of American citizens had zero emergency savings.
- People ages 30 to 49 are the smallest amount likely to possess emergency savings.
- One person out of each five people near retirement age has zero money saved.
- Make a financial commitment that you simply can keep, albeit it means starting small, like $50 from every paycheck or ablation your gym membership for an additional $100 a month.

Get this account isn't for celebrating on the latest Apple product or a Michael Kors wallet. Be deliberate about only using your savings for necessities. Whenever you're taking money out, do your best to replenish the withdrawal promptly.

Unfolding compatible savings habits empowers you to leverage time, age, current sources, compounding interest, investments, and tax-advantaged savings.

Saving tips:
DO found out some of your paychecks to attend savings automatically.
DON'T bequeath a savings account as your last financial precedence.

Debt
The aim of personal debt in America over the past four decades shows a slow but steady climb.

A December 2014 Federal Reserve System study revealed the typical United States house ought:
$15,611 in credit card debt
$155,192 in mortgage debt
$32,264 in student loan debt
In February 2018, Experian published its year-long national average Vantage Score, a representative credit score of 675, up from 666 in 2014. Still, it's much less than the 800 rating that qualifies to drive the most straightforward interest rates when it grows the opportunity to shop for a house or car.

The report also said the everyday consumer features a credit-card balance of $6,354.

Consumer Debt Over the Years

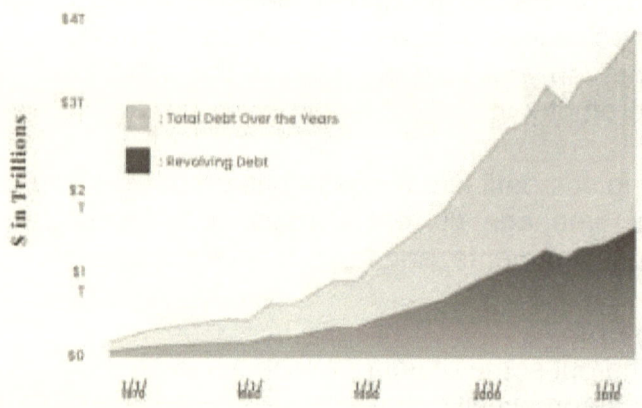

Credit Scores
A credit score is often a powerful indicator of your financial well-being. Equifax, Experian, and TransUnion are the first credit bureaus and assign ratings starting from 300 (high risk) to 850 (low risk). The bureaus determine scores supported by a bunch of things that reflect your spending habits.

Never underestimate the importance of credit scores. Once you're spending money with plastic and paying bills regularly, you start your records. This record of how often you acquire, how quickly you repay, and how much you owe can follow you throughout your life.

Credit Score Checklist
Make sure you recognize where you stand and address the blemishes on your credit reports.
You can obtain a replica of your credit report free of charge once per annum from each credit department.

Developing a high credit score can encourage you to get approval for low-interest loans, credit cards, mortgages, and car payments. Once you seem to maneuver into an apartment or get a replacement job, your credit history could also be a deciding circumstance.

On the opposite hand, getting late payments on bills, missing payments, piling on debts, and regularly maxing out your credit card may severely lower your credit score. Even as an excellent score can offer you access to loans, jobs, and more, an occasional credit score can prevent you from borrowing more, paying low-interest rates, and even getting into certain situations.

Using Credit Responsibly
Using credit cards may be a way of life for many Americans. For remarkable, it's a means for developing credit and borrowing money for better purchases. For others, it's a continually refilling debt relied on for almost every purchase.

How many credit cards does one ought? Experian's eighth anniversary State of Credit Report, announced in February 2018, confers consumers have an aggregate concerning three credit cards.

Discovering how to utilize these devices intelligently has a meaningful influence on your destiny, as inherent employers may review your credit history. And credit scores are often accustomed to qualify you for better interest rates when it involves loans, mortgages, and applying for more credit.

Choosing the proper card

Several credit cards want you to reach a minimum credit score for approval. The top your score, the more perks you'll qualify for, like low-interest rates and a high credit limit. If you're a student, you'll be eligible for specific rates. Choose before you apply for a card what your plan for using the card is going to be. Concentrate on introductory promotions, which can expire after six months to at least one year of owning a card.

Making a Game Plan for Credit Use
Plan before you spend. You'll be able to become a responsible credit card owner by marking your calendar to avoid missing or late paying credit bills. Another precaution against getting into a borrowing hole is ensuring you are not spending money you can't repay and keeping your balance well below the limit for your account. Ask questions. Are there points you'll earn for regular use? Is that the Annual Percentage Rate affordable? What quite limits will you have? Determine what the fine print means before racking up debt you won't be ready to compensate.

Paying Off credit card Debt
Acquiring command of your credit card debt claims to take a proper check out what balance you owe. Take a deep breath and evaluate what you'll afford. You likely will have to be compelled to define a long-term strategy for chipping away at the entire amount you owe while ensuring you don't dig yourself deeper into debt. Check with creditors to seek out if they will work with you to form an idea that works. Only check out consolidation and settlement as a final resort.

Student Loans

Student loan debt is near as routine today as an automobile loan or credit-card mortgage. Few college graduates leave school without some kind of student loan to repay.

Most students don't ask if they'll attend college, but rather where they're going to go. And it's going to not be until a couple of decisions later that they consider the way to afford to tutor. Years later, when academic ends and real-world living begins, the afterthought of student loans takes its toll, so the bills start rolling in.

Student Loan Facts
- Forty million Americans have a minimum of one outstanding student loan.
- Americans owe $1.2 trillion in student loans, making up 6 percent of the entire mortgage or debt.
- The average borrower who graduates from the university owes $29,000.

Giving Interest to Loans While You're Still in a class

In addition to signing the note for your loans, take the time to look at exactly when your initial amount will be due and how much it'll be. Put that future date and price on paper, and within the time between now, begin saving money to repay your loans. If you work a couple of hours during the week, on the weekends, or only on holidays and summers, you'll begin your post-college years with a surplus of cash to go directly toward loans.

Do's & Don'ts
- DO determine when your balance period ends.
- DON'T miss your initial payment because you skipped checking your calendar.

Staying on top of things once you Leave or Graduate

When the time to start out paying comes, you've got options for repayment. The federal offer long run payment also plans as graduated repayment options, which permit you to bulk up your income and obtain some work experience under your zone before making higher monthly payments.

From there, your following action will be paying payments on time and reducing the principal if possible by paying quite the minimum that's due. For public service careers, you'll qualify for loan forgiveness.

Do's & Don'ts
- DO make quite the minimum payment to scale back your principle.
- DON'T skip payments or accrue late fees.

When repayment Isn't an Option

During certain seasons of life, your income could also be critically limited, and affording student loan amounts just isn't feasible. Fortunately, loan servicers are knowledgeable that situations like this happen and have precautions to assist learners in getting through these challenging times. Qualifying conditions, like unemployment or health problems, can cause you to be eligible for deferment or forbearance, which will temporarily postpone or reduce payments. Contact your loan servicers to seek out your options. If you only ignore loan bills, your account may receive delinquency or default status.

Do's & Don'ts
- DO communicate with lenders if you're unable to form amounts.
- DON'T neglect scholar loans when you're coping financially.

Real Estate

Having a property may be a reasonable goal for an excellent financial statement. Homeownership not only develops a way of accomplishment and pride but also build equity. It's also a serious financial undertaking and a long-term investment.

For many people, buying a house is the most important purchase they're going ever to execute. Perversely, more and more personalities find themselves compelled to place off this purchase. Scholar loan debt, underemployment, rising home prices, and stringent mortgage standards prevent people from buying their own homes until later.

Before signing a mortgage, confirm to calculate all costs and leave some savings untouched for after your purchase. Homeownership often comes with a slew of added expenses like taxes, insurance costs, emergencies, and necessary repairs. You would like to possess quite enough to make it by barely. Often getting approval for a reasonable mortgage rate requires a couple of more years to save lots of up for a bigger deposit.

The planning level before buying a home is lengthy. Prospective buyers work effortlessly to urge to an area where they will find their permanent home. The method is long and involved, demanding that most people create up their credit scores, save for a deposit, and plan to a stable job location. Earn an income that qualifies for an oversized enough mortgage, choose an honest realtor, find an appropriate place to measure, find a home inspector then have a proposal accepted.

Home Ownership in the US
- The average buyer searches for ten weeks and views ten homes.
- The median price of a single-family range in 2018 was $261,600.
- The average price of a replacement single-family range in 2018 was $299,400.
- In April of 2014, homeownership for all ages fell to 64.8 percent, the bottom it's been since 1995.

Foreclosures and Short Sales

A foreclosure occurs when a borrower cannot make mortgage payments, and therefore the lender is legally given the proper to require possession of the collateral property. A brief sale occurs when profits from selling a home are less than debt remaining on a mortgage. During this case, the lien holder often agrees to release the debtor of the rest of the loan.

On the other phase of the coin is uncertainty for buyers attending to get a home at a lowered rate. While it'd take more paperwork and a few hoops working with a bank to urge the sale approved, these homes often discounted the maximum amount of $60,000. Has the home inspected before proceeding with the acquisition may require extensive repairs, remodeling, and insurance?

Business Finance

Start-ups are sweeping the state. With the burgeoning tech industry and, therefore, the DIY convenience of using the online as your storefront, entrepreneurial ventures became commonplace. A University of Phoenix survey discovered 63 percent of grown-ups in their 20s desire to run their businesses.

Small Business Facts
- Approximately 400,000 new businesses begin per annum.
- The SBA determines small companies as those with but 500 representatives.

Top fastest growing sectors in 2014
- Electronic shopping and mail-order houses
- Software publishers
- Computer systems design and related services

Start-ups & Small Business

Business owners use their savings, mortgages, stocks, and other references for start-up funds. It's essential to research your business and make a concept that describes how you'll keep profitability. Some personalities rush into starting a business without sufficient knowledge and looking out a way for long-term progress. Seeking an exciting business idea and not analyzing all the prices concerned can make your desires short-lived.

Start-up Facts
- There are considerably 28 million small companies within us.
- One-third of the newest companies terminate within two years and half-close within five years.
- The Small Business Administration states that around 10 to 12 percent of small businesses with representatives close per annum.

After commencing a business, the struggle has only started. Lingering competing in your industry needs retaining a sight fixed on trends and adapting to developing consumer demands. Developing your marketing strategy to growing your client reach the business of managing a business requires consistent devotion.

Startups and Closures

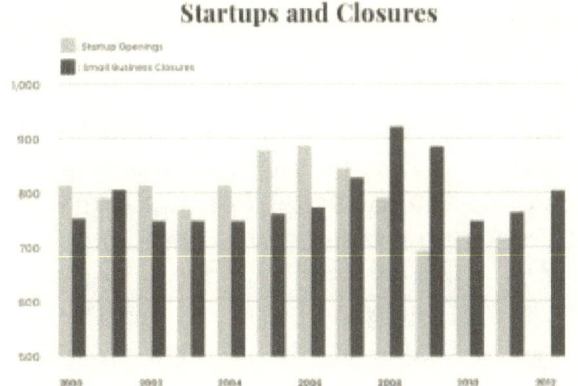

Share of Owners

Age	Under 35	15.9
	35 to 49*	33.2
	50 to 88*	50.9
Gender	Male	64.0
	Female	36.0
Race	White	85.4
	Non-white	14.6
Ethnicity	Hispanic	10.3
	Non-Hispanic	89.7
Veteran*	Veteran*	9.1
	Non-Veteran*	90.9

Venture Capital

One approach entrepreneurs succeed in their financial difficulties when rousing is by gathering working capital, which refers to money from investors hoping to take advantage of partial ownership and, therefore, the long-term, high-potential growth of the latest companies.

This capital is often an essential tool for handling start-up costs, as a brand new venture's size, assets, and growth phase can prevent it from promptly growing.

While banks could also be unwilling to increase credit to companies without a vital record or commitment, angel investors and venture capital firms are often responsible for requiring a chance on a brand new product or service. If there's a right pro formal, an in-depth program for operating the business, investors will be more likely to require on the chance.

Retirement
The promptly you begin saving for retirement, the more possibilities you'll need to gain the available resources. The typical lifespan has been steadily increasing. Within us, the average prospect is 78.74 years (World Bank). Personalities are serving backward in life and living longer, both of which influence what proportion you'll be ready to save and how much you would like to last your entire lifespan.

Your bank account, bank, investment portfolio, and employer can all be resources that help you steel yourself against the longer term.

Retirement Facts
- The average period of retirement is 62.
- The average range of retirement is 20 ages.
- According to the core for Retirement Research, approximately a 3rd of all homes nearing retirement haven't any retirement savings.

Annuities and Retirement

People curious about adding security to their retirement portfolio often address annuities, which they will purchase with one premium or a series of incentives. Insurance companies announcing annuities ensure their pay-outs, hence the safety claim.

The other retirement benefit that annuities have: their capital investment grows over time, and taxes get suspended until the investment starts paying out—the IRS (Internal Revenue Service) tax beneficiaries on the annual allowance alternatively of the whole's worth account.

A secondary annuity market also exists for people that want to shed their annuity or structured settlement immediately rather than waiting thereon to pay off years from now. This market allows annuity owners to live their money contracts. The cash value for such a purchase is smaller than it might be if an owner persisted in the investment. Still, even those that once wanted a retirement investment find themselves needing money now and not later.

For instance, some people got to pay off unforeseen medical bills or family crisis expenses. Others require to pay off student loans or get divorced and make their long-term asset a free one. A seller can prefer to sell some or all of their payments, using some money and saving the remaining income.

Why an annuity for retirement?

Anyone can purchase an annuity, and you'll shop among a spread of them. You'll get a contract that sets up distributions to be paid out immediately, in several months or years, or a few years within the prospect.

Possibilities include a fixed annuity, which affords a stable playout, or variable investment, which fluctuates supported market changes. Owners also can buy riders, like the power to form early withdrawals or the guarantee that payments last throughout the owner's entire lifespan.

Getting Started

Begin by observing what proportion you think that you'll need and planning a retirement budget. Fidelity financial corporation urges pre-retirees to possess eight times their annual salary saved by retirement. This general guideline can offer you a rough idea of what you'll need, but to urge a more precise understanding, take a glance at each part of the image.

Questions to ask

- At what age does one expect to prevent working?
- Do you decide to work part-time during retirement?
- What quite pre-existing health concerns will you would like to hide during retirement?
- What does reasonably retirement benefit your company offers?
- Will your business give you a pension?

These are merely some examples of the questions you would like to respond to as you collectively put a retirement strategy. Use resources just like the AARP non-profit organization website to seek out calculators for estimating expenses. You'll study topics like how inflation will impact your money's worth and how you'll expect your health cost to extend with age.

Do's & Don'ts
- DO consider down-sizing and keeping the cash you save to supplement retirement income.
- DON'T ditch 401(k) savings once you move to a replacement job.
- DO lower uncertainties as you age, like driving from stocks to bonds.
- DON'T put retirement savings as a low-level preference only because it appears to be within the far future.

Current Assets

Next, check out the resources you have already got. It's never too early to start a savings account. Although your bank may offer accounts with low-interest rates, you'll use the decades between now and retirement to slowly build your savings. To ensure you're dedicating some of your income to retirement, line up automated transfers accurate from your paycheck into your savings.

Get an assessment of your stock portfolio, and the process assets will mature by retirement age. Use tax-advantaged accounts like 401(k)s (A 401k is a qualified retirement plan that provides eligible apprentices to invest and save for their retirement on a deferred tax authority). If your employer offers a match plan, attempt to budget so that you'll put in maximum contributions to urge the foremost from this account. The worth of 401(k)s has been increasing in recent years, partially thanks to the stock exchange.

Looking into the longer term

Appraise other sources of retirement pay. The Social Security Administration grants an estimator for learning what proportion your monthly Social Security payments will be. You'll notice that the longer you await Social Security payments (before full retirement age), the more your monthly payments will be.

If you're a veteran, teacher, or another government worker, you'll have pension payments you'll calculate. Your retirement benefits can significantly vary, looking at your occupation and employer. Confirm you're conscious of and participating in any employer-offered retirement plans.

As you age, periodically gauge the worth of your portfolio. You'll get to adjust your funds, accounting for market lows or stagnant investments. The older you're, the more you'll want to place money toward risk-averse investments like bonds instead of varying stocks. Additionally, if you happen behind in your retirement savings account deposits, you'll fit for immense catch-up enrichment, which might typically be quite the yearly maximum.

This guide can assist you in measuring your savings progress.

Timeline for Retirement

- At age 50

Begin making catch-up contributions, an additional expense that over 50 can combine to 401(k) and other retirement statements accounts.

- At 59½

No more extended tax penalties on withdrawals from retirement statements accounts, but neglecting money in averages longer for it to grow.

- At 62

The minimum age to collect Social Security gains, but delaying proposes a much more significant monthly profit.

- At 65

Qualified for Medicare

- At 66

Eligible for total Social Security gains if birth in the year between 1943 and 1954.

- At 70½

Begin practicing minimum withdrawals from most retirement statements accounts by this age; contrarily, you will be charged heavy tax penalties within the future.

"Real riches aren't about money. Real riches are: not going to gatherings, not spending time with jerks, not being secured in status games, not feeling like you need to state 'yes,' not stressing others were claiming your time and vitality. Real riches are about financial independence."

Financial Independence - A Reliable Guide to Accomplish It in Levels

What is financial independence? It's a state where one's assets generate enough passive income to pay money for life's specified expenses.

Personalities also consider this phase of independence as financial freedom.

In this phase of independence, personalities needn't work (do a job) to earn income. What they consider is effortless automatic income (called passive income).

When it involves the monetary aspect of life, I believe the essential need for anybody should be "attaining financial independence." this is often not a simple goal. It'll take time to attain. Together, they realize the necessity of 'financial independence' takes steps to know it from that day itself. This chapter will assist you in trying to that.

A PHASE OF FINANCIAL INDEPENDENCE

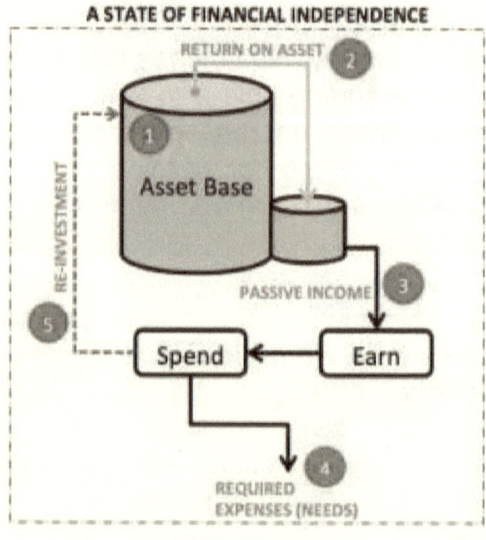

A STATE OF FINANCIAL INDEPENDENCE

What shown within the above flow chart may be a state of financial independence?

Asset Support: These are those assets that have accumulated over time in a sort of investing. These assets are often house property, stocks, deposits, annuity, etc.

Return on Asset: The "Assets" accumulated above generate regular returns. These returns are often in cash (like rent, dividend, interest, etc.) or capital appreciation (profit booked). Let's say; these returns have gotten credited periodically in an exceeding bank account statement.

Passive Earnings: These recurrent returns are available for consumption. It's a sort of income. Because the revenue so generated is occurring automatically, it's called passive income.

Required Expense: These expense requirements sufficed by consuming passive earnings. The more profound will be the "required expenses," minor will demand passive income.

Re-Investment: It's also a crucial ingredient to take care of the state of financial independence. Re-investment increases the dimensions of asset support. The larger will be the asset support, and more will be the Return from these assets. Increasing returns are vital to negate the effect of inflation.

To reach the state of monetary independence primary step is to start out accumulating assets. These assets successively must generate income (passive income).

The passive income will look out of various needs of life.

PROCESS: TO REALIZE FINANCIAL INDEPENDENCE

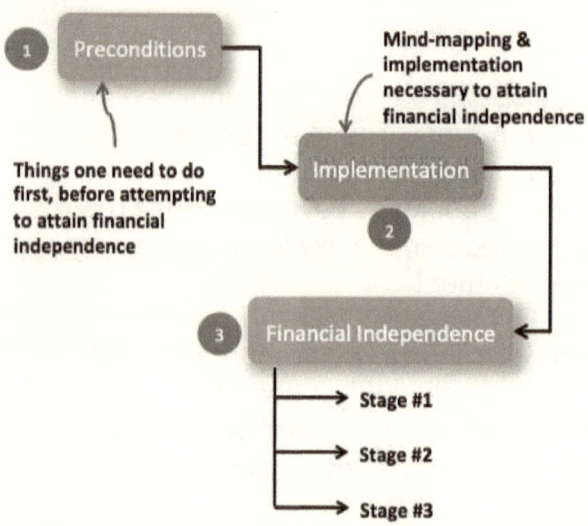

It is crucial to develop a process to attain financial independence. Why?

Because it's a challenging goal to attain, and following a process makes it easy and quantifiable. How?

Preconditions: Few things must perform before one even attempts to achieve financial independence. What are these things? These are such activities that improve one's financial health. These improvements successively help one to climb the height of financial freedom.

Implementation: this is where the focus conception of growing financial independence (asset building & passive revenue generation) implement. Here we'll discuss how one must map minds to perform the concept successfully.

Level of Financial Independence: Financial independence may be a dynamic goal. There are three levels of financial freedom. Within the first level, people can independently afford "primary" necessities of life. Similarly, in the second and third levels, expenses of "comfort" and "luxury" in nature are often afforded.

To start the journey of financial independence, one must drive with the "preconditions."

If these preconditions are appropriately implementing, it builds a solid foundation on which the infrastructure of "financial independence" can stand.

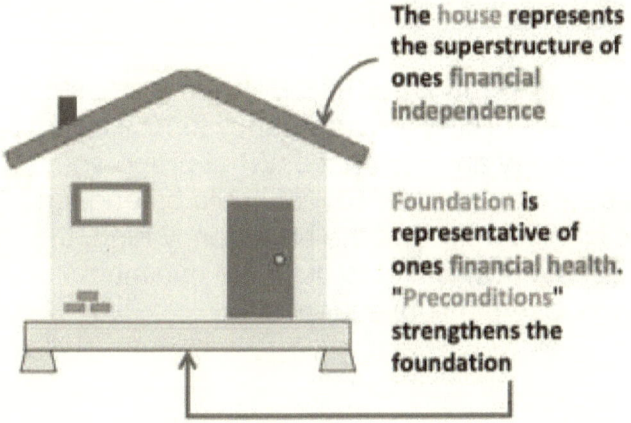

The house represents the superstructure of ones financial independence

Foundation is representative of ones financial health. "Preconditions" strengthens the foundation

1. PRECONDITIONS: TO FINANCIAL FREEDOM

Everyone must aspire to attain financial freedom. But it also essential to understand that this is often not a common goal. For achieving this goal, it's necessary to follow a process.

The process of attaining financial independence commences with the "preconditions." Understanding these preconditions will grow one "financial health."

There are three positions that one must practice carefully:

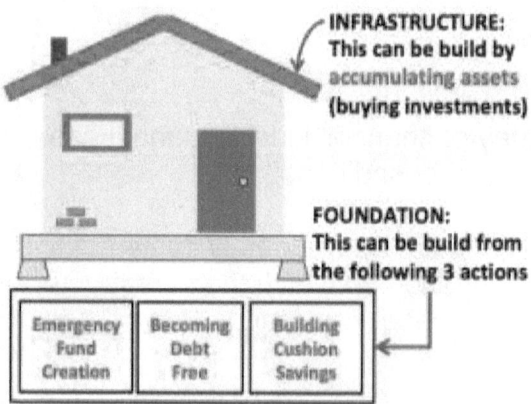

1.1 Emergency Fund Creation: Prepare yourself for the worst. Start building an emergency fund. This fund consists of money and insurance. What proportion of cash, life cover, and health cover should be enough? The more significant is that the emergency fund, the higher. But essential is first to build the minimum balance and take the subsequent step.

SL	Emergency Fund	Monthly Expense	Minimum Size of Fund (Cover)
1	Cash	"E"	6 x E
2	Life Cover	"E"	(10 x 12) x E
3	Health Cover	"E"	15 x E

1.2 Becoming Debt Free: Debt may be a financial burden. The best is to keep the debt burden at zero. Why? Because to succeed in the goal of monetary independence, debt is that the biggest hurdle. Why? Rich people avail loans to leverage their profits. We take a loan to shop for things we cannot afford. That's why it's a hurdle. Set a target to be debt-free. The way to be debt-free? The most accessible rule is to list down all debt/loans that one is carrying. Begin by clearing off the most valuable debt preeminent.

1.3 Make Shelter Savings: Emergency funds and debt-pay-off serve a particular purpose. What's cushion saving? It's that cash which may be wont to run daily chores of life just in case of emergency. What sort of crisis? Unexpected loss or reduction of income. What should be the dimensions of cushion savings? Minimum of 6 months' worth of current expenses. Use? For example: just in case of income loss, a livelihood can temporarily run from cushion savings.

List of Espense	Cusion Savings ($)					
	Jan	Feb	Mar	Apr	May	Jun
Expenditure 1	100	101	102	103	104	105
Expenditure 2	10	10	10	10	10	11
Expenditure 3	200	202	204	206	208	210
Expenditure 4	300	303	306	309	312	315
Expenditure 5	60	61	61	62	62	63
Expenditure 6	40	40	41	41	42	42
Expenditure 7	50	51	51	52	52	53
Expenditure 8	350	354	357	361	364	368
Expenditure 9	150	152	153	155	156	158
Expenditure 10	200	202	204	206	208	210
Expenditure 11	400	404	408	412	416	420
Expenditure 12	65	66	66	67	68	68
	1,925	1,944	1,964	1,983	2,003	2,023

2. EXECUTION: FINANCIAL INDEPENDENCE

Financially, our final goal in life should be to grow economically independent. The way to do it?

The only way to achieve it's by generating "enough passive income." Passive income must equal our expense needs.

So this brings us to the present logical question. Generating enough passive income is enough to attain financial independence? The solution is yes and no.

Yes, because till there's enough passive income, there is often no financial independence.
No, because till we have an accurate "mind-mapping," enough passive income is not generated. If one can first map the minds correctly in favor of financial independence, building passive income streams will happen automatically.

So let's learn the way to try and do mind mapping.

2.1 MIND MAPPING: TO ACHIEVE FINANCIAL FREEDOM

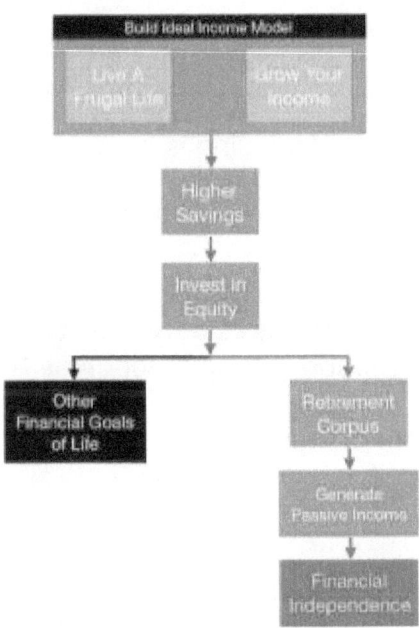

Mind mapping often performs by drawing logical steps during a flow-chart style, explaining the trail to achieve financial independence.

Such a flow chart shows the above. Let me explain briefly the flow of ideas shown within the above mind map.

2.1.1 Ideal Income Model: what's the perfect income model? A status of being where the personality (families) lives a 'frugal living' in tandem with regular 'income growth.'

2.1.2 High Savings: a mix of frugality and increasing income leads to higher savings. How? Because such people grow their revenue at a rate faster than their expenses.

2.1.3 Equity Investing: Personalities must learn to strengthen the facility of their savings. The way to do it? By investing the savings. Where to invest? When the time horizon is long, equity financing is best. Achieving financial independence may be a future goal; hence equity focus is going to be suitable.

2.1.4 Retirement Structure (Asset Support 1): The concept behind investing in equity is to grow asset support. When the asset support is large enough, it shall accustomed build a retirement structure. This structure will then generate streams of passive income. That may eventually cause financial independence.

Other Financial Goals (Asset Support 2): The asset support must accustom to paying attention to different financial aims of related (other than retirement structure).

The most crucial step within the above list is **2.1.4.** it is often the step that's eventually driving us to financial freedom.

But to achieve this step efficiently, all other levels must get equal weightage. Nothing often neglected.

Let's see these steps in additional detail.

2.1.1 IDEAL INCOME MODEL:

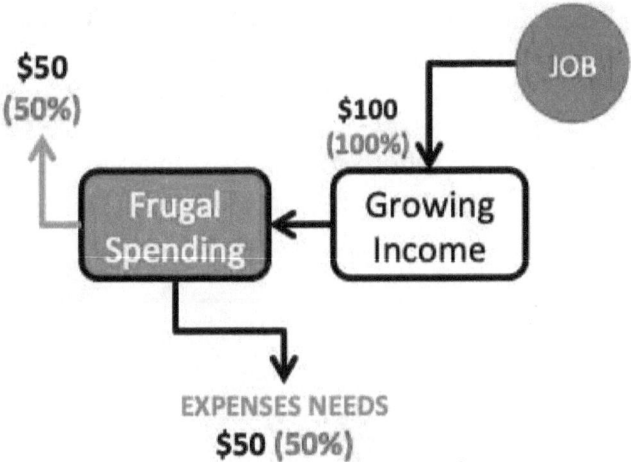

There are two components of a perfect income model:
- Frugal lifestyle, and
- Continual income growth.

How they become components of the "ideal income model"? Because working in tandem, they will transform even a pauper into a financially independent person. How?

What is Frugal Living? Maintaining a lifestyle that is much less than what one can afford. What does it mean? Such people save a better division of their revenue (assume 50%).

Consolidate frugal living with revenue growth, and it enhances a primary approach in achieving financial freedom. How?

EXAMPLE:

Suppose there's an individual who gains Rs. 100,000 per month. He remains frugal (saving 50% of his income). His salary increases to 10% once a year.

Let's see his savings pattern for the next five years.

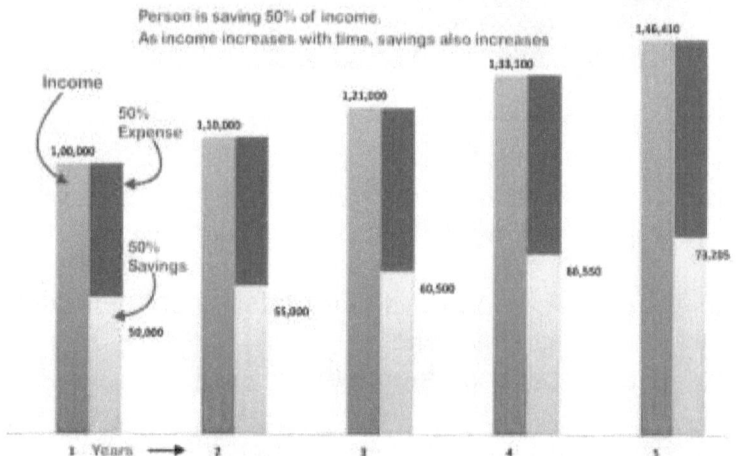

In 5 ages, the savings of the personality raised from Rs. 50,000 to Rs. 73,205 per month.

The person was anyway saving slowly (50%). But because the quantum of savings is increasing per annum, its impact on financial independence is phenomenal. How?

Let's read more.

2.1.2 HIGH SAVINGS:

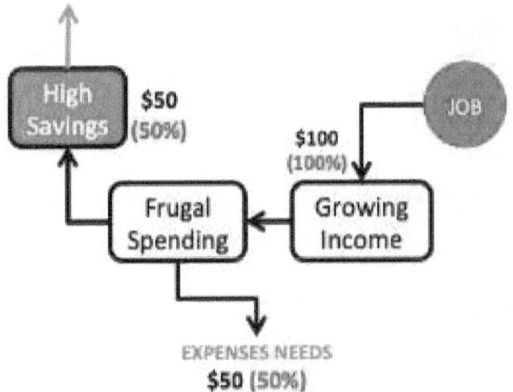

EXPENSES NEEDS
$50 (50%)

Frugality may be a lifestyle that results in higher savings.

In the project of financial independence, savings is that the resources. During this campaign, fewer resources won't serve the aim.

Hence for a standard man, practicing frugality must be an appropriate compromise. After all, financial independence is not a common goal.

Tip: Calculate what proportion you're saving today. Attempt to increase the saving by 1% per month. Keep increasing the savings until you reach the coveted target of fifty. Please note, the beginning is going to be more robust. Once you pass the boundary of 25% savings, everything will start maturing more comfortable.

2.1.3 INVESTING IN EQUITY:

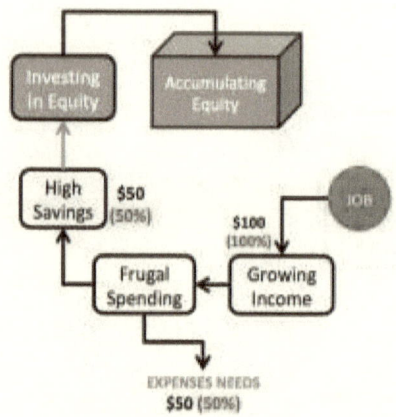

It is a significant milestone within the journey towards financial freedom. It must implement adequately. Why? Because in equity investment, there's a high risk of loss.

Then why to speculate inequity? Because, if appropriately invested, equity can yield high returns. Moreover, investing in equity is additionally convenient.

So, three points that need clarification:

High Return: what proportion of Return should one expect from equity? On a median, 12% p.a. from equity is taken into account competent. But it's also possible to the touch 18%-20% p.a. by practicing long run holding strategy in equity.

We are investing in equity correctly: the way to finance adequately? There are two ways to speculate in equity: (1) direct through stocks, (2) indirect through mutual funds.

Equity is Convenient: Why? Because it's possible to start investing in equity, although one's savings is simply Rs.500 per month. Compare this with gold and property. It'll not be easy to shop for gold or an actual estate property with such low savings.

What should be the target of investors during this level? The investor must target to acquire more assets over time. The way to purchase equity? By buying shares of businesses or lots of equity-based mutual funds. But care must take to shop for only undervalued stocks.

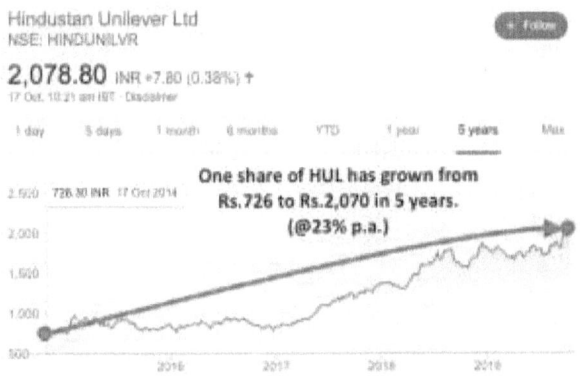

Hindustan Unilever Ltd
NSE: HINDUNILVR

2,078.80 INR +7.80 (0.38%) ↑
17 Oct. 10.21 am IST · Disclaimer

One share of HUL has grown from
Rs.726 to Rs.2,070 in 5 years.
(@23% p.a.)

What is the advantage of equity accumulation? Equity appreciates faster in value. When undervalued equity purchase, it automatically acknowledges with a period.

Assume one purchased one share worth $50. After three years, an equivalent one number share will appreciate becoming $70 (@12% p.a.).

2.1.4 CREATION OF ASSET SUPPORT:
In the above step, what appeared is "equity growth."

The term equity growth depends on the quantum of savings and the quantum of the corpus required.

Suppose one must build Rs.2.0 Crore. His average monthly savings is said Rs. 20,000. Consider return @14% p.a; what proportion of time it'll take him to accumulate two crores? 18.3 Years (use the below calculation).

Once the equity accumulation is complete, the subsequent step is to convert equity within the following two asset supports:

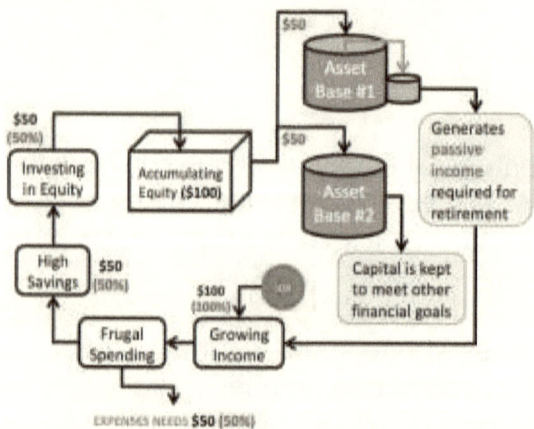

Asset Support 1 (Retirement Structure): It consists of such assets that make passive income flows. It must remember that not all asset types can generate passive income. Assets that are proper for revenue creation post-retirement present hereabouts.

Asset Support 2 (Other Financial Goals): It contains most debt-based assets (like debt mutual funds, deposits, etc.). These are plans like buying a house, car, child's education, etc.; within the pursuance of financial independence, these goals can't compromise. Due importance must even give to them.

Let's review step 2 **(Execution: of financial independence)**.

We have built a mind-map that encourages us to envision the way to convert "income from job" into an "Asset." To attain financial freedom, and we require such assets that generate "passive income." Here, we must not ignore the need for "other financial goals."

This way, one can do financial independence.
But complete financial autonomy can't reach at one go. It is often accomplished only in levels.

Let's know more about the three levels of financial freedom.

3. LEVELS OF FINANCIAL FREEDOM
Cutting down financial freedom in levels can assist in achieving it efficiently.

Financial freedom may be a goal, which is sort of a 42Km long marathon. One cannot sprint and reach the finishing line. It is often achieved only slowly, in levels.

What is logic? When the goal is challenging, it's better to interrupt it down into levels– like taking one step at a time. The way to do it?

Levels: it's an idea like breaking down big goals into smaller milestones.

There are often three levels of financial independence:

MILESTONES TO CLIMB THE PEAK OF
FINANCIAL INDEPENDENCE

Level 1 (Primary Independence): When it involves financial security, people must first cover their necessities (like meals, house, apparel, bills, education, etc.).

Level 2 (Comfort Independence): When their immediate demands are becoming taken care of regularly, people start spending on comfort.

Level 3 (Luxury Independence): After necessities and luxury come luxury spending.

Everyone doesn't spend an equivalent amount on essential goods, comforts and luxury. What's the pattern?

The pattern often formed from looking deep inside one's necessities of life.

Some people can spend as little as Rs. Ten thousand per month to hide their necessities of life. On the opposite hand, there are people for whom an equivalent obligation will need Rs. 20,000.

In turn, these people also will spend differently on their comfort and luxury needs.

Why this difference? It's due to the way they need to have been brought by their parents. For example, a child who has always lived in an air-conditioned home will treat AC's as necessary goods.

Let's see each level of financial freedom in additional detail.

LEVEL 1. PRIMARY INDEPENDENCE.
It is level one (first milestone) of financial independence. What does it stand-up? It tells people first to build enough assets to hide the necessities of life.

What does it mean? Building an oversized enough asset support, which ultimately yields such a lot of income, covers life's fundamental necessities.

Which are the fundamental necessities of life?

Food,
Rent/EMI,
Utility Bills,
Communication,
Education,
Public Transport,
Essential Clothing,
Essential Health,
Essential Emergency Cash,
Essential Maintenance,
etc.

How to calculate the quantum of necessary freedom?
By using this method:

Primary Independence = N x 200

N = Share of monthly income,

which is getting accustomed to buying necessities of life.

Example: Suppose there's an individual whose necessities of life costs Rs. 50,000 per month. This individual will require asset support of Rs.1.0 Crore (200 x 50,000) to succeed in level one. What's the count?

	Monthly Income	No. Months in an Year	Return on Investment (%)	Asset Size
	N	12	6	= (N*12/6)*100 = 200N
Basic Necessities	50,000	12	6	1,00,00,000

How to get the estimate? By investing in Rs. One Crore in an equity option, which yields an annual return of 6% p.a., will generate a yearly income of Rs.6.0 lakhs (or Rs. 50,000 per month).

Why 6% p.a. return and less or less? An appropriate risk-free debt-based investment portfolio can easily yield a median return of 6% p.a.

LEVEL 2. COMFORT INDEPENDENCE.

It is level two (second milestone) of financial independence. What does it stand-up? It tells people to create more assets to cover those requirements of life, which makes them comfortable.

Here one will need to build much bigger asset support than in level 1. This asset support will be so significant that it'll cover both necessities and comforts of life.

Which are the comforting requirement of life? These are such spending that can't be tagged as luxuries, as they incline to become "necessities" in times to return. Few examples show here:

House maintenance,
Wi-Fi Connectivity,
Essential Shopping,
Entertainment,
Person Transportation Expenses,
Child Plan,
Essential Investments,
etc.
How to determine the quantum of comfort independence? By using this formula:

Comfort Independence = N x 400

N = Share of monthly income,
which is getting accustomed to buying necessities of
life.

Example: Suppose there's an individual whose
primary requirements of life costs him Rs. 50,000 per
month. This person will need asset support of Rs. 2.0
Crore (400 x 50,000) to succeed in level two. What's
the estimation?

[Reminder: As per my views, personalities spend
equally on the primary & comfort needs of their life, if
an individual spends Rs.50K on necessities. he's
likely to pay the same amount of cash (Rs.50K) on
satisfaction needs also.]

	Monthly Income	No. Months in an Year	Return on Investment (%)	Asset Size
	N	12	6	= (N*12/6)*100 = 200N
Basic Necessities	50,000	12	6	1,00,00,000
Comfort Needs	50,000	12	6	1,00,00,000
				2,00,00,000

What does this count state? By investing Rs. 2 Crore
in an equity option that generates an annual return of
6% p.a., it will make a yearly income of Rs.12.0 lakhs
(or Rs. 100,000 per month).

Quick Tip: people that spend on their comfort needs
often overspend. Hence it's advisable to create an
expense budget and pay accordingly.

LEVEL 3. LUXURY INDEPENDENCE.

It is level three (final milestone) of financial independence. What does it stand-up? Here, the investor's asset support is so high that each expense requirement of life experience.

Here one will need to build the most crucial asset supports over what has already wiped out stages one and two.

Generally, people tend to spend far more on luxury than on essential goods and luxury needs. Why? Due to two reasons:

- Luxury is expensive.
- Luxury is additionally tempting.

Hence, the dimensions of asset support required to hide the person's luxury needs are sort of high. The proportion often has shown within the chart.

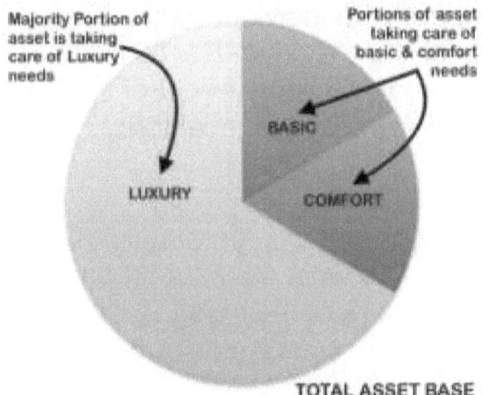

Which are the luxurious requirement of life? These are those spending that individuals generally incur once they have excess take advantage of hand. People usually spend money here to uplift their standard of living.

Purchase of a more substantial home,
You are buying a much bigger car,
Vacation,
Celebrations,
Donations,
You are investing for net worth building,
Shopping,
etc.

How to determine the quantum of luxury independence? By using this formula:

Luxury Independence = N x 1200

N = Share of monthly income,
which is getting accustomed to buying necessities of life.

Example: Suppose there's an individual whose primary requirements of life costs him Rs. 50,000 per month. This person will need asset support of Rs. 6.0 Crore (1200 x 50,000) to succeed in level three. What's the count?

[Reminder: As per my observations, personalities spend double on luxury than what they spend on the primary & comfort necessities of their life.]

	Monthly Income (Rs.)	No. Months in an Year	Return on Investment (%)	Asset Size (Rs.)
	N	12	6	= (N*12/6)*100 = 200N
Basic Necessities	50,000	12	6	1,00,00,000
Comfort Needs	50,000	12	6	1,00,00,000
Luxury Needs	2,00,000	12	6	4,00,00,000
				6,00,00,000

What does this count state? By investing Rs. 6 Crore in an equity option that yields an annual return of 6% p.a. will generate Rs' yearly revenue. 36 lakhs (or Rs. 300,000 per month).

Quick Tip: Personalities who can bear to spend on luxury shall need extra attention to make their asset size grow faster. Why? Because it'll further increase their monthly income.

IMPORTANCE OF OTHER GOALS OF LIFE
Achieving financial independence is a crucial goal. But there are equally important goals:

Car purchase.
Annual Vacations.
Home purchase.
Higher Education.
Marriage.
What about these goals?

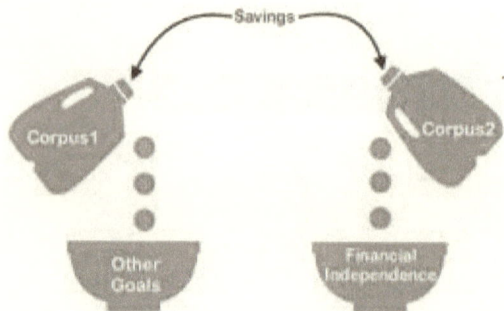

It is relatively essential to achieve other goals along with side financial independence. Why? Because if not done, they're going to eventually eat-away your built 'financial independence corpus' anyway.

So the right strategy is going to be to place money proportionally in each goal separately. The thought is to keep the dream of financial independence isolated from other purposes.

FINAL WORDS

Financial independence achieve when "required" income will still drip-in even once we are sleeping. We should always not be required to figure to get paid to manage our expense needs.

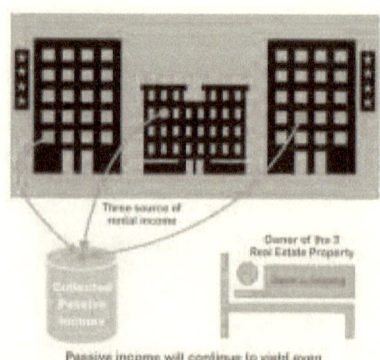

Passive income will continue to yield even when the owner is sleeping

Income generated from a job or business isn't passive income. It's an active income. The thought is to figure and generate active income. Then divert a minimum of 50% of the active income to accumulate equity.

But equity accumulation, not enough. it's more important to convert equity into "passive income-generating assets. "

Which are such assets? Few best samples of such assets are the following:

Asset	Passive Income
Deposits	Interest
Stocks	Dividend
Real Estate	Rent
Annuity	Pension

QUICK ADVICE:
A sure way of growing financially independent starts with living a frugal life; frugality doesn't mean leading a life of misery. It means diverting a much more significant proportion of one's income towards the net worth building.

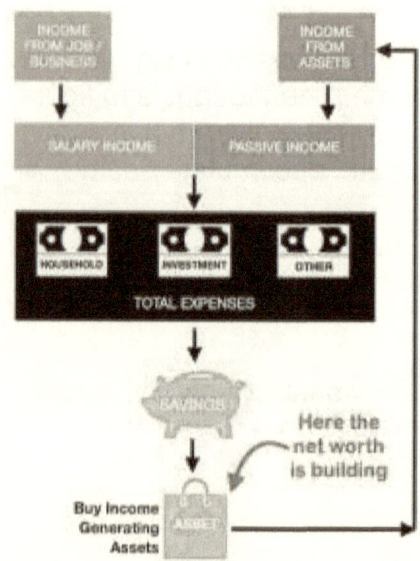

A personality who lives a frugal life assures that an enormous piece of income is out there as savings. It is often a tremendous advantage. Why? Because this available liquid cash accustoms to investment in equity; As equity earns higher returns, such assets can build a sizeable corpus in the long run.

First, a part of this corpus shall accustom to manage "other financial goals" of life. The second part shall use for "retirement" (financial independence}.

Have attractive financing!

Chapter-8: RULE NO.8 TAX PLANNING

"The best is a tax for doing something wrong. A tax is pleasant for doing something right."

"Taxation is the rate which civilized communities pay for the possibility of last civilized."

Everything about taxation planning

1. INTRODUCTION

Before we get into the main points of taxation planning, let's first understand a few fundamental taxation principles—income generated from diversified sources.

The majority earn income from one source, like a job or business.

But some earn income from sort of sources.

For taxation purposes, all incomes categorize into five types.

All types of income attract taxation.

But there are exemptions provided on some sort of income.

Even if the income is taxed or excused, it's essential first to learn to categorize one's source of income.

In the terminology of taxation, categorizing income is usually referred to as "heads of income."

It is essential for the taxpayer first to categorize the income under its right heads.

It becomes exceptionally crucial for those who have multiple sources of income.

In terms of tax planning, it all starts with defining the right heads for every flowing-in income.

2. THE "5 HEADS OF INCOME."
- Income from salary.
- Income from house property.
- Profit from a business.
- Capital gain.
- Other sources of Income.

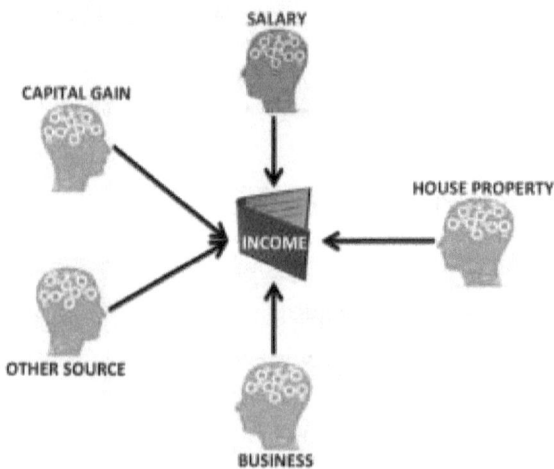

Let's elaborate more on the above five heads of income:

2.1. INCOME FROM SALARY:
When an individual receives a paycheck from a corporation for his job, it's called a salary.

Anybody paying some money to others can't treat it as payment.

There must be a settlement subsisting as per the rule of law, which may prove that:
- The Payer: is that the Employer.
- The Receiver: is that the Employee.

One this is often established; an employee can receive the salary (remuneration's) in the following forms:

Concerning Indian taxation laws, the jargon is like this:
- Payments,
- Expenses,
- Allowances,
- Credits,
- Reward,
- Pension Funds,
- Retirement profits etc.

If one earns money in any of the above modes, its level will be under the top "pay."

2.2. INCOME FROM REAL ESTATE PROPERTY:
The earnings gained by the proprietor of real estate property is taxable.

In case the apartment property is self-occupied, there'll be no income. So liabilities are nothing or zero.

But if the real estate property is let-out on rent, then the income in the owner's hands may become taxable.

Let's see how liabilities on income from house property calculates.

The formula is like this:

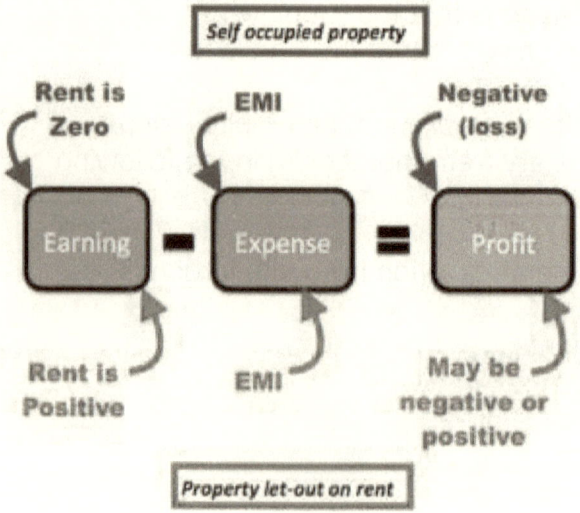

2.3. "PROFITS" FROM BUSINESS:
Please note that the word used hereabouts is profit and no income.

What is the contrast between income and profit?

Income from the company, minus the allowable expenses acquired while driving the company, is profit.

The profit made by the business is responsible for taxation.

To compute; take advantage of the business, the taxpayer needs to remember the allowed expenses available as deductions.

Otherwise, one may find yourself miscalculating one's profits.

2.4. CAPITAL GAIN:
Generally, the valuation of assets appreciates with time.

When the owner sells such an asset, the profit made within the sale is taxable.

Not all kinds of asset sales attract tax.

Personal assets generally don't attract tax. But there are exceptions here also.

Few assets whose profitable sale attracts tax are:
- Immovable property,
- Movable property,
- Jewelry,
- Artwork like painting etc.

As per the tax act, financial gain further categorized into two parts:
- Short term financial gain &
- Long term financial gain.

Depending on the period that the vendor held the asset, the financial gain will be short or long.

Short term financial gain will be applicable if the asset has held for fewer than three ages.

For money assets like ETF's, mutual funds, stocks, etc., short term financial gain will be applicable as long as assets have held for fewer than one age.

All capital profits, not coming under short term financial profit, is chargeable for long-run financial gain.

2.5. OTHER INCOME SOURCES:
There are different sorts of income that don't fall into the above four categories.

Few samples of income sources that can fall into "other income" head are as below:
- Dividend earnings,
- Interest earnings,
- Gifts,
- Provident Fund income,
- Income from games like lottery, racecourse, etc

Till now, what we've seen are the five heads of income.

The one that wants to calculate one's tax liability shall do the subsequent first:
- List down all sources of income.
- Categorize this income within the above five heads.
- Once often done, the following step is to understand the exemption.

What is the exemption? That income cannot attract tax.

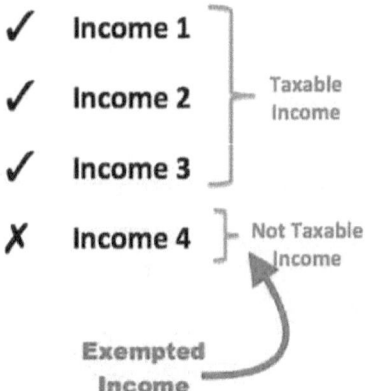

3. INCOME EXEMPTED FROM TAX
People often think that the government will tax all income. But this is often not correct.

There are income types that don't draw any taxes.

Let's see some well-known income types excused from the tax net:
- Agriculture or Farming income
- Pay derived from the employer as LTA (conditions apply).
- Retirement income is a division of reward, pension, leave encasement, compensation gained upon spontaneous retirement (up to prescribed limits).
- Income from policy, including gratuity
- House rent allowance (HRA) up to specific limits.
- Dividend income earned from companies on which dividend distribution tax has paid (conditions apply)

- Long Term Financial Gain (LTCG) tax applicable on selling of stock, total equity mutual funds (conditions apply), etc.

These are few income types that excuse from the taxpayers.

3.1 ALLOWABLE DEDUCTIONS ON INCOME
In addition to exclusion, there are deductions. Deductions also assist us in saving lots of tax.

What are deductions?

They are a few selected "expenses" that reduce our liabilities. How?

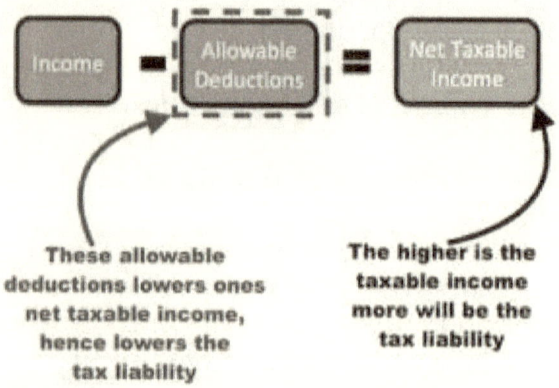

These allowable deductions lowers ones net taxable income, hence lowers the tax liability

The higher is the taxable income more will be the tax liability

But why deductions are allowed? To market some sort of expenses,

The government gives incentives to draw in personalities to acquire these expenses.

This way, they discursively ask themselves to spend money in a certain way.

These allowable deductions successively help people to save lots of tax.

Let's see here a few deductions that folks can utilize to scale back their tax liability:

SECTION 80C:

The allowable amount, which will claim under section 80C, is Rs. 150,000.

Few ordinary expenses that deductions often claimed u/s 80C are as below:
- Life insurance premium purchased family (self, spouse & child)
- Annuity contract payment for family (person, spouse & child)
- Contribution to EPF, pension capital funds, etc
- Benefits from PPF to the families (self, spouse & child)
- Income deposited in Post Office Savings Bank in 10Y or 15Y a/c
- Amount spent to get NSC
- Amount spend to get ELSS Fund
- Amount spend to get pension funds contributed by mutual funds
- Buying of deposits declared by National Housing Bank (NHB)
- Tuition fees paid to high school, college for full-time education
- Principal portion purchased homeownership loan
- Chosen fixed deposits of registered bank
- Investment to Bonds declared by NABARD
- Gains under SCSS

- Investments of 5Y term deposit of Indian Post Office

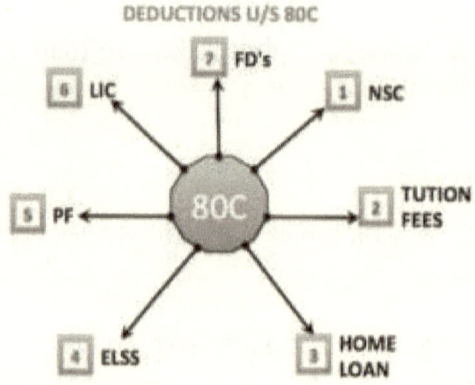

Section 80CCC: Bonus payment towards annuity plan of LIC

Section 80CCG: Bonus payment towards RGESS

Section 80D: Allots deductions for incentive payment upon buying insurance policies

Section 80DD: Allots deductions for an expense incited towards the maintenance of a disabled person

Section 80DDB: Allots deductions for an expense incited towards medical treatment of senior citizens

Section 80E: Allots deductions for an expense incited towards interest payment of education loan

Section 80G: Allots deductions for an expense incited towards contribution to confident public trust

Section 80GG: Allots deductions for an expense incited towards payment of rent if HRA doesn't receive from a company

Section 80U: Allots deductions for expense incited towards maintenance/treatment of self of a disabled person

Section 80TTA: Allots deductions for interest gained from savings bank account up to Rs. 10,000.

But does this statement answer why the government gives such incentives (deductions)?

All these incentives are such it generates a win-win condition for the people, economy, and business.

Speaking generally about these incentives, do the following:
- It causes people to save lots of, invest & insure.
- This way, the government has more free cash.
- The government uses this free cash for the economic process.

4. WHO MUST PAY INCOME TAX?
Anybody who is functioning in India and is making money should pay taxes to the govt of India.

But the liabilities substantially vary counting on who is paying the tax.

As per the taxation act, the taxpayers have been categorizing into the following types:
- Individual

- HUF (Hindu Undivided Family)
- Company
- Firm
- Association of persons
- Local authority &
- Other people not included in the above list

4.1. WHO IS AN INDIVIDUAL?

The following two (2) types of people classified as "individual ":

(1). The person has been residing in India for the last 182 days or more (in the previous year).

(2). The person who has been living in India for the last 60 days or more (in the previous year) and 12 months/More within the four years preceding the year earlier.

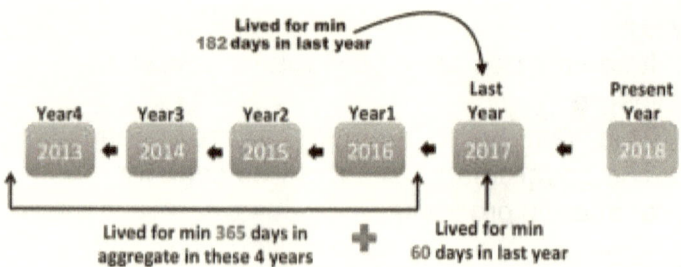

NON-RESIDENT INDIVIDUAL:

An Indian citizen who doesn't qualify for the above criteria becomes an NRI.

NRI status makes the liabilities different than a "Resident Individual."

How NRI's people taxed in India?

NRI's need to pay tax (to India's Government) only on those profits generated in India. Foreign income won't be charged tax in India.

Assume there's an NRI who resides in Europe. But this person has some income-generating ventures and investments in India.

In this case, all income made in India grows taxable for this NRI (as per the legal tax section).

But the investment or venture income earned by NRI's is taxed adversely than a resident person.

Interest received on deposits owned by an NRI in Indian banks (FCNR / NRE) doesn't draw tax.

If an NRI invests or finances in shares, securities, debentures, etc., in India, their short-term gain will tax at a flat rate of 20%.

In the state of long-run financial profit, the rate applicable is going to be only 10%.

4.2. WHO IS HUF?

In an undivided Hindu family (HUF), assets belong to a family and not any specific individual.

In such a case, HUF treats like a persona.

But in fact, the taxation levied on HUF is different from an "individual."

All persons during a family can jointly form a HUF.

But the condition is merely one, and they ought to be descendants from a standard ancestor.

In HUF, spouses and unmarried daughters also can be included.

5. TAXATION SLABS

Gross total income, minus allowable deductions, give net tax payable payment.

On this next tax payable income, one must apply the govt recognized tax slabs.

Once the tax slabs are taxing on the taxable income, one's liabilities are often counting.

Every year within the Union Budget, the Finance Ministry of India sanctions/changes the prevailing tax slabs applicable to a person's earnings.

One may question why there are tax slabs and not one tax rate?

To take charge of the income inequality. How?
The reasoning goes like this; personalities that earn less shall pay lower taxes than high earning people.

More extended tax-burden shall capture on the rich. Why? Because they will manage to pay higher taxes.

Based on this approach, the prevailing tax slabs in India are as below:

AGE < 60 YEARS (MEN, WOMEN & HUF) – FY 2018-2019

Taxable income (TI) in Rs.	Tax Slabs (Applicable Tax Rate)
Zero < TI < 2,50,000	No Tax
2,50,000< TI < 5,00,000	5%
5,00,000< TI < 10,00,000	20%
TI > 10,00,000	30%
50,00,000 < TI < 1,00,00,000	30% (Surcharge of 10% on income tax)
TI> 1,00,00,000	30% (Surcharge of 15% on income tax)

60 YEARS < AGE < 80 YEARS (MEN & WOMEN)

Taxable income (TI) in Rs.	Tax Slabs (Applicable Tax Rate)
Zero < TI < 3,00,000	No Tax
3,00,000< TI < 5,00,000	5%
5,00,000< TI < 10,00,000	20%
TI > 10,00,000	30%
50,00,000 < TI < 1,00,00,000	30% (Surcharge of 10% on income tax)
TI> 1,00,00,000	30% (Surcharge of 15% on income tax)

AGE > 80 YEARS (MEN & WOMEN)

Taxable income (TI) in Rs.	Tax Slabs (Applicable Tax Rate)
Zero < TI < 5,00,000	No Tax
5,00,000< TI < 10,00,000	20%
TI > 10,00,000	30%
TI> 1,00,00,000	30% (Surcharge of 15% on income tax)

6. EXAMPLE OF TAXATION CALCULATION.

Let's take the case of an individual (person below 60 years of age) whose income and other features are below:

- **R**evenue from Salary = Rupees 12,00,000/-
- Interest Gain = Rupees 1,00,000/-
- **D**eduction or Abatement u/s 80C = Rupees 1,50,000/-

What is the net taxable income of this individual?
= 12,00,000(R) + 1,00,000(I) – 1,50,000(D)
= Rupees 11,50,000/-

What are the liabilities of this individual?

Before we calculate the liabilities, let's consider Rs. 11,50,000 into following tax slabs:
- @0% Tax – Rs. 2,50,000
- @5% Tax – Rs. 2,50,000
- @20% Tax – Rs. 5,00,000
- @30% Tax – Rs. 1,50,000

Now, let's calculate the Tax Liability:

First Rupees 2,50,000 = Zero.
Rupees 2,50,000 = (5% x 2,50,000)
= Rupees 12,500
Rupees 5,00,000 = (20% x 5,00,000)
= Rupees 1,00,000.
Rupees 1,50,000 = (30% x 1,50,000)
= Rupees 45,000.

Lump sum Calculated Tax = Rupees (12,500+1,00,000+45,000) = Rupees 1,57,500/-

Total Liabilities = Rupees 1,57,500 + Education Cess.

Education Cess (Cess is a sort of tax charged) = 3% x 1,57,000 = Rupees 4,725/-

Total Liabilities = Rupees 1,57,500 + 4,725 = Rupees 1,62,225/-

7. CONCEPT OF MARGINAL RATE

There is the other concept described as the "Marginal Rate of Tax."

As per this dictate, nobody is tax likewise. How?

Let's see examples:

(1) Personalities below 60 years of age are taxed differently from those above 60.

(2) NRI's are taxed differently than resident Indian citizens.

(3) High earning personalities are taxed differently than low, reaching people.

Let's attempt to explain the concept of marginal rate with a more specific example:

EXAMPLE-1:
Suppose your taxable income (salary) is Rupees 12 Lakhs.

You also invested some money in a deposit where you had earned an income of Rupees 26,000 last year.

How your total income is going to be taxed?

The answer is that the gross income will be tax at the applicable marginal rate of tax.

What does this mean?

The authorities are telling you to compute your liabilities as per your applicable tax slabs.

What is your tax slab?

Salary Portion: Rs.12,00,000

Taxable Income (TI) in Rs.	Tax Slabs (Applicable Tax Rate)
Zero < TI < 2,50,000	No Tax
2,50,000< TI < 5,00,000	5% (5% of 250,000 = 12,500)
5,00,000< TI < 10,00,000	20% (20% of 500,000 = 100,000)
TI > 10,00,000 (Rs.200,000)	30% (30% of 200,000 = 60,000)

Interest Income Portion: Rs.26,000

Taxable Income (TI) in Rs.	Tax Slabs (Applicable Tax Rate)
TI > 10,00,000 (Rs.26,000)	30% (30% of 26,000 = 7,800)

Here you'll note that the interest income charges a 30% rate and not 0%, 10%, or 20%. Often it is what it means by margin percentage or proportion.

The costliest rate applicable for your salary will apply to the interest portion of the security or deposit.

Henceforth tax to be paid on interest earnings is going to be 30% of Rupees 26,000/-

EXAMPLE2:
Taxable income from job Rupees 995,000, interest earned on deposit Rupees 26,000.

What tax will apply to interest returns on bank deposits?

Salary Portion: Rupees 9,95,000

Taxable Income (TI) in Rs.	Tax Slabs (Applicable Tax Rate)
Zero < TI < 2,50,000	No Tax
2,50,000< TI < 5,00,000	5% (10% of 250,000 = 12,500)
5,00,000< TI < 9,95,000	20% (20% of 495,000 = 99,000)

Interest Income Portion: Rs.26,000

Taxable Income (TI) in Rs.	Tax Slabs (Applicable Tax Rate)
5,00,000< TI < 10,00,000 (Rs.26,000)	20% (20% of 26,000 = 5,200)

The costliest rate appropriate for your salary earnings will be related to the interest portion of the deposit. What is the very best rate applied during this example-2? 20 percent.

Hence tax to be paid on interest returns is going to be 20% of Rupees 26,000/-

-	Example 1	Example 2
Salary Income	12,00,000	9,95,000
Interest Income	26,000	26,000
Tax Payable on Interest	30% of 26,000 = 7,800	20% of 26,000 = 5,200

For the same interest income higher earning person is taxed more on it than a lower earning person

8. HOW DIVIDEND OR PROFITS FUNDED BY MUTUAL FUNDS ARE TAXED?

We know that dividends or profits paid by companies are tax-free within the hand of the shareholders.

But not many of us knowledge dividends paid by mutual funds are taxed.

The problem with mutual funds is that they're not of the same type.

So, when mutual funds pay dividends, it's pertinent to know the source of income.

A. EQUITY BASED FUNDS.
These funds feature a portfolio that is 65% or more abundant in equity.

These equity-linked stocks reserve profits and share them to their lot holders as "profits or dividends."

The fund house pays dividends or gains after payment of corporate dividend tax (CDT).

Before Feb'2018, dividends paid by equity-based funds weren't taxable within the hands of investors.

But post-Feb '2018, this dividend income is additionally taxed @10%.

What does it mean?

It means dividends received from equity-based funds aren't tax-free in the hands of the investors.

The investor must pay a 10% tax on their dividend income originating from equity-based funds.

B. DEBT BASED FUNDS.
These funds feature a portfolio that has an equity component but 65%.

These debt funds earn the majority of short term income in sort of interests.

Here Dividend Distribution Tax (DDT) is applicable. The mutual fund business shall repay DDT @28.84% for debt-based.

What does it imply for the investors?

The mutual fund organizations should settle DDT before sharing the profits to lot owners.

So dividends or profits received from debt-based funds are tax-free in the hands of the investors.

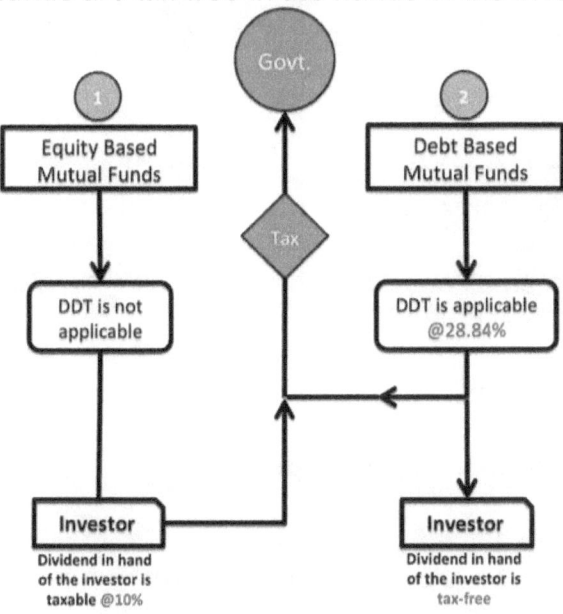

9. HOW IS INTEREST INCOME TAXED?

Interest income is the tax payable at the marginal allowance or rate.

Not all interest is taxable, but the majority is taxable.

The government of India provides some "exemptions "in interest income also.

Example: There are tax-free bonds issued by India's government (Infrastructure bonds, NHAI Bond, etc.).

When NRI parks their money in India as a deposit, the interest earned on such deposits is tax-free.

There is some debt linked financial instruments whose interest income subjected to TDS.

What is TDS? Tax Deducted at Source.

This TDS is collected to make sure that the govt upfront receives some of the tax.

TDS may be a small portion of the tax that an investor shall pay on the accrued interest income.

What does it mean?

Let's reconsider point #7, **Example-1.**

The person who gained interest is Rupees 26,6000. On this interest, the total tax to be paid was Rupees 7.800.

Taxable Income (TI) in Rs.	Tax Slabs (Applicable Tax Rate)
TI > 10,00,000 (Rs.26,000)	30% (30% of 26,000 = 7,800)

Assume on payment of Rupees 26,000 as interest, TDS of Rupees 1,2000 was already deducting.

It determines that the individual's internet tax payable on the interest income will be only Rupees 6,600 (7,800 – 1,200).

10. INDEXATION BENEFIT AND TAXATION LIABILITY?

Indexation can dramatically reduce one's long-run financial gain liabilities.

Indexation is nothing but adjusting one's cost of investment purchase for inflation.

Let's see how this often done:

EXAMPLE:
Suppose you purchased a mutual fund lot @ Rupees 150 in the year 2012-13. This fund offers indexation benefits.

The lots purchased in 2012-13 sold in 2016-17 at a price of Rs.200.

What will be the financial gain during an average case?
What will be the financial gain applying indexation?
Long term financial gain (without indexation) will be Rupees 50 (200-150).

Now let's apply the indexation.

To do this, we'll need to see the value of the Inflation Index (CII) published by India's government.

From this graph, I could get the following information:

Record for the year 2012-13: 852
Record for the year 2016-17: 1,125
Let's consider the way to use indexation to estimate net financial profit.

The actual value of the purchase of a mutual fund lot is Rupees 150

Price of buying a mutual fund lot (applying indexation formula):

Price after indexation = (index in the financial year 2016-17/ index in the fiscal year 2012-13) x Actual price of the purchase.

= (1125/852) x 150 = Rupees 198

Long term financial gain (after indexation) will be Rupees 2 (200-198).

You can see how long-run financial gain has gown down from Rupees 50 to Rupees 2 due to indexation.

Indexation can dramatically reduce one's liabilities.

11. HOW ARE CAPITAL GAINS TAXED?

Equity (Shares & equity-oriented mutual funds):

15% – Short term financial gain tax (STCG)

Conditions apply – long-run financial gain tax (LTCG)
All other securities:

At marginal rate – Short term financial gain tax
(STCG)
10% – long-run financial gain tax (LTCG) – without
indexation
20% – long-run financial gain tax (LTCG) – indexation
Exemptions:

LTCG is exempt from tax on residential property sales
if it reinvested back to shop for or construct another
residential property in India.

The new residential property must purchase within
one year of the sale of the earlier feature.

LTCG is again exempt from tax on residential
property sales if the profit reinvests back to shop for
an NHAI or REC bond.

This bond features a lock-in period of three years.

The maximum LTCG, which will save using the bond
route, is Rs.50 lakhs.

FINAL WORDS

If one knows the critical taxation rules, it's possible to
reduce one's liabilities drastically.

It can do by investing one's money in how that,
besides providing investing advantage, also saves tax
briefly.

As an honest citizen of the country, it's good to pay tax to the govt, but overpaying tax isn't advisable.

When the Government allows us to save lots of on tax, then why to overpay it?

Overpayment of tax often is prevented by doing immaculate taxation planning.

I know that the majority would like to save lots of tax ethically.

But they fail to try and do so in the absence of the right information.

Income Tax Slabs: liabilities comparison Between 2020 and 2019

The Union Budget introduce in February 2020, and a new tax scheme annex. The tax slabs have changed. As opposed to the financial year 2019, the latest tax rates are lower.

But the lower tax rates won't necessarily reduce the liabilities for everybody.

Who will benefit?
Some will have the benefit of the new lower tax rates. Those who don't claim high tax "deductions" will pay less tax within the latest scheme (2020).

Who won't benefit?
Some also will pay more taxes within the new scheme. Those who currently claim high tax

deductions, if they prefer the latest tax rates, agree to pay more than the income tax.

"A succeeding in being successful is notable, but not anything is notable as enjoyable as an income tax." - Al Zayd

"The only component that bothers me more than paying an income tax doesn't enduringly have to pay an income tax." - Al Zayd

NEW TAX SLABS / RATES (2020 VS 2019)

The new tax slabs have more income subdivisions than before. An in-depth subdivision has allowed the minister of finance to pass away better tax rates for "lower-income earners." Let's compare the latest tax slabs (2020) with an old one (2019).

Slabs	Taxable Income (Rs.)	Tax Rates 2019	Tax Rates 2020	Remarks
1	Upto 2,50,000	0%	0%	-
2	2,50,001 to 5,00,000	0%	0%	If taxable income is < Rs.5,00,000 u/s 87A
3	2,50,001 to 5,00,000	5%	5%	-
4	5,00,001 to 7,50,000	20%	10%	
5	7,50,001 to 10,00,000	20%	15%	-
6	10,00,000 to 12,50,000	30%	20%	New rates for
7	12,50,000 to 15,00,000	30%	25%	FY 2020-21
8	Above 15,00,000	30%	30%	-

Surcharge: 0% if taxable income is less than Rs.50 L, 10% if taxable income is more than Rs.50 L, 15% if taxable income is more than Rs.1 Cr, 25% if taxable income is more than Rs.2 Cr, 37% if taxable income is more than Rs.5 Cr. Cess: 4% Cess is applicable on all income tax payable.

By watching the above tax rates, it's like 2020 rates are lower, right? But this conclusion is often inaccurate. Why? However, even with lower tax rates, some personalities will find themselves paying more tax.

Let's know more about this ambiguity.

LOWER TAX RATES – BUT HIGH LIABILITIES, WHY?

What is the explanation for 'lower tax rates' not converting into 'lower tax liability'? It happens because the deductions allowed till 2019 removed in 2020

Tax liability calculated supported one's taxable income. Gross income minus deductions are tax payable income. If a person cannot profess deductions, an expected tax income will increase. Hence even with lower tax rates, personalities might end up paying higher taxes.

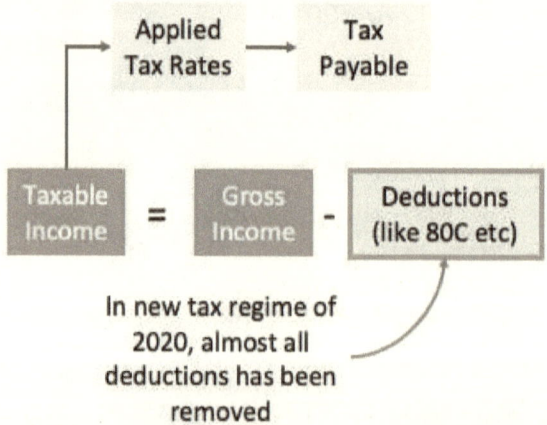

WHICH DEDUCTIONS HAS REMOVED?

Almost everything removes. See a listing of few standard deductions applicable for the 2019 tax scheme but aloof from the 2020 plan:

Deduction Heads	Deduction (Maximum Amount)
HRA	Minimum of (a) Total HRA received from your employer, b. Rent paid less 10% of (Basic salary +DA) c. 40% of salary (Basic+DA) for non-metros and 50% of salary (Basic+DA) for metros
Standard Deduction	Rs.50,000
LTA	100% Travel expenses incurred during leaves.
U/s 80C (LIC, EPF, ELSS, NSC, PF, NPS etc)	Rs.1.5 Lakhs
U/s 80D (Medical Insurance)	Self (Rs.25K or Rs.50K for senior citizen), Parents (Rs.25K or Rs.50K for senior citizen)
Sec 24 (Home Loan Interest on self occupied property)	Rs.200,000
Sec 80E (Education Loan Interest)	100% interest paid in a FY
Sec 80G (Donations)	100% Amount paid
Sec 80TTA (Savings A/c Interest)	Rs.10,000
Sec 80EE (Home Loan Interest - Affordable homes)	Additional Rs.50,000

- ## 80C/80CCC (Rs.1.5 lakhs)

Life Insurance Premium
PPF (Public Provident Fund).
PDF (Employees' Provident Fund).
FD (Tax saving fixed deposits)
NSC (National Savings Certificates).
ELSS (Equity Linked Saving Schemes).
Repayment of homeownership loan Principal
Tuition Fees (for child)
SCSS (Post office old person Savings Scheme).
NPS (National Pension System).
Stamp duty charges for the purchase of a brand new house.
Contributions made to annuity plans.

- ## 80CCD(1b) (Rupees 50,000):

Contributions to NPS. (over Rs.1.5 Lakhs).

- **80D (Rupees 25K+30K):**

Health Insurance Premium (self+Parents).

- **Sec 24 (Rupees 200,000):**

Interest paid on homeownership loan of self-occupied property.

- **80EEE (Rupees 50,000):**

Interest paid on the homeownership loan for the first-time buyer.

- **80TTA (Rupees 10,000):**

Interest income generated from a bank account.

- **80GG:**

HRA received from the employer.

- **80G:**

Contributions made to the charity.

- **80E:**

Interest paid towards the repayment of education loan (self, spouse, child).

- **80GGC:**

Contributions made to a political party

*There are a few deductions that remain under the **new tax scheme:***

- **Sec24:**

Homeownership loan interest deduction on loose let property up to Rupees 2.0 Lakhs
(Note: interest deduction on a self-occupied property isn't acknowledged).

- **80CCD (2):**

Organizations augmentation to NPS of an employee (Max: 10% of Basic+DA)

NEW TAX SCHEME IS OPTIONAL?

Yes, the new tax scheme of 2020 is optional. It means it's the taxpayer's discretion to continue paying tax as per the old plan (2019).

The taxpayer can choose from the old and new tax scheme reckoning, which is best suited to him/her.

How to know which tax scheme (old or new) is more apt for us? It can be what we are going to discuss during this chapter.

But to create the understanding more accessible, I suggest you use my tax calculation for comparison. The estimate will show ends up in a comparative form between old and new tax scheme. It'll make a choice easy.

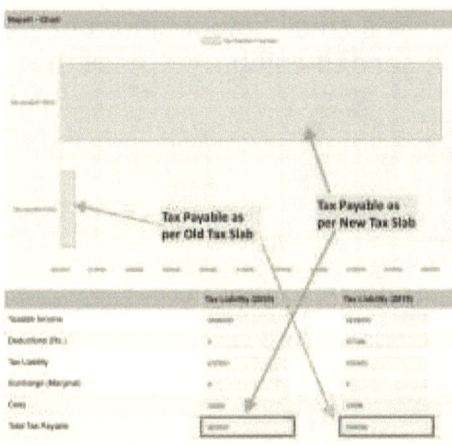

NEW TAX SCHEME (2020) VS OLD (2019)

Tax rates proposed in the new tax scheme are lower. But with these lower tax rates, tax-saving deductions 'can't be applied. It makes the new scheme tricky for people. Generally speaking, the "old tax scheme with deductions" is best than the new tax rates of 2020.

There are two sets of individuals who pay tax.
First: Are those who have just started employment. These personalities have invested less or zeroed in tax saving options. Hence they can't claim tax deductions. For such people, a new tax scheme is best.

Second: Are those who have grown and have generously endowed in tax saving options. These personalities claim high deductions in their tax returns. Hence their tax payable income is comprehensively less than their gross income. For such people, the old tax scheme is best.

I would prefer to elaborate a small amount more for people falling within the second category. Check the below infographics:

Gross Income	New (2020)		Old Regime (2019)	
	Deductions	Tax Liability	Deductions	Tax Liability After Deductions
5 Lakhs	N/A	0	0	0
6 Lakhs	N/A	23,400	0	23,400
7 Lakhs	N/A	33,800	50,000	33,800
8 Lakhs	N/A	46,800	87,500	46,800
9 Lakhs	N/A	62,400	1,12,500	62,400
10 Lakhs	N/A	78,000	1,37,500	78,000
12 Lakhs	N/A	1,19,600	1,43,666	1,19,600
14 Lakhs	N/A	1,68,000	1,83,334	1,68,000
15 Lakhs	N/A	1,95,000	2,00,000	1,95,000
20 Lakhs	N/A	3,51,000	2,00,000	3,51,000
30 Lakhs	N/A	6,63,000	2,00,000	6,63,000
40 Lakhs	N/A	9,75,000	2,00,000	9,75,000
50 Lakhs	N/A	12,87,000	2,00,000	12,87,000
1 Crore	N/A	31,31,700	2,00,000	31,31,700
2 Crore	N/A	31,31,700	2,00,000	31,31,700

Value of deductions (tax savings) which will make old tax regime at par with new tax regime

DEDUCTIONS MAKING NEW & OLD TAX SCHEME AT LEVEL

The above infographics highlight the minimum deductions' worth, making old and new tax schemes at the level. What does it mean? To know this, let's see the following examples:

- **Gross Income = 6 lakhs:**
When income is said six lakhs, the total liabilities in both cases are Rs. 23,400. People opting to remain with the old tax scheme needn't claim any deductions.

- **Gross Income = 7 lakhs:**
Suppose there's an individual who pays a premium (Rupees 50,000 p.a) on the insurance scheme. The personage can claim a deduction of Rupees 50,000 u/s 80C. After alleging the said deduction, old and new tax schemes will generate equivalent liabilities (of Rupees 33,800). If the amount of deduction will increase, penalties in the past tax scheme will further go down.

- **Gross Income = 14 lakhs:**
Suppose an individual claims a reduction of Rupees 183,334 p.a. on account of interest spent on homeownership loan (u/s 24b). For this personage, after alleging a minimum deduction of Rupees 1.84 Lakhs, old and new tax schemes will generate equivalent liabilities (of Rupees 1,69,000).

- **15 Lakhs < Gross Income < 2 Crore:**
For this group of individuals, they have to say a minimum deduction of Rs.2,00,000. Post claiming the said deduction, the liabilities of old and tax scheme will become equivalent.

(Note: Please note that the deductions highlighted within the above table are the minimum values. If the number of deductions increases, liabilities in the old tax scheme will further go down.)

EXAMPLE: TAX CALCULATION [2020]

Particulars	Old Tax (2019)		New Tax (2020)	
	Rates	Rs.	Rates	Rs.
Gross Income	-	8,00,000	-	8,00,000
- Standard Deduction (50K)	-	-50,000	-	N/A
Deductions:		-	-	-
- U/s: 80C	-	-25,000	N/A	N/A
- U/s: 80D	-	-10,000	N/A	N/A
- U/s: 24B	-	-52,500	N/A	N/A
Total Deductions	-	-87,500	-	0
Taxable Income	-	6,62,500	-	8,00,000
Tax Slabs:	-	-	-	-
- Upto 2,50,000	0%	0	0%	0
- 2,50,001 to 5,00,000	5%	12,500	5%	12,500
- 5,00,001 to 7,50,000	20%	32,500	10%	25,000
- 7,50,001 to 10,00,000	20%	-	15%	7,500
Tax Payable	-	45,000	-	45,000
Cess	4%	1800	4%	1800
Total Tax Payable	-	46,800	-	46,800

It is an example of an individual having a gross income of Rs. 8 Lakhs. In the old tax scheme, the person can claim a standard deduction of flat Rs. 50,000. Additionally, to the present, he has also claimed a deduction of Rs. 87,500. It brings down his taxable income to Rs.6,62,500. In this manner, he can pay an equivalent tax as he would have paid; he opted for the new scheme.

Particulars	Old Tax (2019)		New Tax (2020)	
	Rates	Rs.	Rates	Rs.
Gross Income	-	20,00,000	-	20,00,000
- Standard Deduction (50K)	-	-50,000	-	N/A
Deductions:				
- U/s: 80C	-	-1,00,000	N/A	N/A
- U/s: 80D	-	-25,000	N/A	N/A
- U/s: 24B	-	-75,000	N/A	N/A
Total Deductions		-2,00,000	-	0
Taxable Income	-	17,50,000	-	20,00,000
Tax Slabs:				
Upto 2,50,000	0%	0	0%	0
- 2,50,001 to 5,00,000	5%	12,500	5%	12,500
- 5,00,001 to 7,50,000	20%	50,000	10%	25,000
- 7,50,001 to 10,00,000	20%	50,000	15%	37,500
- 10,00,000 to 12,50,000	30%	75,000	20%	50,000
- 12,50,000 to 15,00,000	30%	75,000	25%	62,500
- Above 15,00,000	30%	75,000	30%	1,50,000
Tax Payable	-	3,37,500	-	3,37,500
Cess	4%	13,500	4%	13,500
Total Tax Payable	-	3,51,000	-	3,51,000

It is an example of an individual having a gross income of Rs. 20 Lakhs. Additionally to the quality deduction, he has also claimed an additional deduction of Rs. 2,00,000. It brings down his taxable income to Rs. 17,50,500. In this manner, he can pay an equivalent tax as he would have paid just in case he opted for the new scheme.

Particulars	Old Tax (2019)		New Tax (2020)	
	Rates	Rs.	Rates	Rs.
Gross Income	-	50,10,000	-	50,10,000
- Standard Deduction (50K)	-	-50,000	-	N/A
Deductions:				
- U/s: 80C	-	-1,00,000	N/A	N/A
- U/s: 80D	-	-25,000	N/A	N/A
- U/s: 24B	-	-75,000	N/A	N/A
Total Deductions		-2,00,000	-	0
Taxable Income	-	47,60,000	-	50,10,000
Tax Slabs:				
- Upto 2,50,000	0%	0	0%	0
- 2,50,001 to 5,00,000	5%	12,500	5%	12,500
- 5,00,001 to 7,50,000	20%	50,000	10%	25,000
- 7,50,001 to 10,00,000	20%	50,000	15%	37,500
- 10,00,000 to 12,50,000	30%	75,000	20%	50,000
- 12,50,000 to 15,00,000	30%	75,000	25%	62,500
- Above 15,00,000	30%	9,78,000	30%	10,53,000
Tax Payable	-	12,40,500	-	12,40,500
Surcharge	-	0	-	7,000
Cess	4%	49,620	4%	49,900
Total Tax Payable	-	12,90,120	-	12,97,400

It is an example of an individual having a gross income of Rs. 50.1 Lakhs. Additionally to the quality deduction, he has also claimed an additional deduction of Rs.2,00,000. It brings down his taxable income to Rs.47,60,500. In this manner, he can pay an equivalent tax as he would have paid; he opted for the new scheme.

CONCLUSION

New tax rates proposed within the union budget of 2020 show lower rates, but additionally, to the rate cuts, allowable deductions have also been removed (including the state deduction of Rupees 50,000).

In India, where most houses spend money on tax savings options to scale back their tax burden, our FM's move was unsolicited.

The new tax scheme has kept optional not to cause a significant disruption because of the proposed tax rules. It suggests that the old tax rates alongside deductions will still exist.

So if the new scheme isn't tax-friendly, who will choose the new tax rates? Those who currently claim little deductions will have the benefit of the new tax rates.

"Income tax is the most trustworthy intelligent fiction composed today." - Al Zayd

Chapter-9: RULE NO.9 RETIREMENT

"Retirement resembles a never-ending get-away in Canada. The purpose is to enjoy it the fullest, however, not wholly that you run a lack of money."

Retirement Planning: A comprehensive lead about a way to have it off

There are two retirement planning levels; one is the accumulation level, and the other is the distribution level. Both must immaculately implement to create it successfully.

Retirement planning is vital. Why? Because this is what's getting to give us financial independence after we've retired from our jobs/work.
The planning will make sure of the availability of the specified fund when it's time to retire. In India, most service-class retired people depend upon annuity to require care of their income needs post-retirement. But this is often not enough to guide a real life.

It means people need a much bigger retirement pension. The way to do it? By building some externally.
Internally our retirement pension is made through EPF, NPS, PPF, etc. In addition to those, external contribution to the retirement corpus is additionally necessary. It makes the need for retirement planning even more essential.

The planning for retirement must perform once we are still earning (is in the job). A way to do it? By diverting sufficient savings to an honest retirement linked investment plan. Which may be a good plan? That's what we are going to see during this chapter.

"Retirement will be with enough possibility to do all things that you don't need anything except a peaceful life."

WHAT IS RETIREMENT PLANNING?

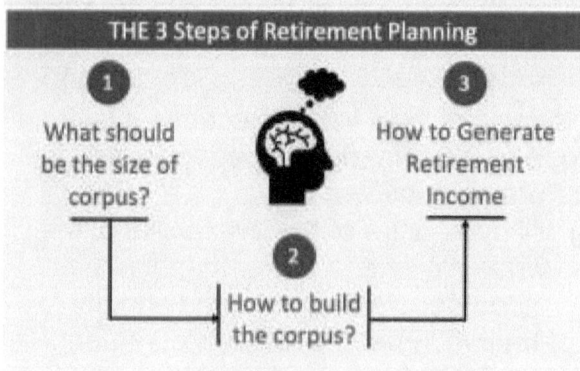

When we state retirement planning, it consists of three significant steps:

First Step: This can be the foremost essential step. It starts with estimating what proportion of retirement corpus will be necessary for a person to guide a real retired life. In simple words, we must decide the dimensions of the retirement corpus here.

Second Step: Once the dimensions establish, the second step is knowing what proportion of monthly savings will be necessary to create the estimated retirement corpus. Often, savings alone won't be enough; the investment must practice alongside it.

Third Step: This is often the ultimate step. It's about investing wisely in the built retirement corpus. There's a difference between investments practiced in the second and third steps. The 2nd step, it's performed to create the corpus. Within the 3rd step, it delivers to get a fixed income.

To successfully execute these steps essential to first judge one's present financial heath. If one's current health is robust, smaller savings will be necessary to make the specified retirement corpus.

But if one's financial health isn't secure, more considerable savings are going to be needed. Why? Because the dimensions of corpus to create will be more significant. The person's economic health interpretation gives us a target of what proportion to save lots of and invest monthly. Once the goal is about, it's also necessary to understand where to speculate the money.

HOW TO PLAN FOR RETIREMENT?

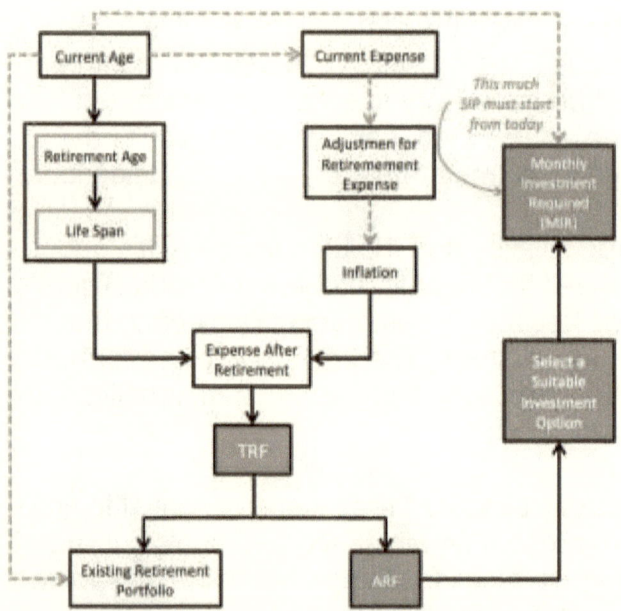

The above flow graph abstracts how a person can prepare for retirement. This flow graph is more useful for personalities who want to understand the plan rule to go behind retirement planning.

We can also read a few Q&As about the above flow chart, further clarifying its utility. Let's see how this flow chart answers a few crucial questions on retirement planning. It's the answering of those questions which can eventually help us to plan well for retirement:

HERS ARE THE Q&A'S:

Q1. Once you want to retire: It's the primary question of retirement planning. Answering this is often important because the further away is that the more comfortable the retirement date, the easier it will be to make the corpus. When the goal is way, even smaller monthly investments can build a given corpus.

Q2. How long spun the retirement corpus must endure: This question said to lifespan? People that expected to measure longer after retirement will need a much bigger retirement corpus.

Q3. What will be my expenses and costs subsequent retirement: Personalities frequently underestimate or overestimate this condition. My calculation determines the minimum future fee necessary supported by a rule of thumb. It considers a person's expenses post-retirement to be nearly 35-45% of the current payment.

Q4. What's the current retirement portfolio's size: Check the current balance in accounts like EPF/PPF/NPS? Enter the worth within the calculation. As per recent trends, we will estimate that our savings parked in EPF, PPF, etc., will fetch on the brink of 7-8% returns in times to return.

Q5. How briskly the expense grows with time: Over a long period of your time, one's expense growth will match the speed of inflation @6% p.a.

Q6. Where to speculate to create the corpus: this is often a goal that is exceptionally far-off in the future. Hence can take the freedom of 'equity-based investing.' I might wish to use SIP in multi-cap funds to make my retirement corpus.

Q7. Where to speculate retirement corpus: Here, the money can't invest too conservatively or too aggressively. Here one must specialize in 'regular income generation. Once the main target is true, subsequent attention-point must get on 'yield' and 'diversification.'

Q8. What shall be the dimensions of retirement corpus (TRF): This is often the leading decisive issue. One can practice my retirement planning calculation to hold a rough estimation of the total retirement pension (TRF).

Q9. What's the Monthly Investment Required (MIR): this is often that monthly investment, which is essential to build the entire retirement corpus.

Based on the above flow chart and, therefore, the Q&A's, here is my retirement planning calculation:

RETIREMENT PLANNING CALCULATION
I'll suggest you use the retirement calculation. The calculation will highlight what proportion you want to invest more and monthly to make an honest retirement corpus.

–	Current Age	Years	24
–	Retirement Age	Years	60
–	Life Expectancy	Years	80
–	Current Monthly Expense	Rs.	100000
CRF	Current Retirement Fund	Rs.	500000
–	Expected Growth of CRF	%	8.0
–	Average Inflation Till Life Time	%	6
–	Expected ROI Till Retirement	%	10
–	Expected ROI After Retirement	%	8

CALCULATE

TRF	Total Retirement Fund Required	Rs.Lakhs	
ARF	Additional Retirement Fund	Rs.Lakhs	
MIR	Monthly Investment Required	Rs	

This retirement planning calculation provides three critical answers:

Total retirement pension Required (TRF): Supported these expenses calculation will forecast future costs (after retirement). Supported this forecast and ROI levels, and the count will estimate the entire retirement pension required. The dimensions of this retirement pension are going to be enough to manage retirement expenses.

Addition retirement pension to make (ARF): Suppose one must build a retirement corpus of, say, rupees 2 Crore (TRF). They supported his current retirement portfolio rupees 80 Lacs are going to be complete automatically. It means the person must make only a further Rupees 1.2 Crore (ARF).

Monthly Investment Required (MIR): this is often the most To-Do for the user of this calculation. It is often the quantity that one must invest monthly to make a corpus as big as ARF.

The logic supported in which the above retirement planning calculation works is going to explain below. Why it's essential to know? Because it'll build a concept process that eventually benefits the planner.

Notes: An informed planner can build a substantially more significant retirement corpus than an informal investor.

WHY MAKE RETIREMENT PLANS?
Because it's necessary, retirement may be a phase of life where one has left the work and is no longer

working. It eventually results in a stoppage of average income in sort of paycheck etc.

People generally retire from a job at 60 years aged. It is often an age where the person might not be physically as able as before. Hence, if an individual can rest and still generate regular income at this phase of life, it'll be ideal.

How may this happen? The generation of regular income without working for it is that the purpose of retirement planning.

The primary step of retirement planning is to reach a secure retirement planning with a calculation. This calculation won't only ask essential questions but also will give critical answers.

A useful retirement calculation guides one to the proper set of answers associated with retirement corpus building.

ACCUMULATION AND DISTRIBUTION PHASE.

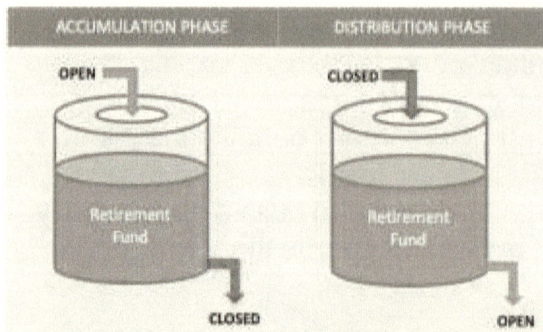

To get retirement planning effectively, one must understand these two levels of retirement planning.

Accumulation level: During this level, people save and invest money to make their retirement corpus. The length will be the build-up level, the easier it'll be to make a sufficiently big retirement corpus. Hence experts recommend starting early. Required corpus for retirement is usually an enormous amount. Therefore, starting soon will make life easier for the investor.

Distribution level: During this level, people withdraw money from their retirement corpus. As necessary, it's to create the amount, and it's equally essential to utilize the funds even more wisely. A way to use it wisely? By investing the built corpus in such how that it generates consistent income.

LONGER ACCUMULATION PERIOD IS FAIR

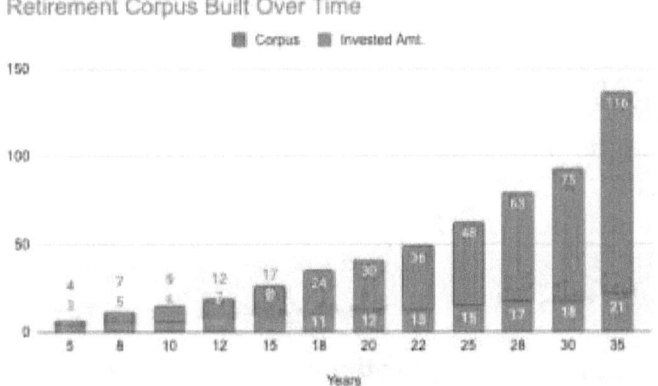

Retirement Corpus Built Over Time

Longer is that the accumulation level, the higher; why? However, in such a condition, even smaller SIP's can ultimately develop a large retirement corpus. We'll use an instance to know this matter.

Example: Financing Rs. 5,000 monthly for 35 years, generating a profit of 8.5% once a year

The above chart may be a graphical representation of this instance. The blue portion indicates the entire amount invested as of date. For example, the amount of three reported in blue is Rs. 3 Lacs spent till the 5th year. Similarly, the amount 11 indicate in blue is Rs. 11 Lacs invested until the 18th year.

The red portion indicates the size of the retirement corpus as of date. For example, the amount four shown in red is the corpus' size as Rs. 4 Lacs till the 5th year. Similarly, the amount 24 indicates in red is that the corpus' size is Rs.24 Lacs until the 18th year.

You will note that within the initial years (till 10th year), out of the entire retirement corpus developed, the principal amount (amount invested) rules size as the sum of the corpus amount. Example: 5th Year: When the total retirement corpus is Rs. 4 Lacs, the principal amount is Rs. 3 Lacs.

But after the 10th year, the compounding effect starts to require its duty. **Example**: 18th Year: When the complete retirement corpus is 24 Lacs, only 11 Lacs is the principal amount. Similarly, in the 35th year, when the entire retirement corpus is 116 Lacs, only 21 Lacs is the first.

What does it imply? The red part gets huger in later years. It determines the invested capital grows faster within the later years. Hence the longer the cash stays invested, the more significant is that the benefit.

2. WHY BEGIN EARLY?

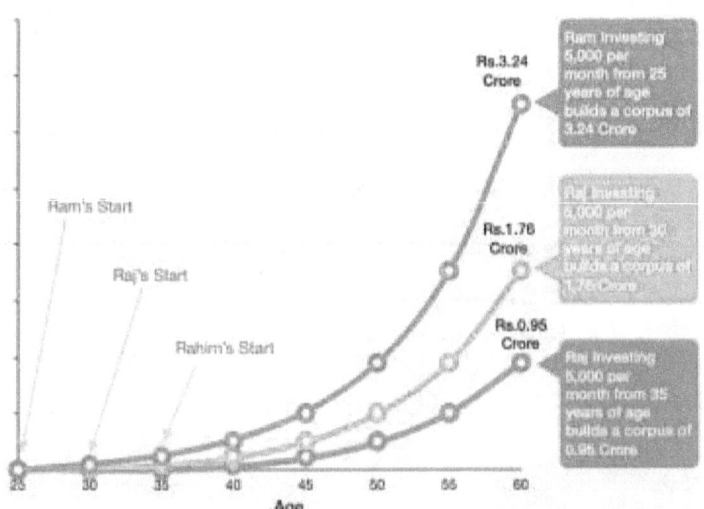

Assume there are three buddies Ram, Raj, and Rahim. Each of them is 25 years aged. These three buddies chose that they might prefer to retire at the age of 60 with a wholesome retirement corpus.

Ram Commences a SIP of Rs.5000 monthly in an equity mutual fund shortly after making this choice. His mutual funds generated a return of 12% p.a. over the next 35 years. By the time Ram was 60 years old, his SIP forms a retirement corpus of Rs.3.24 Crore.

Raj Started a SIP of Rs. 5000 monthly in an equity fund when he reached 30 years aged (5 years after Ram). By the time Raj was 60 years old, his SIP had built a retirement corpus of Rs.1.76 Crore for him. Due to 5 years delayed start, Raj's corpus amount is merely 50% of Ram's.

Rahim started a SIP of Rs. 5000 monthly when he reached 35 years of age (10 years after Ram). By the time Rahim was 60 years aged, the dimensions of his corpus were only 95 Lacs. Although Rahim has also waited invested for as long spun as 25 ages, his start was ten years suspended than Ram, Rahim's corpus is solely 20% of Ram's.

The lesson to find out from this instance is that one must start as soon together realized the necessity of investing. The idea shall be to offer our money a long-time to remain invested. The longer it will say invested, the bigger it'll become eventually.

INITIAL YEARS ARE TOUGH

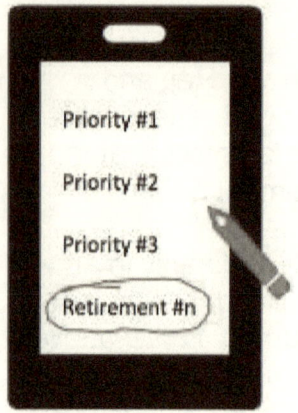

When one first starts to set aside money for retirement, it'll desire a burden. It is often natural. Including a replacement activity in life is usually not smooth. What's the reason? Current priorities overshadow the longer-term requirement of retirement.

Allow me to clarify now more because it'll assist in surmounting the barriers of rousing. Assume one's current preferences are a child's education, parent concern, house purchase, entertainment, dining out, etc. These are the immediate needs of life. Among such requirements, retirement planning becomes hard to execute.

Our mind indeed sees immediate financial goals as necessary. But it's also true that retirement also needs excellent practice. But the way to plan for retirement linked savings when immediate ones look much more important? The concept is straightforward.

Begin Base: Begin turning only small sums of cash monthly into retirement connected plans. If allotted funds may be a difficulty, you'll start with as low a denomination as Rs. 500 monthly. More critical at this level is to begin investing for retirement.

Increase Gradually: Once you've got started and contributed a minimum of 12 SIP's to your mutual fund, you're able to take the subsequent step. Increase the contributions gradually (every year). What proportion to increase? Match the share pay-hike you bought that year.

HOW TO CALCULATE SIZE OF THE SPECIFIED RETIREMENT CORPUS?

How big should be one's retirement corpus? The corpus should be large enough so that it generates enough income to support retired life. Two essential questions require answering at this step:

a) What proportion of income needed after retirement?

b) What shall be the retirement corpus dimensions necessary to get the specified payment (in ques a)?

(A) INCOME NECESSITATED AFTER RETIREMENT

I'll bestow to you my formula using which we will discover the necessary income after retirement. But before we see this formula, acknowledge me to define a term that I've used in this ratio:

Replacement Ratio (Rr): The method of income replacement ratio is straightforward. Assume a person's current average monthly expenses are Rs. 100,000. He has planned his retirement well. During this case, after retirement, his income-need will be Rs. 45,000 (45% of present average spending). The worth of 45% is what I call the "replacement ratio"—[Notes: People tend to spend much less after retirement. If you would like, you'll select an extraordinary replacement ratio for yourself.]

Now let's see the formula:

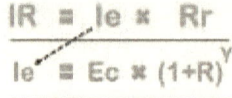

$$IR = Ie \times Rr$$
$$Ie = Ec \times (1+R)^Y$$

IR =	Income required after retirement
Ie =	Extrapolated income requried just before retirement
Rr =	Replacement ratio (45%)
Ec =	Current Expense
R =	Average expense growth rate (per annum) in next "Y" years
Y =	Number of years remaining before retirement

Let's understand the utilization of this formula with an example:

Ram and Raj are two friends. They need to calculate their retirement income. Their present monthly cost is Rs. 80,000 (Ram) and Rs. 68,000 (Raj). Ram is 29 years aged, and Raj is 25 years aged. It indicates Ram has 31 years ere retirement, and Raj has 35 years. Furthermore, we consider that the next 30-35 years' inflation rate will be an average of 6% p.a.

Let's put these values within the above formula and see what numbers these two friends get as an estimate for their "required income" post-retirement.

		RAM	RAJ
Ec	Rs./month	80,000	68,000
R	% p.a.	6%	6%
Y	Years	31	35
Ie	Rs./month	4,87,048	5,22,654
Rr	%	45%	45%
IR (1)	Rs./month	2,19,172	2,35,194
IR (2)	Rs./annum	26,30,059	28,22,331

What will we deduce from this example? An individual, 25 years aged, who consumes Rs. 68,000 monthly today will necessitate earnings of Rs. 2,35,194 monthly at the retirement (Age: 60 years – 35 years from now).

So during this case, where will the income come from that? It'll generate returns from the invested "retirement corpus." What shall be the dimensions of the corpus? It is what we'll see next.

(B) SIZE OF RETIREMENT CORPUS

Let's attempt to estimate the dimensions of retirement corpus by continuing with the above example (Ram & Raj). We've already calculated that Ram's retirement income claim is Rs. 2.19 Lacs monthly (or 26.30 Lacs per year). Raj's income claim is Rs. 2.35 Lacs monthly (or 28.22 Lacs per year).

Before proceeding, we must also factor-in a crucial assumption. It's associated with life expectancy. Suppose both Ram and Raj expect to survive till 85 years aged. It indicates the retirement corpus should produce income for the succeeding 25 years after their retirement.

In this case, what should be the dimensions of the retirement corpus? To calculate the measurements, we will use the "Present Value" formula of Excel.

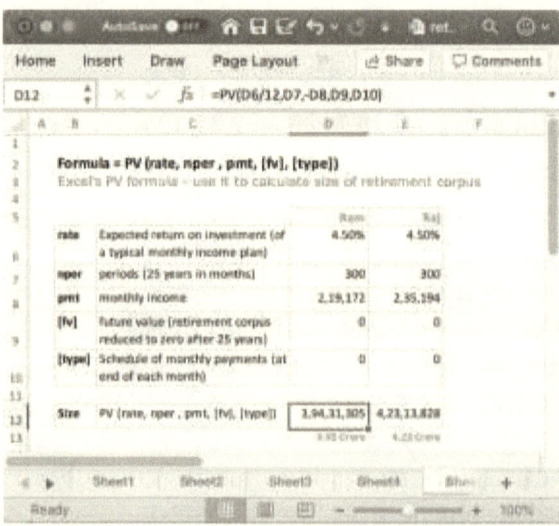

What is considered here during this equation are the following:

Rate: Required return on investment is 4.5% once an age. I've believed that a standard monthly income plan (MIP) will generate this much return after 30-35 years from now.

[fv]: I've assumed that the retirement corpus's long-term benefit is nothing zero. Why? However, after the failure of 25 years, I've concluded that the total retirement corpus will get spent. Hence the remainder becomes nothing zero.

[type]: I've concluded that the monthly payments will commence generating at the head of every month. If the cash invested during a MIP on 1st-Jan, then the primary income will start flowing-in from 31st-Jan.

Using this formula, the dimensions of the retirement corpus for Ram are Rs.3.95 Crore, and Raj is Rs.4.23 Crore. Check the calculation down within the above screenshot.

HOW TO BUILD THE RETIREMENT CORPUS?

Ram and Raj now feature an amount. They know that Ram must make a retirement corpus of Rs. 3.95 Crore and Raj Rs. 4.23 Crore. But the process of making this corpus? Two figures have got to be simplified first to answer this question:

1. What proportion to invest: Ram and Raj must invest a particular amount of cash monthly to obtain Rs' corpus. 3.95 and Rs. 4.23 crore, individually. We must perceive that Ram & Raj has 31 & 35 years, respectively, for corpus growth. To know the quantum of investment, we will use the "PMT" formula of excel (shown below). Using this formula, we all understand Ram will get to fund Rs. 15,582, moreover Raj 11,053 monthly to obtain the corpus.

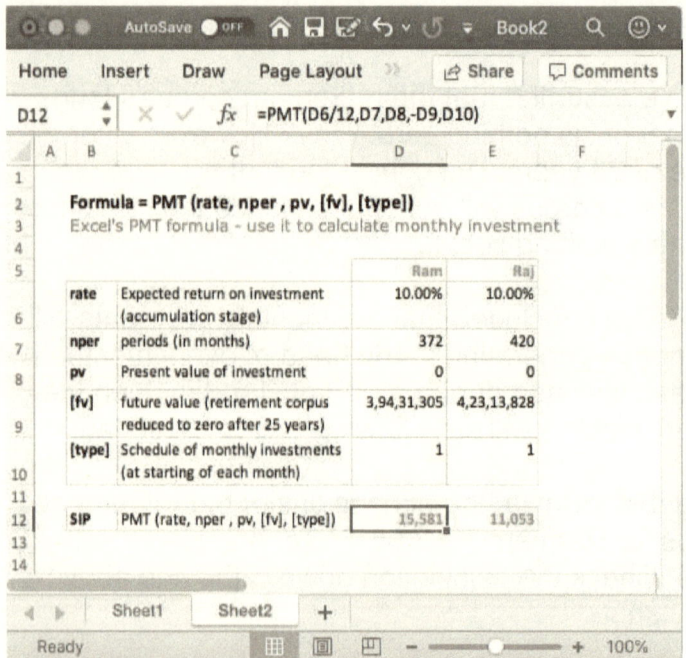

2. Where to invest: The proof must take from point-1 earlier. The anticipated return on investment is 10% once an age for both Ram and Raj. It expects profits generated by the investment portfolio must be 10%. What shall constitute an investment portfolio within the accumulation level?

To satisfy the aim of 10 percent per annum, returns portfolio planning must be investment prevailing.

WHERE TO SPECULATE MONEY IN ACCUMULATION LEVEL?

In the growth phase, the purpose of the planner should get on a corpus structure. The faster and easier the corpus created, the higher. In my opinion, here, the person should consider growth investing. Generally, people attempt to play safe here too.

But considering that one has such an extended time horizon available for investing, going all guns blazing shouldn't be an enormous worry. People that are farthest faraway from retirement (like people in their 20's and early 30's) should consider growth investing over the other options.

Here, I will attempt to list down all "traditional" investment options that an individual can use to speculate their money in the accumulation level of a retirement plan:

A. TRADITIONAL RETIREMENT PLANS

Employee Provident Fund (EPF): Most salaried status personalities already contribute to EPF/PF. During this scheme, the workers mandatorily contribute 12% of their basic salary and allowances. Employee's also can voluntarily help quite 12%. The employer's contribution restricts to 12%. The rate of interest provided by EPF is about 8.6% once a year.

Employee Pension Scheme (EPS): This appears as a combination pack with the EPF. In EPF, 12% contributed by the employer. Out of this 12%, 8.33% diverted to EPS. Moreover, the GOI of India also helps EPS. Additionally to the employer's contribution of 8.33% to EPS, GOI (Central) also contributes 1.16% of employees' basic salary towards EPS. The rate of interest offered on EPS is the same as EPF.

Reward: An company should mandatorily pay a benefit to the worker. If an associate has achieved five years of consecutive services, he/she becomes qualified for a reward. The worker can claim gratuity while leaving the duty. Insurance corporations, like LIC, ICICPRULIFE, KOTAK, etc., contribute a collection reward scheme.

VPF: this is often an acronym for the Voluntary Provident Fund scheme. Once we have options like EPF, why VPF is required? In EPF, the share contribution restricts to 12%. However, in VPF, one can contribute 100% of their paycheck. One has got to ask HR to boost an invitation for a VPF account. VPF offers the same interest as EPF.

PPF: Publicly Provident Fund scheme (PPF), like VPF, can contribute from as low as Rs. 500 monthly. But in PPF, there's a higher contribution limit. The more upper limit is Rs 1,50,000 once an age (Rs. 12,500 monthly) with a 15 age lock-in period. Today, the interest granted by PPF is on the edge of 8.7%, formerly a year.

B. NON-TRADITIONAL RETIREMENT PLANS

National Pension System (NPS): NPS is a retirement linked investment scheme that each individual above 18 years of age can utilize to make their retirement corpus. NPS is a relative replacement retirement savings plan made available by India's government in the year 2009. I consider it as an efficient tool for building a large retirement corpus with ease.

Mutual Fund's Pension Plans: Once we have already got great traditional retirement plans and NPS, why to think about mutual funds? Because just in the case of NPS, people oblige to use a 40% fund to shop for an annuity. The annuity successively generates regular income. But only in the case of a retirement savings plan of mutual funds, buying an annuity isn't compulsory. One also can plan to choose a scientific withdrawal plan post-retirement – which can yield better returns.

Hybrid Mutual Fund: I would go full throttle when it involves building a retirement corpus. Traditionally people choose more reliable alternatives like PEF, VPF, NPS, etc. But when time compass in hand is so widespread, why to perform secure? But this is often also an indisputable fact that one cannot afford to play when it involves retirement planning. There must be a resourceful balance between aggression and performing securely.

I believe hybrids funds grant such a dividend. These funds provide 10%-12% returns in the long run.

WHERE TO SPECULATE MONEY WITHIN THE DISTRIBUTION LEVEL?

At the distribution level, the funds of the retirement corpus must invest conservatively. It is often necessary because the family depends on the accumulated retirement corpus's income during this level.

Over and above this, the priority is to keep the corpus amount intact to the maximum amount possible. Distribution level can further subdivide into sub-levels:

Level 1: This represents the first ten years of retirement. Here the retiree is predicted to be more active. Hence, the risk profile is higher. During this level, the person can maintain partial exposure to equity.

Level 2: This represents a level where the person has already lived the first ten years of retired life. During this level, the person anticipates becoming less active. The danger profile of the person is low during this level. I feel, during this level, equity exposure shall be almost zero.

Investment diversification must even maintain within the distribution level. The retirement corpus must be dispersed equally in multiple income-generating roots. Ideally, income should flow-in from various sources rather than one or two options. Here we'll see a listing of few proven investment options suitable for the post-retirement phase:

1. Annuity: Retiree can purchase an annuity. It is often a safe investment option. It'll generate regular income.
The Schedule of income generation is usually monthly, quarterly, half-yearly, and yearly.

2. SCSS: People of only 60+ years aged can invest in SCSS. One can open an SCSS account with the Indian Post Office. The cash invested in SCSS features a lock-in period of 5 years. The utmost amount one can spend in SCSS is Rs. 15 Lacs per account. Presently SCSS offers an inexpensive rate of interest of seven .4% once a year.

3. POMIS: This is regularly a savings scheme proposed by Post Offices. POMIS attains for "Post Office Monthly Income Scheme." It is often wont to generate monthly income. Its lock-in period is five ages. Here the merest investment amount is Rs. 1,500. The maximum limit which will invest in POMIS is Rs. 9 Lacs (joint account). Soon POMIS allows a rate of interest of 7.7%, formerly a year.

CONCLUSION

Retirement planning is an essential priority of private finance management. It'll not be wrong to mention that retirement planning should be the amount one priority of all. Why? Because financial stability in adulthood may be a necessity.

How to plan for retirement? I exploit my retirement planning calculation to work out 'how big should be my corpus, 'and 'how much should I be investing 'on a date to succeed in the goal.

It is an easy tool but effective associated with retirement planning.

"The difficulty with retirement is that you, in no way, get a weekend or day off."

"The best ideal possibility to begin contemplating your retirement is earlier than the director does."

Early Retirement: The Way to Retire Early from Job

When my father was working, he began searching for answers for early retirement at an old age. It took my father on the edge of 28+ years to retire from his job at the goal of retirement.

How he did it? Why he did it? How can you also plan and retire early from a job?

Probably these are the questions that you, too, are seeking the answers to; author Al Zayd shares his father's experience during this chapter. The author's father addresses some rules and consultations. I hope it'll assist you also.

1. The way to Commence?

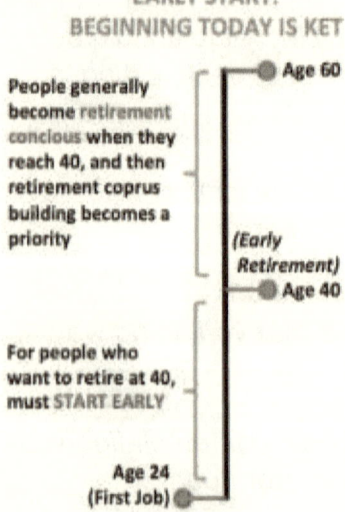

EARLY START:
BEGINNING TODAY IS KET

People generally become retirement concious when they reach 40, and then retirement coprus building becomes a priority

Age 60

(Early Retirement)
Age 40

For people who want to retire at 40, must START EARLY

Age 24
(First Job)

An early start is vital.

Generally, people start considering early retirement in their 40's. But to retire early, one must also begin soon.

How to start? Expose yourself to the concept of 'financial independence.'

I examine it during a book called Rich Dad Poor Dad by Robert Kiyosaki. Read every page of it. It's worthwhile.

This book has the power to tune one's mind in favor of financial independence.

According to my, there can't be a far better start than this.

2. WHY EARLY RETIREMENT is hard

Early retirement is more difficult due to our psychological limitations than financial.

We just don't let our jobs go. We stay glued to our position.

PEOPLE   JOB

What is the justification? We are saying, "There is not an alternative. " Cliche.

For learning to swim, it is essential first to enter the water. You'll fear the more severe, but one has got to face it to overcome it.

New-born babies welcome during this world by cutting the epithelial duct.

It may look extreme, but it's an essential requirement to create the baby self-sustainable.

Likewise, we must evade our umbilical cords (called the birth cords or funiculus).

You will feel the pain. You'll also cry out for a few days, but it'll eventually getaway.

How to do it? Take a test.

3. TAKE A TEST

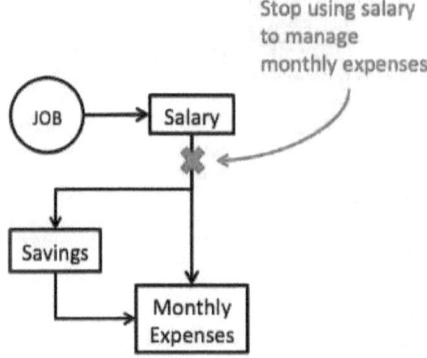

Why is this test required?

Because it'll confirm if one features a mindset to become financially independent,

Yes, financial independence (early retirement) may be a challenging goal to follow.

There will be instances where dropping on this goal will look a great deal easier than continuing.

So before starting – ask yourself to require this test. It'll provide you with a concept of the magnitude of the task at hand.

3.1 What's the test?

The test is to go-lean and begin leading a frugal lifestyle for the next two months.

Spend only on those items which are essential and necessary for survival—cut-off all other expenses.

How to manage monthly expenses? Fund them from your savings.

But what if the saving isn't significant enough?

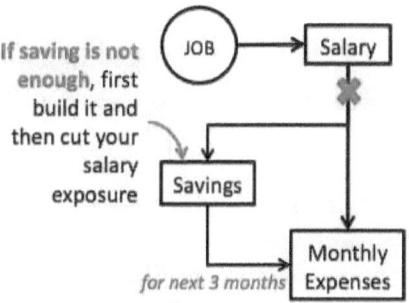

Give yourself time, build savings, then take the test.

My humble suggestion is to take this test a minimum of 3 times before taking the subsequent step.

Tip: attempt to take these three tests within one year.

4. CONTROL EXPENSES

Once you've got given the tests, you'll get a feel of your salary dependency.

To reach the goal of 'early retirement,' the only way is to interrupt this dependency.

How to do it? By balancing one's expenses over income.

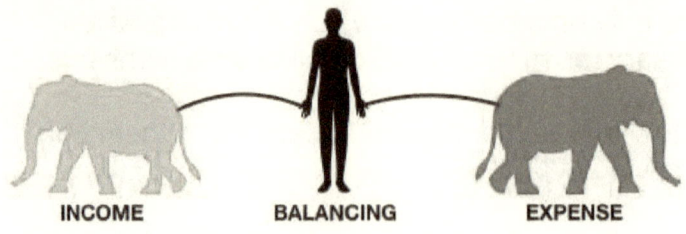

INCOME   BALANCING   EXPENSE

Note: *To retire asap, "learning to spend only the maximum amount as we will earn" is the solution.*

The skill prevails in learning your expenses (spending habits). Why?

Because our spending habits don't seem to be as controlled as they must be in control,

But when preference is "early retirement," spending must restrain.

How to execute it? Through budgeting and tracking expenses.

Commence with budgeting expenses.

4.1 BUDGETING EXPENSES

I remember I head to serve an expense budget way backward in the year 2008.

EXPENSE LINES	BUDGET	BUDGETED CASH FLOW PER MONTH					SAVINGS				
		SALARY		OTHER INCOME							
		SELF	SPOUSE	BONUS	RENTAL INCOME	INCOME		JAN	JUNE	FEB	TEN
	2,01,500	1,14,500	58,300	60,300	7,500	20,700	4,97,700	6,500	11,700	0	0
ESSENTIAL											
BILL PAYMENTS											
ELECTRICITY	2,000	800	100	800	550	250	8,000	1,200	8,500	0	0
INTERNET	1,500	1,500	0	0	0	0	7,500	0	0	0	0
COOKING GAS	700	700	0	0	0	0	4,500	0	0	0	0
CABLE TV/DTH	500	500	0	0	0	0	2,500	0	0	0	0
CAR WASH	500	500	0	0	0	0	500	0	0	0	0
MOBILE	500	500	0	0	0	0	4,500	0	0	0	0
PROPERTY TAX	1,000	1,000	0	0	0	0	3,000	0	0	0	0

I was living in a new city (metro), and expenses suddenly skyrocketed.

In those moments of realization, I learned about budgeting expenses.

My wife and I prepared a listing of all expenses.

We categorized them as supported its recurrence – consumed daily, weekly, monthly, yearly, etc.

Once the data was active, we decided to guess what quantity was its monthly cost.

Example:

SL	Expense type	Expense	Unit Cost	Monthly Cost
1	Daily	Bus	50.0	1,000.0
2	Weekly	Grocery	1,000.0	4,000.0
3	Monthly	Electricity	1,000.0	1,000.0
4	Annual	Med. Premium	16,000.0	1,333.3
5	Biennial	Vacation	38,000.0	1,583.3

It was a specific task to perform.

It took us about 3-4 days to organize the entire data (with monthly costing).

Once the data set, it became our budget.

The monthly costs specified against each line item were our upper limit.

We decided to keep our expenses within these limits.

But the way to assure compliance? By tracking all expenses.

4.2 TRACKING EXPENSES

Preparation of expense budget was still a neater work. What's even tougher was expense tracking.

It is a particular activity, and it must do on day to day.

But people that judiciously track their expense know its sublime power.

I've been tracking all my expenses for, eventually, ten years.

DATE	EXPENSE CATEGORY	NOTE	Online / Cash EXPENSE (in Rs.)	Credit Card EXPENSE (in Rs.)
01-Jan-16	Utility Bills	Electricity		$20.00
02-Jan-16	Utility Bills	DTH		$6.00
03-Jan-16	Utility Bills	Gas		$6.00
04-Jan-16	Utility Bills	Phone		$15.00
05-Jan-16	Food Bills	Grocery & Veg		$30.00
06-Jan-16	Food Bills	Snacks - ATM	$5	
07-Jan-16	Food Bills	Lunch - ATM	$2	
07-Jan-16	Household Expense	Maid	$60	
08-Jan-16	Entertainment Expense	Movie		$10.00
08-Jan-16	Entertainment Expense	Movie Popcorn		$25.00
09-Jan-16	Clothing Expense	Child's Uniform		$45.00
10-Jan-16	Education Expense	School Fees	$75	
11-Jan-16	Investment	Mutual Fund	$200	
12-Jan-16	Investment	Stocks	$60	
13-Jan-16	Loan EMI	Home Loan	$900	
14-Jan-16	Transportation Expense	Petrol		$23.00
15-Jan-16	Medical Expense	Crocin for Self	$5	
16-Jan-16	Medical Expense	Vaccination	$9	
17-Jan-16	Fixed Deposit	$90		

It's been one of the most vital forces which helped me to retire early from the office.

Should I not trace my expenses, I would've never realized that overcoming job dependency is feasible.

Advice: Use a mobile app to start tracking expenses. Once you begin becoming familiar with data feeding, switch to Excel.

5. MAKE EARLY-RETIREMENT A NON-NEGOTIABLE GOAL

Start telling yourself this a minimum of once before getting to bed. *I can sacrifice my office job, but I'll not give up my aim to retire early.*

Keep feeding your confidence by chanting such slogans.

Is it needed? Yes, it's. Why?

Staying in a job and continuing to earn a similar way may be a lot easier.

What is more difficult?
For taking a step to elevate oneself to financial independence,

What is the difficulty?
For Fulfilling the priority of early retirement alongside the work,

So, the way to do it?

Take the subsequent step – quantify early retirement.

6. QUANTIFY EARLY RETIREMENT
What it means by quantifying retirement?

I was checking what proportion of money you would like to retire early. How to do it?

By looking deeper into one's standard of living, there are few steps to try.

6.1 STEP A: CATEGORISING EXPENSES
In point number 4 (above), we've already listed expenses and done its budgeting.

Here we'll further categorize these expenses within the following heads: essentials, comfort & luxury.

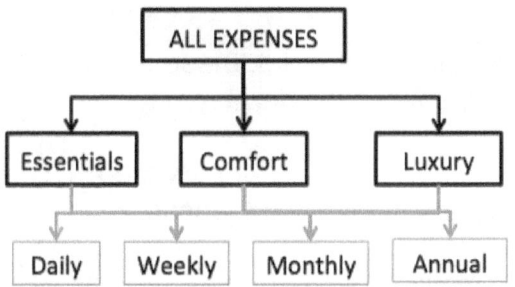

Essentials: These are those spending that can't negotiate. Few examples: supermarket, bills, expenses, loan EMI's, transport, etc. These are such expenses that, regardless of what, will still yield. These expenses fix in nature. In other words, these are unavoidable expenses.

Comfort: These are those spending that isn't unavoidable. But because they need to become a part of our habit, they're hard to give up. There are a few examples: miscellaneous shopping, multiplex expense, dining out, etc. These spendings are generally variable. Few months they're going to below, then a sudden jump. In most cases, it's impossible to form these expenses zero. But there's an enormous margin of savings here.

Luxury: India's socio-economic class generally spend less on these things. But whenever it appears, it picks away bulk savings. There are a few examples:

feasting in an exceeding star hotel, extended holiday, vehicle purchase, home furnishing, etc. Generally, luxury shopping has worn out amount. The potential to carve-out savings is the highest here.

Personalities manage to overspend on comforts or luxuries.

When the priority is early retirement, these two expenses must bring down considerably.

The idea is to overcome expenses step by step. The first focus should get on essential expenses.

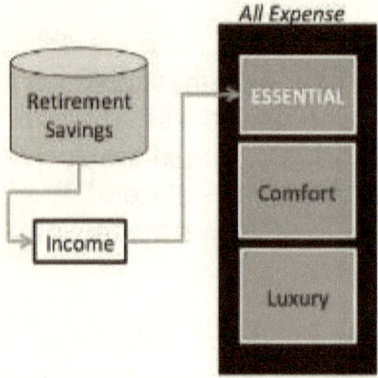

6.2 STEP B: CALCULATE THE RETIREMENT CORPUS STRUCTURE

How to execute it? Let's determine this with an example.

Assume Jack consumes Rs. 2 lacs monthly to maintain his everyday expenses.

Out of Rs. 2.0 lacs, 35% is 'compulsory' expense (no compromisable spending).

35% of Rs. 2,00,000 = Rs. 70,000

Jack expects to retire early.

How can Jack make an income of Rupees 70,000 monthly?

From retirement gains raised by Jack,

How much retirement profits are going to be enough to make Rs. 70K monthly?
Rs. 1.4 Crore
[Return = 6%,
Time = N/A,
Inflation = N/A]

USE CORPUS CALCULATOR

Monthly Income (Rs.)	70000
Expected Return p.a. (%)	6
Time for Retirement (Yrs)	10
Avg. Future Inflation (%)	8

CALCULATE

Retirement Corpus (Rs.Lakhs)

ADJUST FOR INFLATION

Suppose Jack (age: 30 years) isn't able to retire immediately.

He needs ten more years to retire (he will retire at 40).

In this case, Rs. 1.4 Crore won't be enough. Why?

Because of the inflation of current expenses,

How to estimate retirement corpus during this state? Use the above calculation with the following information:

- Current Income Requirement (Rs.): 70,000.
- Return on Investment (% p.a.): 6.
- Time for Retirement (Years): 10.
- Average Inflation in expected ages (% p.a.): 6.

Acknowledging the above estimates needed retirement corpus is Rs. 2.5 crore (ten years from presently).

Hence, Jack must build an Rs. 2.5 Crore in the next ten years to retire early (at 40 years of age).

7. DEDUCE A MONTHLY INVESTMENT PLAN

Why are we discussing an investment plan?

Let's take Jack's example moreover for better knowledge.

In 6.2 before, it had been explicit that Jack wants Rs. 2.5 crore afore contemplating early retirement at 40 (in the succeeding ten years).

How will Jack build the corpus of Rupees 2.5 crore in 10 years? Jack has two alternatives:

Savings Route: Jack must build Rs. 250 Lacs in 10 years. It means monthly Jack must save Rs. 2.08 Lacs. In this manner, in 10 years, Jack will accumulate Rs. 250 Lacs (Rs. 2.08 x 12 x 10). But Jack's income is merely Rs. 2 Lacs monthly. He can't follow the savings route and build Rs. 250 Lacs.

Equity Investing: If Jack invests Rs. 84,000 monthly in the equity-based mutual fund for the next ten years (@16.5% p.a. return), he can build Rs. 250 Lacs. You'll also check the numbers using the below calculation.

MONTHLY INVESTMENT CALCULATOR

Corpus to be Built (Rs.Lakhs)	250
Current Savings (Rs.Lakhs)	0
Expected Return p.a. (%)	16.5
Time (in years)	10

CALCULATE

Jack must use the ability to compound (investing).

This way, his monthly investment load is going to be substantially reduced.

Jack, who spends Rs. 2 Lacs monthly, with some effort, can save 84,000 monthly for onward investing.

The amount of Rs. 84,000 monthly reduced if Jack has some existing savings (say Rs. 10 Lacs).

In this case, what is going to occur the finance load on Jack?

Use the above calculation with the following metrics:

- Corpus to be built (Rs. Lacs): 250
- Current Savings (Rs. Lacs): 10
- Expected Returns (% p.a.): 16.5
- Time for Retirement (years): 10

Jack's investment load is going to be Rs. 68,500 monthly.

THE FINANCE PLANNING FOR JACK

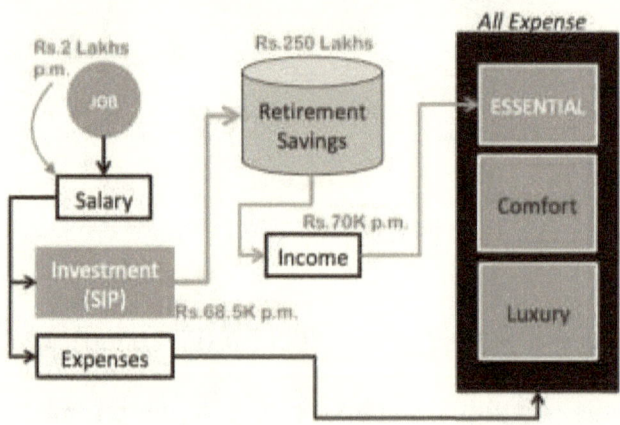

He will finance Rs. 68,500 monthly for the next ten years in an exceeding vehicle that may generate a return of 16.5% p.a. to make a corpus of Rs. 250 Lacs.

Such specific calculations help in the creation of a practical roadmap for early retirement.

Is this enough? One can do financial independence just by investing? Yes, and No.

Yes, because, mathematically, nothing else is required.

No, because I felt the necessity for more. What did I do?

8. HOW MY FATHER SECURED MY EARLY RETIREMENT?

When he started implementing my investment plan, everything was going perfect (It was those years of 2009-10).

The market was bullish. Everything that used to be touching was giving some returns.

But soon, he faced reality. He could see his portfolio size not growing as fast.

For the next 3-4 years, the business was either inactive or too subtle.

But I nevermore quit my SIP contribution. I chose my mutual funds and persisted adhered to them.

I still recognize, 'HDFC Top 200 fund' was one of my select in those days.

In those moments of uncertainty, I thought concerning alternative income formation.

Since then, my focus has tended from capital recognition to regular income formation.

I started growing a die-hard fan of passive income roots.

I also decided to start my full-time blog, which eventually became a good revenue generator.

When my book's earnings grew more stable, I started diverting most of my income to reduce my debt burden.

I still remember how fanatic I used to be towards living a loan-free (zero EMI) life.

Advice: From my personal experience:
- Continue your SIP, regardless of what.
- Invest in passive income generation.
- Try to build an alternate income source.
- Become debt-free as soon as possible.

FINAL WORDS

We all desire to retire early from our office jobs to conduct a freewheeling life. But to make this dream a reality, we shall get enthusiastic about its realization.

The next step is to line forth and write down a few steps about how you're progressing to reach this ultimate goal. Always remember that planning for early retirement link with one's ability to guide a financially independent life.

If one can become financially independent, the dream of early retirement will automatically become a reality.

"Retirement is fantastic on the off chance that you have two rules – plenty to stay on and plenty to live."

Chapter-10: RULE NO.10 NEVER GIVE-UP & NEVER QUIT YOUR GOALS

What you're thinking about today is what you dwell on tomorrow.
What did you think about yesterday? What are you pondering today? What are the thoughts that you believe just most often?

Question yourself these proposals and determine the answers because the thoughts you're thinking about today would most likely be what you may live tomorrow.

Does this sound complicate? No, this can be quite simple.

The thoughts you most frequently affect and shape your life. Repeating similar ideas repeatedly a day would eventually change your behavior, actions, and energy if you think that an equivalent reasonably thought today and tomorrow. After tomorrow, in time, your life would start mirroring these thoughts.

Don't Limit Your Thinking
Most people believe their current life, their problems, their worries, and the items that disturb them or which they are doing not. Doing so, day after day, turns this manner of thinking into a habit and how of life.

Limiting the scope of your thinking to a limited circle limits your life. You define the mind, and you can't see beyond these thoughts, and thus, cannot dream, think and aspire for a life beyond your current circumstances.

If you think that equivalent thoughts day after day, you limit yourself to the same situations and circumstances and never rise above them

Your Thoughts of Today Are the Life you may Live tomorrow

What does the above statement mean? Now, after reading the primary part of these chapters, you already know.

It means the thoughts you think that today affect your future. It means if you continue thinking within the same opinions, nothing will change, and you'll be creating and recreating similar circumstances and situations.

It also means if you have a vision in your mind of an individual lifestyle, and if you repeat this vision day after day, eventually, your image would turn out to be a reality.

Always remember the thoughts that you simply think today will affect your tomorrow. If you're considering your problems, worries, and how difficult life is, this is what you'll create and continue creating. You'll keep complaining about your experience, and your enthusiasm would improve.

You need to urge down from this merry-go-round and alter your thoughts. Only by changing your dreams, your life would change for the higher.

Are you satisfied together with your thoughts? Does one like what you think that every day? If you don't just like the mental scenarios you create in your mind and mirror your current circumstances and don't like them; you would like to vary the mental images.

Stop letting your current negative thoughts shape your future. You would like to interchange these thoughts with better and more positive reviews. It may not happen overnight. This process will take time, but you'll eventually rise above your current mindset and gain the ability to shape your life.

You might accept as accurate with what you readjust. Still, you will take action, continue thinking limiting thoughts, and keep creating and creating similar situations, problems, and worries in your life?

Take the primary step today, right now, and appearance at your thoughts. Be more conscious of your dreams, and you'll most likely discover that you are merely limiting your beliefs. You think that about your current circumstances, current life, current job, and current financial situation.

The next step would be to think bigger, determine what you want and the way you would like your life to be, and begin thinking of it as possible and attainable.

Remember, your thoughts of today are the building stones of your tomorrow.

Two of the foremost helpful techniques for changing your thoughts and changing your reality are affirmations and visualization. You would admire to seek them if you never did before.

Obtain the Courage Never to Quit and Never Give Up!

Succeeding Your Problems into Perspective

Life always appears to grant us countless challenges and problems on the day-to-day. It throws left hooks once we were expecting the right ones; it gives us apples once we desire oranges; it even presents us with seemingly awful surprises that we weren't expecting. It bloats us with non-resourceful passions that lead to fasten us down to a lifetime of mediocrity and unhappiness.

Despite all this, it's not such a lot of what happens to us that makes a difference; instead, what we do with what happens to us determines where we'll find ourselves, what we'll have, and the way we'll be transformed by our experiences.

An IQ Matrix and final words delve into the small print of the issues and obstacles that we face on a day to day, providing us with a way to urge through all-time low moments of our lives when everything seems to be falling on top of our heads.

Throughout these final words, we'll first identify the various faces of the obstacles, problems, and challenges you may face daily. After this, we'll glance at the explanations behind barriers and what they mean to your life and future endeavors.
Thirdly, we'll develop a resilient mindset to help you break through any challenges that life presents you. And eventually, we'll discuss how to create unstoppable momentum, which will guide you towards attaining your most passionate goals and objectives.

Never Give Up. Here Come the Obstacles

It is effortless to strive towards attaining our goals and objectives when the oceans are calm and nothing appears to be standing in our way. However, if we don't seem mentally prepared the instant something begins to stir the waters and rock the boat from side-to-side, we start to panic and struggle to affect our chances. We perceive these difficulties and challenges as larger than life and way beyond our capabilities and means.

These events may alright find yourself overwhelming us and causing great heartache and hardship. As a result, we may find ourselves quitting and throwing within the towel of defeat, all because our resolve wasn't strong enough to handle the burden related to our journey towards attaining our objectives.

Within this final section of the book, we'll see the possible obstacles that will interchange our way as we progress along the trail towards fulfilling our dreams. These obstacles necessarily are available in four distinct forms:
- From within ourselves
- Extending from our decisions and actions
- Directed by people
- Originating within circumstance

Let's now get a more in-depth aspect of each of those in additional detail:

The Obstacles Within Us!

Probably the most robust and most challenging obstacles that we face come from within ourselves. These obstacles are extremely challenging to beat because, in many instances, we blind to their existence.

Your first objective is to spot these obstacles and endeavor to know how they affect your life and perception of reality. Secondly, you want to learn to cope with them in an efficient and resourceful way that may once more help move you in the right direction.

Let's now take a better look into each of those obstacles in an exceedingly little more detail.

Lack of Desire

A lack of desire means you merely don't have enough emotion behind your actions. It means the goals and objectives that you only are working towards aren't yet emotionally sturdy sufficient. As a decision, when barriers come your way, you'll not have the emotional reservoirs available to cope with these challenges successfully. You'll, therefore, likely succumb to your predicament without putting up a fight.

Lack of Self-Belief

When belief is lacking, you have little or no confidence in achieving anything of consequence in your life.

The very second a barrier grows running across your way, your lack of belief will manifest in two ways.

First, it'll manifest as a scarcity of belief in yourself. Intrinsically, you do not believe that you are ok or worthy enough to attain your aims and goals.

Secondly, your ineffective belief practices result from not having sufficient confidence in your personal ability to overcome any obstacle in your path. As a result, you need the will-power to persevere when things get a bit severe and moderately unfamiliar.

Lack of Commitment
A lack of commitment is somewhat associated with a scarcity of desire. However, it just stems from your inability to manufacture enough reasons to maneuver you through the obstacles that interchange your way when it involves commitment.

If you're unable to come up with enough reasons to get you through an obstacle, you may likely quit when the going gets tough.

It is also essential to understand that your commitment levels are directly connected to your initial expectations once you began your journey towards attaining your objectives. If you're not meeting your expectations along your route, then your commitment will waver, and you'll be more likely to quit within the appearance of adversity.

Asking too Many Why Questions
'Why' proposals are self-sabotaging programming means that focus you on your inadequacies and weaknesses.

When things start to induce a bit challenging, and externally it begins to seem as if you're struggling against a hopeless situation. Then 'why' questions will place the finishing abilities on a journey full of regret and unfulfilled purposes. The moment you begin asking yourself.

- Why does this always happen to me?
- Why do I nevertheless fail?
- Why is that ever so difficult?
- Why is life still against me?

It is the instant you ought to effectively close up your bags and leave the large Brother House. ☺

These questions are self-sabotaging forces that may put you into a state of regret and emotional weakness. Avoid them at the least costs.

Focus on What 'Don't Want.'
Whenever you specialize in your problems, obstacles, and uncontrollable circumstances, you're at that moment, focusing on belongings you don't want in your life.

It said that whatever you concentrate on will expand and envelop you during a new reality. Therefore, if you still focus on what you don't want, this may effectively expand the things you are doing not need in your fact.

All your decisions, actions, behaviors, and thoughts will build a non-resourceful case of weak-thinking, which will likewise sabotage your progress towards achieving your goals and objectives.

Being Riddled with Negative Emotions

Negative emotion is primarily a sentiment that places you into a non-resourceful state, discouraging action and effective decision making.

The sentiments of anxiety, worry, uncertainty, overwhelm, violence, and guilt all work collectively to create a robust self-sabotaging cocktail that may hypnotize you into a state of self-pity. That may likewise prevent you from achieving your goals and objectives.

Being Riddled with Fears
Over time, our negative emotions usually turn out to be uncontrollable worries that direct and dictate our daily decisions and behaviors. These worries will take you of your life essence and desire to move past the obstacles that successfully interchange your approach.

The worries of rejection, responsibility, success, and failure will purge and drain your energy of life if you want to achieve your purposes and goals.

Being Riddled with Apologies
All the above stated self-sabotaging might efficiently serve the reasons that we build up within ourselves over time.

There would be no reason to create excuses if the forces mentioned above weren't directing our behavior. Yet, it's essential to know that our apologies are blessings in disguise in some ways, as they supply us with an insight into the self-sabotaging forces that are dominating our current reality and process of thinking.

Please pay attention to the reasons you continuously make and identify where exactly they originate. Identification is that the commencement that may set you on target towards taking control of your emotional responses. Ask yourself:

Do my excuses come from a scarcity of desire?

Do they are available from a scarcity of self-belief?

Do they manifest as merely a scarcity of commitment to my role?

Am I making excuses because I'm asking too many 'why' questions?

Do my excuses come from the very fact that I'm focusing on what I don't want?

Or do they come from my negative emotions that are manifesting as fears?

Obstacles Manifesting through Our Actions

There is another assortment of barriers that usually disclose through our everyday decisions and behaviors. These aren't many such obstacles that come from within ourselves, but rather, obstacles from a scarcity of judgment, understanding, insight, and knowledge.

The first step is to spot these obstacles, while the second step is to include strategies that may allow you to correct your course-of-action and set you on target towards achieving your purposes and goals.

Rushing Decisions
In many cases, we undermine our success and develop unnecessary barriers because we rush our decision-making manner.

We rush the results of our decisions due to a scarcity of time or external pressures or circumstances. And therefore, the consequences of such inefficient decision making can sometimes cost us quite the refraining method from choosing within the first situation.

Making Incorrect Decisions
We often make incorrect decisions because of a scarcity of understanding of a situation or a shortage of experience or resources.

In this instance, we take the time to carefully consider our decision-making process and come up with conclusions that we feel will best help us maneuver forward along our journey towards attaining our objectives. Yet, a scarcity of judgment can cause the creation of unnecessary obstacles that could've avoided if we had taken a somewhat different way.

Sabotaging Habits
Our habits are, in reality, the everyday decisions we make, and therefore the actions we take that manifest within the outcomes we experience within our lives.

Action related self-sabotaging habits such as laziness and procrastination are ongoing obstacles that several people fight against on a day-to-day basis. A number of these habits are so deeply ingrained in our psyche that it's difficult for us to know how to overcome them.

Obstacles Created by personalities.

Today we are faced with barriers that are created by the decisions and efforts of personalities.

It is not such a lot of people responsible for creating the obstacles within our lives, and it's instead of our approach and the way we affect others that manifest the truth we experience. Nevertheless, for this discussion, let's overlook that experience and look at how others lead and make interpersonal barriers to attain our goals and objectives.

People Not Cooperating

When people don't cooperate or don't see things from your perspective, this could cause arguments and non-resourceful nowadays spent trying to convince others that your ideas and methods are worthwhile and will implement.

If you would like to achieve life, you want to obtain the cooperation of people who can assist you along your journey. You must, in essence, become an individual of influence.

People Sabotaging Your Progress

Sometimes people may purposefully attempt to sabotage your progress by doing things that may throw you off target to serve their interests. It is often difficult to manage if you have little experience understanding human behavior's psychological tendencies.

People Incorrectly Influencing Your Decisions and Actions

Although some people may have the best possible intentions for you and your future, this doesn't mean that their suggestions will be of the most significant benefit for your future endeavors.

Other people might not have the proper perspective or insight into a situation that might make them influential mentors when influencing your decision-making process. You must, therefore, be wary of the recommendation that individuals offer you. By taking the incorrect advice on board, you'll find yourself creating more obstacles than you handle.

Obstacles Springing from Circumstance

Finally, let's take a fast cross-check of the possible barriers that crop up out of your life's changing circumstances.

It is essential to recollect here that it's not what happens to us that creates a difference; instead, we reply to what happens that determines how successful we are at overcoming the challenges in our lives.

When Things Don't Go As Planned

In this scenario, you've meticulously sorted out every detail along the trail to achieve your purposes and goals. However, for one cause or another, something unforeseen happens, and your plans throw wandering and into another unexpected direction that brings stress and distress.

When Difficulties and Uncertainty Develop
In this situation, you successfully managed to handle the issues and obstacles that stood in your way. However, each time you tend to place a barrier to rest, another problem pops up, creating an excellent greater sense of uncertainty. The more issues you successfully affect, the deeper you dig yourself into further problems and challenges that you appear to possess without stopping.

When Circumstances result in the looks of defeat
The above two scenarios of constant problems and uncertainty may, in essence, lead you to believe that failure is merely moments away. However, the truth of the case could also be somewhat different than what you would possibly imagine.

Within the final section of the book, we'll consider this in a complete aspect.

Intellections Behind all the Hindrances We Face
Hindrances are often only momentary roadblocks along our journey. For the foremost part, they're nothing quite interpretations that we make about people, events, ourselves, and circumstances. Moreover, obstacles show us great lessons and help us understand our situation, others, ourselves, and the world.

Did you recognize that each obstacle that you face has an underlying reason for appearing within your reality?

This section will consider a number of these reasons and identify what they mean to your life and predicament.

Life may be a Magnificent Journey.
Life itself may be a journey of self-discovery and not just a mere combination of remote destinations. It's a never-ending journey with many unexpected turns, twists, and surprises that make it worthwhile and fun.

When you face obstacles and challenges in your life, it's essential to know that you are on a journey in which nobody's event or circumstance determines how your trip will pan-out over every week, month, year, or longer.

Let's take a glance at the journey of life in an exceedingly little more detail.
- Uncertainty is Required to create Strength of Character.
- Life presents us with constant challenges to develop the strength of character.

Reflect on your past for an instant, and identify the challenges that you just successfully faced.
Therefore, the adversity that you overcame. Ask yourself:
- How did these circumstances improve me as a personality?
- How have they progressed and developed my character?
- Would I be the equivalent person I'm today without having passed through these experiences?

- How have my prevailing opportunities and decisions grown as a result of these life circumstances

Life Moves through Cycles of Changes, just like the Seasons.

Nature experiences cycles of change that we call seasons. These phases of development move through scenes of birth (spring), growth (summer), conversion (autumn), and hibernation (winter). We all acknowledge that summer must end, even as very much like we recognize the very fact the winter won't last forever.

It's essential to know that the road towards attaining your purposes and goals also moves through spring phases.

You have your seasons, which give birth to new and creative approaches. The summers arise and extend those ideas in actions in which allow you to obtain fantastic rewards. Then there are your autumns, which bring new obstacles and challenges that encourage a change of plans, character, and circumstances. Eventually, we have the winters that allow us to enter into long periods of hibernation and deep self-reflection into our life circumstances, future goals, and objectives. When our winter is over, we enter the spring season, bringing new ideas that are encouraged throughout our Winter hibernation staging.

The seasonal periods of life won't always drive during this appropriate combination or order; however, at any moment in time, remember that you only are indeed moving through a cycle. And regardless of what that cycle is, rest assured that this particular season won't last forever, regardless of how grim your current predicament could be — as long as you persist — there'll always be a light-weight expecting you at the top of the tunnel.

Life may be a Journey of Wonders Hiding Around Every Corner.
When it involves life, we never understand what's disappearing around the edge.

Our barriers may currently be confounding our perceptions; however, our opinions don't structure our reality. What seems to be an intense amount of problems may only be quite temporary. If you persist just a touch longer, you'll find that great opportunities and wonders are expecting you only round the corner. You merely never know.

Life may be a Journey of Opportunities as Concealed as Hindrances.

The amusing thing about life is that it seldom features a habit of bestowing us with a myriad of opportunities presenting ourselves to unimaginable hindrances.

Remember, what you concentrate on becomes your reality. If you're continually looking for problems and focusing on what you don't want, then that's all you'll perceive within your reality. However, on the opposite hand, if all you're looking for are answers, solutions, and opportunities, you'll always turn lemons into lemonade.

You must effectively teach yourself to look for the seeds of opportunity in every apparent problem that crosses your path. By undertaking this deductive process, you'll create a healthy habit that may allow you to identify what others fail to note.

Life Requires New Learnings and Experiences
We do not exist only for the sake of existing. Instead, we live because we are here to find out, experience, and mature as productive and intelligent personalities.

Every hindrance or problem we encounter has been granted to us to interpret life lessons that may allow us greater clarity of thought as we progress forward along our journey towards attaining our goals and objectives. Therefore, don't look down and frown on the issues you face, instead turn your frown ☹ upside-down and take time to find out from your challenges in ways that will expand your thinking and improve your predicament.

Other People Are hoping for You.
You can never quit and never give up because if you consider it, and there is a mess of people hoping to excel and achieve your aims and goals.

Understand your children, parents, siblings, relatives, spouse, co-workers, friends, the people you care about most, etc.; what proportion is each of them hoping to achieve this field of endeavor? If you are doing not do that for yourself, then a minimum of success for them.

It is also necessary to recognize that others are continually watching and observing our standard of living decisions and behaviors, whether we all know it or not.

As a mentor to the youth age, you want to find it within yourself to set a real example, to get down specific habits and foundational principles that you would like these younger minds to cultivate within their personalities. I know it's an enormous responsibility; however, their development and future circumstances may vary by the decisions you create today.

Obstacles leave Personal Growth.
Did you recognize that you will never achieve the goals you're working towards if you're incapable of learning from the issues (lessons) that life throws your way? You'll never even get about achieving your objectives if, whenever a problem arises, you opt to seem the opposite direction or quit.

Life may be a journey of learning and personal growth that guides you toward your next stepping stone. Yes, this guidance is with obstacles and problems. However, these challenges are there to check our resolve and help us deserving of experiencing the goals we strive for it.

From this second on, only view hindrances as opportunities for growth, and you'll drive forward towards your aims and goals with accelerated speed and precision.

Time is Required to Succeed
Today more than ever before, we board a society that riddles with instant gratification. We want fast food, love, money, and success. Yet, this may never eventuate for many people, as success, love, and cash only accompany time.

Before you ever plan to hand over and quit, consider that you may have a bit of overtime before things fall under the place the way you would possibly have envisioned them. It, therefore, doesn't hurt to develop touch patience.

Time is Required to make a robust Support Network.

To achieve any goal or objective, you would like to believe people both directly and indirectly.

Suppose you're struggling with an oversupply of obstacles. In that case, it could mean that you don't yet have an excellent support network in situ that may assist you in maneuvering through these problems efficiently and efficiently.

Take an outing to build up your network of support by zoning in on those who will naturally compliment your strengths and support your weaknesses.

Time is Required to gather Resources.

You will currently be battling many problems and obstacles because you haven't yet built enough resources to assist you with these provocations.

Get time to research and create the resources you may have to get through your current hindrances and problems. Once you have your list collectively, reach out to the world, and infer them to help you overcome your challenges.

Time is need to Master Life.

Mastering life involves teaching yourself the talents, strategies, techniques, and acquiring the tools you would like to achieve your goals and objectives successfully.

Take a while out to study the obstacles you currently face and determine the talents, strategies, techniques, and possible tools you will need to maneuver you through your current problems and circumstances. Mastering these skills, procedures, policies, and tools might take time; however, sometimes, they will pay on a great cause that may further your progress as you quicken your decisions.

Time Needed to Mature and Gather Prospect

Sometimes you will have the support network in situ. You'll even have the required resources and skills needed to beat the obstacles that you currently face. However, you still be stifled by their persistent aggravating methods that sabotage your journey at every step. During this instance, the ingredient that's lacking is just time.

We all require time to mature and accumulate perspective concerning our current life state and circumstances. In some cases, others will not be available to assist us, and that we will get to take time to reflect and gather personal insights that will only claim from our own experiences.

The key here is to take outing for deep self-reflection quickly. Reflect on your situation, concentrate on solutions, and find answers that you might not be conscious of before.

A Mindset Grounded in Determination

Knowledge alone is not sufficient. Instead, we must encourage a mindset of decision that may help us endure the most formidable challenges along our journey towards attaining our goals and objectives.

Within this final section of the book, we will discuss the aspects and characteristics of a naturally processed mindset to successfully overcome the hurdles and hindrances that unexpectedly take us off guardian.

Encourage and include these principles in your everyday habits and actions. You'll develop the killer instinct that may create unstoppable momentum as you progress toward attaining your goals and objectives.

The Language of Determination

Whether we all understand it or not, the language we use daily features a profound and lasting impact on our ability and willingness to persist through the obstacles and problems we face today.

The words you articulate, the tone of voice you engage, and the questions you ask yourself when coping with challenges are critical in determining your decisions and actions.

Using Passionate and Positive Words

The words you express to yourself and others must be of a positive nature that's further supported by a passionate disposition.

The keys to talk in ways that will move you emotionally and motivate you to take action that enables you to overcome the obstacles that interchange your direction

Asking Solution-Focused Questions

In a preceding section, we considered the negative power of asking why questions. Now we'll temporarily deal with the motivating force of asking how problems.

We must prepare ourselves to continuously ask how questions concentrate on finding solutions and answers to the issues that we currently face in our lives.

These sorts of questions will allow you to interrupt through obstacles with ever greater ease and regularity with practice. They're the questions that may cause creative answers and unlock hidden doors of opportunity that you may haven't expected ever endured.

Here is a listing of solution-focused questions that may serve you with breaking through obstacles and challenges:

- How am I able to make this work?
- How am I able to turn this case around?
- How am I able to strengthen my resolve?
- How am I able to turn this into a chance to maneuver me forward?

The Beliefs Growing from Persistence

Unless you think in yourself and your abilities, you'll necessarily struggle to urge through the obstacles and challenges that present themselves in your life.

The first Key's always believe in a positive outcome, regardless of how grim the circumstances may appear. Remember that what seems to be one-way to you may appear to be completely different from somebody else. Therefore, you must acknowledge that appearances are subjective. You've got the facility to visualize things in ways that will further your success and help you overcome the obstacles you face.

The second Key's to believe that you have the required courage and skill to induce through the challenges that life throws your way. Whether you currently have the skills and methods necessary to drag this off makes no difference. It mostly stems from how resourceful you're when the issues of life come knocking on your door.

The Traits and Attributes you want to Cultivate
The accompanying is uncommon traits and associates that you should improve to help you grow a mindset grounded in perception.

High Wish to Succeed
Personalities who never give up grow within their hearts a burning desire to succeed regardless of how dire their circumstances could seem. Their willingness to follow is so strong that now and then, they'll even become unreasonable when working their way through obstacles.

These people's desire to succeed is robust because they need found effective ways to stay motivated when the chips are down. They also happen to ask the pertinent questions at the correct times that focus them on finding a more fabulous array of reasons to stay moving forward even when the outlook appears to be bleak.

Wholehearted Engagement

Personalities who never give up have a steadfast commitment to their purposes and goals. Commitment generally arises from an empowering set of beliefs that keep their gaze locked on their target until successfully achieved.

To create an unwavering commitment, one must become clear about the goals they're working hard on. Hence, these sorts of people set smart goals that may still propel them forward despite the challenges in their process.

Unstoppable Confidence

Personalities who never give up grow a mindset of unstoppable confidence. These personalities don't take no for a solution. They see possibilities where others only perceive problems; they create the first use of each situation and keep moving forward regardless of how the circumstances appear to get on the surface and despite other people's pessimism and objections.

Courage should build by developing an empowering, confident attitude that pierces through hindrances like a blade through a roll of sustenance.

Self-Reliance

Personalities who never give up are self-sufficient and self-reliant individuals. Even though they still build their support network of contacts, they're, in essence, responsible only to themselves and their most wanted goals and objectives.

These people take responsibility for their losses also as their gains wholeheartedly, without making excuses.

Because they're self-reliant, this makes them far more resourceful than other individuals. They always know where and how to seek the resources, tools, strategies, techniques, and skills they have to help them maneuver through each obstacle they confront. They're, in essence, considerably like lions trapped against the corner of a cage. You'd never bet against them once they have their backs against the wall. Self-reliance is making upon the basis of faith.

Cultivation of Curiosity
Personalities who never give up have an unquenchable curiosity that encourages questions that most people would never consider asking.

They understand that curiosity brings practical problem solving and inventive thinking approaches to the lead of their minds. With these powerful means at their action, no hindrance or challenge can interchange their behavior. If they happen to induce fastened, then this only serves for a fleeting moment while their curiosity-driven frame-of-mind progresses into action.
Curiosity is making upon the inspiration of asking useful proposals.

Unfaltering Faith
Personalities who never give up have a confident expectation that naturally breaks through barriers and obstacles standing in other people's way. However, don't mistake their optimism for stupidity within the face of overwhelming evidence to the contrary. If it had been only optimism that drove their behavior, it might be easy to create this assumption. However, confidence coupled along with all the opposite

qualities listed here manifests finely. A tuned biological machine sees each situation's vivid reality because it appears from a mess of perspectives. Simultaneously, maintaining the flexibility of thought may take them over the obstacles that dwell in their wake.

Faith is an outcropping of confidence that arises from a deep desire and self-belief.

Patience through Thought and Action

Although this may not be obvious to a stranger, people who never give up are incredibly patient.

They need to wait and see because achieving one's goals and objectives take time. One needs time to accumulate new skills, tools, support, strategies, techniques, resources, and insight to develop an inspiration that may successfully guide them toward attaining their dreams and aspirations.

Patience may be a characteristic that constructed upon the foundations of cultivating the habit of delayed gratification. This often tricky for many people to achieve because of our society, unfortunately, builds upon convenience stores. Yet, it's only through patience that we'll obtain long-term pleasures instead of short-term fleeting moments of gratification that means little or no within the broader scope of our goals and objectives.

Breaking through all Hindrances that interchange your approach

Having encoded a decision focused mindset into your brain, you're now able to take the ultimate step, which is creating unstoppable momentum through action and thought that might propel you at ever-increasing speeds towards the attainment of your purposes and goals.

In this final section of the book, we'll take a more in-depth look into the straightforward actions you ought to choose, which will help you interrupt through the obstacles that interchange your way.

The Key to making momentum Begins along with your approach.

The manner you approach the obstacles that interchange your way will mostly determine how effectively and efficiently you progress through the issues currently confronting your reality.

Any action you are taking must, in essence, confront the obstacle in a versatile, curious, and proactive manner that's fun and moves through a process of standard small actions.

The hurdles we encounter in life can become somewhat baffling very quickly. Unless we physically take the time to approach these specific fashion obstacles, we risk de-motivating ourselves and stifling our future actions.

By following these guidelines, you'll find that your actions are more straightforward, and you'll confront less resistance as you progress towards the attainment of your purposes and goals.

Setting Smart and Effective Goals

Goals and Aims are the physical manifestations of our desires and aspirations.

Dreams and aspirations are lovely and pleasant ideas that we confine our minds. They're mostly feel-good visualizations. However, they need no concrete basis. On the opposite hand, setting smart goals takes your dreams and aspirations and brings them to the physical world.

Without goals, you'll haven't any direction. You'll mostly find it challenging to develop unwavering commitment and motivation, and you'll fall under the obstacle traps that we mentioned within the primary section of this book.

Goals adequately lay down the bases for everything and are the driving forces that will encourage you to overcome any challenge that stands in your way.

Without goals, you're much more likely to quit than once you have them laid go in front of you.

If you miss this step and easily ignore the importance of the goal-setting process, you'll be a leaf blowing within the wind — with direction and tiny hope; you'll drift from situation to situation without ever accomplishing anything essential or valuable.

Building Your Support Network
We discussed a bit earlier that it takes time to make and grow a support network of individuals going to be there for you once you need them most.

As you're working your way through your challenges, you'll effectively get to be building and growing your support network throughout this process. Your problems will naturally cause solutions within the very unlikely of places. In and of itself, you want never to

doubt anyone's resources, skills, or the help that they may necessarily provide you with when the chips are down.
Always keep an open mind and still build your support network of individuals even when there are no apparent challenges along your path.

Acquiring New Proactive Habits
Proactive habits are regular actions you're taking and behaviors you adopt that keep moving you toward attaining your goals and objectives despite any obstacles that are currently blocking your path.

Proactive habits might be an example, asking practical solution-focused questions, taking the time to try and do your homework before undertaking specific actions, or just making an attempt to awaken at an equivalent time each day, etc. It doesn't matter what habits you develop, as long as they move you toward attaining your required outcomes.

On the opposite hand, if you are currently not focusing on habits that will sabotage or hold you back from reaching these goals and objectives, you want to work on breaking yourself freed from their grasp immediately. Otherwise, they're going to sabotage your progress still when unexpected obstacles cross your path.

Cultivating Foresight and Identifying the chances that Lie Ahead
Finally, to successfully overcome your obstacles, you want to develop the habit of utilizing foresight to spot the changes that will lie ahead. After all, it's better to prepare for potential problems than to overlook possible scenarios that might ensue naively.

It would help if you effectively utilized foresight to spot problems that will lie along your path and the knowledge and skills you will have to compel to master to reduce the resistance and friction that future obstacles may present.

If you take one approach from this writing, life isn't about what happens to us but rather how we perceive and what we do with what happens.

Ending Thoughts

As a concluding thought, I'd thought I endow you with a brilliant poem that was once addressed to me by my mum to help develop the attitude of persistence within my mind.

The author says a person's heart and determination speak louder than words. I hope you enjoy it.

When things fail as they often will,

When the way you're stepping seems all uphill.

When the funds are low, and therefore the debts are high,

And you would like to smile, but you've got to sigh.

When stress is pressing you down a bit,

Rest if you need to, but don't you quit.

Success is failure turned inside out,

The bright side of the seeds of doubt,

And you'll be able never to tell how close you're,

It may be near when it seems thus far.

So, persist with the fight when you're hardest hit,

It's when things fail that you must not quit.

Quotes

"Business loyalty starts with management loyalty. Your management has to understand that if employees are doing the work they employed for and do with a reasonable amount of competence and efficiency."

"Business opportunities are like metro, and there's continually some other one coming."

"*Make money from money, and this will only happen when you invest money wisely.*"

A Thank You Letter to My Readers

Thank you, everybody, for reading my third book, Zayd's Rules: Business & Money for Life'; keep showing your support.

And the foremost necessary Thanks. Thank You to my parents, my loved ones, friends, co-workers, and every person who has supported me. You've motivated me to chase my dreams. You've got brightened dark days. You helped me believe that I will do something and set my mind; you have helped me accomplish what I once thought.

For that and all of you - I will be able to be forever grateful.

- Zayd Haji

AL ZAYD CORP
BUSINESS & MONEY. FOR LIFE.

It brings me enormous joy and great pleasure while observing the overall performance of AL ZAYD CORP—GROUP OF COMPANIES. It has been an eventful year when we delivered and showed what courage and determination could achieve. We believe you must bring one must be full of passion if you want to thrive in today's bizarre world. These elements brought us to discover Al Zayd Corp in 2018. Al Zayd Corp Group Of Companies. **True to its spirit of uniqueness in concept.**

Al Zayd Corp believes that passion is relay back to our readers & clientele through innovative and exciting content. Explore our site and all that we offer, perhaps–Al Zayd Corp works on converting visitors into customers. Since then, the blog has been thriving and has quickly gained a loyal following. We invite you to browse our site, learn about our passions, and explore.
Al Zayd Corp has successfully ventured into multifarious activities–Content Writing, Visual Capitalist, and Visual Publicist Services. Indulge you with addictive blogs on Finance and Market content that influence you to bookmark.
Al Zayd Corp caters to all the needs and primary requirements of a wide range of graphic design services. In addition, Al Zayd Corp promotes content writing and visual publicist service on our social media channels, and blogs are the ultimate online resource for promoting your product or content. Delivering expertise and advice can reach many audiences with a loyal and trusted following.

PASSION
Passion is our strength.

HUMANITY
We provide involvement & support to our clients.

PROFESSIONALISM
We strive to perform at the highest service level.

Al Zayd Corp is the new-age creator in the industry. Al Zayd Corp serves organizations to reach their absolute potential by gathering great ideas and using technology. We want all our clients to believe occupied with us. We greet the opportunity to gain what drives them and look forward to delivering their business to the following level.

JOIN OUR BLOGGING TEAM.

Welcome to the complete list of all the blog sites on the web where you might consider starting a blog.

The goal is to give you a list of all the categories out there so you can start researching the best grades, objectives, requirements, etc. We are going to keep adding to it and updating it each week. Join us to start blogging.

For Joining Us contact the Al Zayd Corp Team alzaydcorp@outlook.com
We are developing a blogging team with various categories of blogs. We are passionate about Finance and the Market. Whatever you have a passion for, you can blog about it. If you try to blog about something you're not passionate about, you'll undoubtedly fail.

ABOUT AUTHOR

Zaid Haji (born on EID-Al-Fitr, February 1, 1998) is an author and writer known for his finance and market blogs.

Zayd Haji – A businessperson whose passion got to found Al Zayd Corp. Al Zayd Corp is a group of companies that have successfully owned blogging and financial activities. In addition, Al Zayd Corp has successfully projected services into various ventures—Visual Capitalist and Visual Publicist.

Zayd Haji has 3-years of experience in financial analysis and financial content writing. A graduate of Pune University, he has a Bachelor of Business Administration Finance. In addition, he is pursuing a Master's in Banking and Financial Management from NMIMS University. Zayd Haji has worked with firms in the most miniature stages of their development, from start-up to maturity.

Zayd Haji's infographics provide a quantitative and qualitative assessment of the market, companies, demographics, and special attention to segments and buying patterns. In addition, the databases and sources used in his financial analysis are beyond Google, ensuring detailed reports and concise.

Solutions offered; Equity Research graphics considering Market Analysis, Financial Investment visuals, and graphic designs. If you're wise to create visuals by researching the financial market or competitive social media graphics for building business, we are happy to guide you with your venture.

"A book is the only place that makes your imagination grow spacious. Reading will help one relieve their stress and gain knowledge." – Zayd Haji.

"It is in your moments of decision that your destiny is shaped and stored in a Diary, full of experiences and memories." — Zayd Haji

"A brand for a firm is like respect for a person. You earn reputation by seeking to do tough tasks well." — Zayd Haji

"Lifestyle change and changes as you become mature and work hard for success." — Zayd Haji

"Learn from morals; morality starts from where we change our vision to make ourselves and others happy." — Zayd Haji

"Motivation keeps coming from the inner core and reason of life; Don't gamble on the future, act now, without delay." — Zayd Haji